JOURNAL OF THE CEYLON BRANCH OF THE ROYAL ASIATIC SOCIETY, 1919 VOLUME XXVII - EXTRA NUMBER

MALDIVIAN LINGUISTIC STUDIES

JOURNAL OF THE CEYLON BRANCH OF THE ROYAL
ASIATIC SOCIETY, 1919 VOLUME XXVII - EXTRA NUMBER

MALDIVIAN LINGUISTIC STUDIES

WILHELM GEIGER.

EDITED BY

H. C. P. BELL

GYAN

Published by

Gyan Publishing House
5, Ansari Road
Daryaganj, New Delhi-110002
Phone: 011-47034999, 9811692060
E-mail: books@gyanbooks.com

Distribution Network
gyanbooks.com
India, USA, Canada, UK, Australia, France

ISBN : 978-81-212-3745-1 (PB)
First Published, Colombo, 1919

2nd Impression 2020

Printed at: Gyan Press, Delhi.

Maldivian Linguistic Studies
Author: Wilhelm Geiger

JOURNAL

OF THE

CEYLON BRANCH

OF THE

ROYAL ASIATIC SOCIETY,

1919.

VOLUME XXVII. — Extra Number.

MÁLDIVIAN LINGUISTIC STUDIES.

BY PROFESSOR WILHELM GEIGER.

Translated from the German by Mrs. J. C. Willis.

EDITED BY H. C. P. BELL, C.C.S.,

Honorary Secretary (Retired).

COLOMBO:

H. C. COTTLE, GOVERNMENT PRINTER, CEYLON.

1919.

CONTENTS.

SECTION I.

SECTION II.

PAGE

SECTION III.

APPENDICES.

PLATES.

PREFACE.

THE MÁLDIVE ISLANDS have been a Dependency of the British Government in Ceylon since 1796, continuing to pay Annual Tribute. But comparatively little is known, even at this day, about the Group, and still less regarding the Language, which is peculiar to it.

The recognized authorities on the MÁLDIVIAN LANGUAGE, up to the close of last century, have been few indeed—François Pyrard (1615), Willmott Christopher (1841), and Albert Gray (1878).

But between 1900 and 1902 were printed, in the *Sitzungsberichte der Kgl. Bayer, Akademie der Wissenschaften*, of Munich, three learned Papers by Professor Wilhelm Geiger, entitled *Máldivische Studien*, I. (pp. 641–684, with one Plate, headed *Máldivische Alphabete*), II. (pp. 371–387), III. (pp. 107–132), which have very materially advanced our knowledge of the Structure of the Language.

The importance of these unique "Linguistic Studies" induced the Council of the Asiatic Society of Ceylon to apply to Professor Geiger and the *Deutsche Morgenlandische Gesellschaft*, at Halle, for permission to publish an English Translation in its Journal. This permission was courteously granted; and in 1913 a Translation of the three Parts of *Máldivische Studien* was completed for the Society by Mrs. J. C. Willis.

The marked and consistent ability displayed throughout by Mrs. Willis, in her translation of highly technical matter, can only be properly realized by those in a position to compare the German Text with its excellent English version.*

---

* A bound copy of the German Text is in the Colombo Museum Library.

The difficult nature of the letterpress, its occasional turgidity (necessitating exceptional pains in translating. to reproduce the writer's full meaning), added to puzzling abbreviations, have not deterred Mrs. Willis from preparing for the Society, with infinite patience and meticulous care, an eminently satisfactory rendering, which reproduces the more or less specialized phraseology of the German original with admirable fidelity and success.

Mrs. Willis's good wine needed little or no bush. Nathless, to ensure as accurate a presentation as possible of certain passages in the German, perchance open to possible doubt, the entire manuscript was carefully revised by Mr. John Harward, M.A., President of the Society, who managed to snatch time, amid his arduous official duties as Director of Education, to compare the English Translation closely with the German Text, and insert in places valuable emendations making for additional clearness.

Mr. Harward found himself unable to see the Translation through the press before leaving Ceylon in 1916, to seek needed and well-deserved rest, on retirement from the Government Service, after a lengthened period of strenuous and invaluable work.

His mantle, as Editor, has ultimately fallen on an *ex*-Honorary Secretary of the Society, to whom the Fates in 1879 granted a short visit to the Máldives, and the opportunity subsequently of making a partial study—uncompleted, owing to his transference to the charge of the Archæological Survey—of the Islands, their History, Customs, Trade, and Language.*

Despite admitted limitations for the adequate fulfilment of such a task, he has ventured, *faut de mieux*, with some diffidence, to essay, on behalf of the Council,† the somewhat invidious task of editing the Translation of the "Studies" for publication in the Society's Journal.

---

* Embodied in a Monograph on "The Máldive Islands" (Ceylon Government Sessional Paper XLIII., 1881 ; issued 1882).

† Resolution of Council, Ceylon Asiatic Society, March 11, 1918.

The "editorial functions" in the issue of this English version of Professor Geiger's work have, on the whole, been comparatively light, and to a great degree confined to formal details: to wit, the splitting up of some of the long wearisome paragraphs of the original text; the occasional insertion of desirable words within brackets to help the sense; adding sub-heads to ensure enhanced clarity and convenience; and transposing to more suitable positions Notes which in the German (*i.e.*, Section I.) are lumped together at the end.

Every endeavour has been made to retain, as far as practicable, the Professor's own spelling of Máldivian, Siṇhalese, and other Oriental words; whilst making it consistent with the System of Transliteration adopted by the Ceylon Government and the forms of diacritical type available in the founts of the Ceylon Government Printing Office. Fortunately few changes proved to be needed; and those almost entirely for the better.*

To Mr. C. H. Collins, B.A., C.C.S., Honorary Secretary of the Society, to Mr. H. C. Cottle, the Government Printer, and to I. Abdul Hamid Dídí Effendi, Máldivian Government Representative in Ceylon, the Editor owes a special meed of thanks.

Mr. Collins fell in most cordially with the Editor's proposal to issue the "Studies" as an "Extra Number"† of the Society's Journal, and in the form in which it is now presented: further, he generously denied no expense for the preparation of the several Plates necessary to a proper understanding of the printed matter. In addition, Mr. Collins's

---

* Professor Geiger used R, C, J, with small v above, and final N with super-script dot. These have been supplanted in the English Translation by Ṛ, C, J, and Ṅ; but want of semi-nasal (*saññaka*) type has necessitatod the employment of the *bindu*, or full *anuswára*, in such words as *iṇdagena*, *hoṇda*, &c.

For extra clearness MÁLDIVIAN words have been printed in SMALL CAPITALS, whilst *Siṇhalese*, &c., appear in ordinary *italic* type.

† The only other "Extra Number" of its Journal issued by the Ceylon Asiatic Society also related to the *Máldive Islands*. It was published in 1882, as part of Volume VII., and contained "*Ibn Batúta in the Máḷdives and Ceyḷon*," translated from the French by Albert Gray, late of the Ceylon Civil Service.

knowledge of German has been more than once very readily lent to the better solving of a knotty passage.

To Mr. Cottle it is entirely due that the "Studies" make their appearance in that unrivalled excellence of type and general finish which distinguish publications emanating from the Ceylon Government Press.

Without his ungrudging advice, and personal aid, this "Extra Number" could not possibly have been issued in its present neat dress and completeness.

Finally, from Abdul Hamid Dídí Effendi the Editor has received most generous, self-denying, and invaluable help in elucidating obscurities in Máldivian texts, sentences, &c., and in throwing a flood of brilliant light on the modern Máldive Alphabet.

Of the Author's own masterly achievement of a hard task, his "Studies" assuredly "give ample room and verge" for unstinted praise.

If, perchance, there asserts itself unmistakably "the Teutonic literary temperament," so-called, for setting store disproportionately large by the meritorious lexicographic work due to a special *protégé*, Hasan-bin Adam, at the cost of belittling, or wholly ignoring, the efforts of other no less worthy labourers in the field—efforts, in the case of the stand-out "pioneers," Pyrard, Christopher, and Gray, which, without doubt, cannot but have greatly simplified the Professor's researches—if at times an undue tendency to "magnify the *ego*,"

> I am Sir Oracle,
> And when I ope my lips let no dog bark,

is amusingly pronounced—let not, on that account, full justice be denied to the real "merits" of a great scholar, even though one may be not altogether "careless his faults to scan."

Any learned savant, be he of whatever race, who, like Professor Geiger, actuated by worthy motive, and despite very considerable drawbacks, has toiled to give a clear lead to students in the study of a tongue still almost unknown, can claim the right, in all fairness, to generous acknowledgment for sterling work.

Having, like Dr. Samuel Johnson, "set limits to" his "work," which was "ended though not completed," the Professor offers a just plea for considerate treatment at the hands of critics :—

> The principal object of my "Máldivian Studies" must be to put in motion an energetic beginning to Scientific Investigation of the Máldivian Language on the very spot ; where alone it can really be carried out with satisfactory results.
>
> The foregoing Notes on Máldivian Grammar give us, of course, only a general and incomplete picture of the Structure of the Language. They are a first attempt, and should be judged as such.
>
> He who knows the many purely external difficulties and obstacles with which one meets in the East in researches which lie at the foundation of work such as mine ; he who has experienced how the best intentions and the most enthusiastic zeal are constantly checked and crippled by a thousand petty trifles, will judge the deficiencies of my work kindly.
>
> Knowledge must be indulgent. It may be an easy thing to point out and criticise this or that defect ; but of greater worth than criticism is energetic co-operation.

A final word touching the four APPENDICES, and PLATES II. to IX.

For thus supplementing Professor Geiger's TEXT, and PLATE I. issued with it, the Editor, whilst accepting full responsibility, does not feel that any apology is due, in view of the special reason justifying its compilation stated in the preamble of each Appendix.

It is hoped that these Addenda, which render the "Studies" more comprehensive, may help further to facilitate prosecution of research by those interested in the semi-unknown Máldivian Language.

H. C. P. BELL.

New Year's Day, 1919.

ADDENDA ET CORRIGENDA.

Page 1, footnote †; page 2, line 24 and footnotes * and †; page 8, line 13; page 9, footnote ‖; page 54, line 2: *for* "1883" *read* "1882."

Page 6, footnote ‡: *for* "1882, Extra Number, VII.," *read* "Vol. VII., Extra Number, 1882."

Page 8, footnote *: *for* "J. A. Young" *read* "I. A. Young"; *for* "Mittheilungen" *read* "Mitteilungen."

Page 25, footnote †: *omit* "indeed not improbably"; *add* "See Appendix C, page 159."

Page 27, footnote *: *for* "all" *read* "whole."

Page 28, line 12 of the footnotes: *omit* "either"; *read* "as a nasal or mute, or without parentheses in the *middle* when used to double, or nasalise, the connected consonant."

Page 49, footnoto †: *for* "1837" *read* "1838."

Page 57, footnotes ‡ and §; page 58, footnote †; page 66, footnote *; page 117, footnote *: *for* "(ʌ̊)" *read* "ʌ."

Page 58, line 11: *for* "*vadinu*" *read* "*vaḍinu.*"

Page 79, footnote *: *for* "GORUNU DOREVE" *read* "GORUNU-DÓREVE"; *omit* "= GOVERNOR-TURAI (English + Tamiḷ)."

Page 92, footnote *: *for* "BAHI(G)" *read* "BAHIA."

Page 126, line 1: *for* "KALUBILI-MAS" *read* "KAḶUBILI-MAS."

Page 129, footnote *: *add* "A record has since come to light showing that Lieutenant Young, still ill, reached Ceylon from the Máldives, in a sailing vessel, in *1835*. This, therefore, settles the question."

Page 130, line 9: *add* "This Tower is built on a peculiar plan, but very strong. The centre is taken up with solid masonry, much in the form of an immense screw, the spiral ascent winding round this centre pillar until a trap door ends the staircase, where the centre pillar and the top of the outer case of the Tower unite, and together will stand for ages."

Pages 141 and 145, last paragraphs: *for* "Indian" *read* "India."

Page 157, line 29: *for* "*Scripts*" *read* "*Script.*"

Page 160, footnote †: *for* "T" *read* "Ṭ."

Page 170, footnote †: *for* "HITI-GAS-DARU-GÉ" *read* "HITI-GAS-DAṚU-GÉ."

ADDITIONAL ERRATA.

Page 25, footnote ‡: *add at end*, "B., *Ed.*"

Page 125: *for* "1313–1314" *read* "1343–1344."

MÁLDIVIAN LINGUISTIC STUDIES

By Professor Wilhelm Geiger.

SECTION I.*

INTRODUCTION.

The Máldives † are a large group of many islands which extend in the Indian Ocean from 7° 6′ North latitude to 0° 42′ South latitude, and from 72° 33′ to 73° 44′ East longitude. Together with the Lakkadives and the Chagos Islands they belong to a submarine mountain chain, on the summits of which the coral polyps have built their reefs.

---

* *Máldivische Studien I. (mit einer Tafel).* Von W. Geiger. Vorgelegt von E. Kuhn in der Philos.-Philol. Classe am 1. Dezember, 1900. München, 1901.

† H. C. P. Bell, Ceylon Civil Service, *The Máldive Islands: an Account of the Physical Features, Climate, History, Inhabitants, Productions, and Trade* (Sessional Paper XLIII., 1881). Colombo, 1883.

This valuable compilation, which contains the whole of our knowledge of the Máldive Islands up to the year 1883, has become very scarce. Even in Colombo it was impossible for me to get hold of a copy. I finally came into possession of one which formerly belonged to Dr. Rost.

I may perhaps be permitted to borrow from Bell's work some notes on the Geography and Ethnography of the Máldives, as a general explanatory Introduction to my "Studies." I have not, of course, neglected to go back to the sources from which Bell himself drew.

The islands are grouped into "Atolls"—the Máldivian word, as is well known, has passed as a termination into geographical science—and these Atolls, as a rule, are surrounded by a barrier reef, which protects them from storms and waves. In the Northern Atolls, however, the reefs are washed away

The form of the individual islands is circular or oval. They are only of very small extent, the length and breadth seldom exceeding an English mile. The soil of the islands consists of sand; and in most islands there is thick jungle, from which the crowns of the coconut palms lift their heads proudly in all directions.

The principal Island is called MÁLÉ. It belongs to (a double) Atoll (North and South) of the same name, and from it the whole Archipelago has probably received its appellation. On Málé is the residence of the Sultán. The number of its inhabitants is from 2,000 to 3,000.*

The climate of the Máldives does not seem unpleasant, for the excessive heat is tempered by sea breezes; but it is extremely unhealthy. Foreigners are usually attacked, within a short time, by severe abdominal disorders, which, if the individual does not at once leave the Islands, seem in most cases to run a swift and fatal course.

As regards the inhabitants of the Máldives, it is impossible to determine their total number. Bell (in 1883) estimated them to be at least 30,000: in former times there were doubtless many more. The gradual decline in the number of the population seems, however, to have recently come to a standstill, or even to have been succeeded by an increase.†

---

* Bell, *loc. cit.*, 1883, p. 53. The Census of 1911 (p. 500) gives the total as 5,236 inhabitants.—B., *Ed.*

† Mr. Gray (*Journal, R.A.S.*, 1878, new series, X., p. 197) puts the population of the group at 20,000. Mr. Bell (*The Máldive Islands*, 1883, p. 53) considered this "perhaps too low an estimate, and a total of at least 30,000 may, with more probability, be assumed." Mr. Bell adds, "that the population was in former days larger is admitted by the Islanders themselves, who point with melancholy significance to islands in nearly every Atoll now lying waste, where homesteads stood of old. It is, however, satisfactory to find good grounds for the belief

The fact can scarcely be disputed, that, at a period of time still unknown to us, the Máldives were colonized from Ceylon, or, as also may be possible, were colonized at the same time as Ceylon, by Áryan immigrants who came over from the Continent of India.

The first view seems the more probable to me, owing to reasons which appear on a study of the character of the Máldivian language. This, in fact, shows a number of features which are characteristic of the Siṃhalese language, and which have not arisen in the Prákṛit foundation of Siṃhalese, but seem to have originated on Ceylon soil itself. In course of time the Áryan stock of the Máldivian population would be much mixed with Drávidian and Arab blood; so that the physical type of the Máldivians can no longer be considered a unit.

The fact that there is no trace of Buddhism on the Islands* must not surprise us too much: Islám has totally ousted this religion.

---

that the gradual depopulation—mainly attributable to the proverbially unhealthy climate—has not merely been arrested, but that, from the closer connection now yearly being established with the outside world, and the increased facilities for obtaining yearly necessaries of life, a steady re-action is setting in." (*Census Report*, 1911, p. 499.)

This Census made the total population of the Máldive Islands to be "72,237 (males, 39,244; females, 32,993)," pointing to 50,000 rather than 30,000 as nearer the mark in the Eighties.—B., *Ed.*

* See Bell, *loc. cit.*, p. 74, *Buddhism on the Máldives.*

Mr. J. Stanley Gardiner (*The Natives of the Máldives*, Proceedings, Cambridge Philos. Society, XI., Part I., 1900) unconsciously plays the rôle of "Balaam" in an endeavour to condemn the theory of Buddhism formerly existing on the Máldives :—

"Mounds in *Landu* and *Miladu* of Miladummadulu Atoll, as also in Haddumati, Suvadiva, and Addu Atolls, and Fua Mulaku Island, suggest by their form a comparison with the dágabas of Anurádhapura.

"*Gang*, in Haddumati Atoll, was evidently a great religious centre, having ruins of fourteen of these, some with smooth sides of squared stone.

"One, in *Landu*, appears to have had a kind of pit or well in the centre, formed by squared blocks of Porites, and covered by two large flat masses. Within this, in 1848, were found a number of gold or brass ornamental discs.

The colour of the skin of the males is usually a dark copper; some of the women are decidedly pretty.

As regards the character of the Máldivians, I give some statements from the Report of the two Englishmen, Lieutenants Young and Christopher, of the Indian Navy, who, in the course of a Survey of the Máldivian Archipelago in the years 1834–1836, spent several months at Málé:—

"They are a quiet, peaceable race, hospitable and kind to strangers, though suspicious and distrustful of them. Unacquainted, indeed, with the practice of the higher virtues, but equally unfamiliar with vice in its darker forms, with desires and wants circumscribed and limited, and the means of satisfying them attainable without much labour, they have little incitement to increased exertion for the purpose of augmenting their productions; and hence, in all probability, the little attention paid to the improvement of their resources, and the absence of all care regarding the amelioration of their condition. The apathy and indifference evinced by them on these subjects seem, however, to result in a great measure from feelings of contentment, though of a spurious kind." *

The religion of the Máldivians is Muhammadan. According to Gray they embraced this religion about the year 1200. Native tradition indicates Yúsuf Shams-ud-dín, from Tabríz, in Persia, as the apostle of Islám in the Máldives. He died in Málé, and his grave there is held in great honour.

"At *Fua Mulaku* a few oval six-sided beads, either of an extremely hard clouded glass or of crystal, were found.

"The presence of an immense *Bó* tree (*M. boi gas*) at *Málé*, and another in *Fua Mulaku*, is of no importance; no traditions cling to them. The tanks resemble those of Anurádhapura, but there is no particular Buddhist type.

"Indication of Buddhism might, indeed, be gleaned from the above, but I found no other evidence in its support."

"Mounds," with possible relic chambers ("pit" or "well"), which "suggest" the "*dágabas* of Anurádhapura"; "tanks" which resemble the *pokuṇu* of that old Siṇhalese Capital; buried metal, "ornamental discs," and "oval beads," glass or crystal—to say nothing of the unexplained presence of two *Bó* trees (one at Málé, the chief Island itself)—are about as promising "indication of Buddhism," judged by Ceylon archæology, as one can well hope to find where Muhammadanism (with its iconoclastic zeal) has existed for some eight centuries.—B., *Ed.*

* *Transactions of the Geographical Society, Bombay*, I., p. 66.

But although Islám is the official religion, the old animistic nature-worship, the belief in demons and spirits, in exorcism and magic, plays the most important part * in the life of the people.

" The belief in the existence of spirits and supernatural beings, who interfere, sometimes visibly, in human affairs for purposes of evil, as also in extraordinary phenomena supposed to afford intimation of pending calamity, is universal among the Islanders. . . . . They believe also in the auspiciousness, or otherwise, of certain days for particular transactions, no undertakings of any importance to individuals, or to the public, being entered upon without the priest being consulted to determine that point. During recitations in Arabic of passages from the Korán, which is a common practice, incense is kept burning, and when this takes place on board a boat, the crew are always careful to fumigate the rudder-head and tiller before the fire is extinguished. . . . . Many individuals on the islands gain their livelihood by writing charms, which are supposed to possess much virtue, not only as a preventive against, but also a cure in most diseases. In order to produce a curative effect the ink of a freshly-written charm is washed off in water and drunk as a medicine." †

So far as is known to me, the ancient historical writings of the Sinhalese give no information about a colonization of the Máldives by that people; neither do they mention any sovereignty which they at times exercised over the Islands.

The first allusion to the Máldives is found in Ptolemy (the Second Century A.D.), who places a group of 1,378 little

---

* Geiger writes "*die wichtigste rolle.*" This is over-stating the case. Gray (*Journal, R.A.S.*, 1878, new series, X., p. 180) puts it better :—

" The picture presented by the modern religious state of the two branches of the Sinhalese family is curious indeed. The one (Sinhalese) has held to the cosmopolitan principles, the atheistic creed and the simple worship of the Buddhist faith; the other (Máldivian) has adopted the exclusive monotheistic and ceremonious faith of Muhammad. These religions have not, however, altered to any extent the characteristics of the race, and both have suffered *the co-existence of the older worship of demons and of the elements*—a common inheritance of both branches of the family, but an alien to both their creeds."—B., *Ed.*

† *Transactions of the Geographical Society, Bombay*, I., p. 76.

islands to the west of *Taprobané* (Ceylon).* There can scarcely be a doubt that by these the Lakkadives and Máldives are meant. After Ptolemy, and with reference to him, Pappus of Alexandria speaks of 1,370 small islands which are near *Taprobané*, and dependent on it.

In the Sixth Century, Cosmas Indicopleustes, who got his information from Sopater, mentions a large number of islets in the neighbourhood of Ceylon where fresh water and coconuts are to be found throughout.† His statement is indeed striking; for on almost all the islands known at the present time there is fresh water, and the richness of the Máldives in coconut palms is a well-known fact.

The first visitor to the Máldive Islands to whom we are indebted for a more accurate description is the famous Arabian traveller of the Fourteenth Century, Ibn Batúta.‡ He remained eighteen months on Málé, and gives us a tolerably detailed account of the condition of the Islands, of their conversion to Islám, of their government, and of their trade with India, China, and Yemen.§

In the Sixteenth Century the Portuguese made many attempts to bring the Máldives under their dominion. Finally, their independence was acknowledged in a Treaty; in which, however, the Portuguese reserved to themselves the exclusive right of trade with them.‖

Almost thirty-five years later, on July 2, 1602, a French ship, with a band of adventurers on board, was driven ashore among the Atolls. The crew were taken prisoners: some died in consequence, others succeeded in escaping; only four remained, among them François Pyrard de Laval.

---

* Forbiger, *Handbuch der alten Geographie*, 2 Aufl., II., p. 524; Lassen, *Ind. Altertumskunde*, 2 Aufl., I., p. 246.

† Tennent, *Ceylon*, 1859, I., p. 538, note ii.; p. 543.

‡ *Ibn Batúta in the Máldives and Ceylon.* Translated from the French of MM. Defrémery and Sanguinetti by Albert Gray. *Journal, C.A.S.*, 1882, Extra Number, VII.

§ Bell, *The Máldive Islands*, p. 25.

‖ Regarding this Treaty, see the Hakluyt Society's *Pyrard*, Vol. II., Appendix B.—B., *Ed.*

Pyrard stayed five years in the Máldives. By his wise and tactful conduct he gained the favour of the Sultán, so that he had a tolerable amount of liberty, and could carry on trade. Finally, when the Máldivian kingdom was plunged into the confusion of war, he regained his freedom.

In 1607 the "King of Bengal" undertook an expedition to the Máldives. His fleet attacked Málé suddenly, without encountering serious resistance, and returned with rich booty. On the Bengal ships Pyrard and his three companions left the Máldives.

Four years later, after many other adventures, Pyrard once more safely trod the soil of his native land.

Pyrard's work, *Voyage aux Indes Orientales*, which is very scarce, appeared for the first time in the year 1611, the second edition in 1615–1616, the third in 1619.* It contains the most complete description of the Máldive Islands which has hitherto appeared, and still serves as a valuable source of information.

The Dutch followed the Portuguese in the Government of the East Indian world; and were followed by the English at the close of the Eighteenth Century. After the latter took possession of Ceylon, the sovereignty which the Dutch had wielded over the Máldives passed automatically to their successors.†

---

* Pyrard's *Voyage* was translated into English, for the Hakluyt Society, from the Third French Edition of 1619, by Albert Gray and H. C. P. Bell, of the Ceylon Civil Service. Two volumes, 1887–1890.

[Of Pyrard's *Voyage*, four French Editions were issued : the first (one volume, 8vo.) in 1611; the second (two volumes, 8vo.) in 1615; the third (two volumes, 8vo., containing the Máldivian Vocabulary) in 1619; and the last (one volume, 4to.) in 1679.—B., *Ed.*]

† "Our (British) influence in the Máldive Islands, as that of the Dutch before us, is *founded on the free will and consent of the Sultáns.* From their confidence in our attachment and our power, they *made themselves the feudatories*, first of Holland, and subsequently of Great Britain, by placing themselves, *of their own accord*, under the protection of the successive Governments in Ceylon ...... The present political status of the Máldives is that of *a semi-sovereign State*, under the exclusive protectorate of the British Government in Ceylon—a relation very similar to that of the King of the Isle of Man with John of England, established by Treaty of A.D. 1212."—Bell, *The Máldive Islands*, Appendix A, pp. 123, 125.—B., *Ed.*

In the years 1834–1836 a Survey of the Máldive Archipelago was undertaken by Captain Moresby, at the instance of the Bombay Government, since such a Survey was urgently necessary in the interests of Marine Commerce.

On this occasion Lieutenants Young and Christopher spent at the Máldives, and almost exclusively on Málé island, two to three months—from June 4 until August 17 and September 9, 1834, respectively. They suffered severely from fever, but were able during their stay to make a series of important observations on the country and people, government and commerce, manners, customs, and language, which they subsequently collected into a *Memoir*.*

This is full, and (until 1883 was) the most recent knowledge of the Máldive Islands available. It must be considered, so far as it goes, credible and reliable, but is, at the present time, scarcely up to date.†

---

* *Memoir on the Inhabitants of the Maldiva Islands*, by Lieutenants J. A. Young and W. Christopher, of the Indian Navy; *Transactions of the Geographical Society, Bombay*, I., pp. 53–86. *Cf.* Captain Moresby's *Report on the Maldivas; loc. cit.*, pp. 102–108.

Among other notices of the Máldives and their inhabitants are M. Haberlandt, *Die Kultur der Eingeborenen der Malediven*, Mittheilungen der Anthropologie; Gesellschaft in Wien, 1888, XVIII., p. 29 *seq.*; Rosset, *Minikoi und seine Bewohner*, Ausland, 1891, LXIV., pp. 16, 35, 67. *Cf. Die Maldiven*, Ausland, 1887, LX., pp. 761–764.

† Bell, *The Máldive Islands*, p. ii.

I.—THE MALDIVIAN LANGUAGE.

After these general preliminary remarks, I now come to the Máldivian Language itself.

Our knowledge of this is very scanty, and almost entirely confined to the vocabulary.

Vocabularies.

We possess two Vocabularies,* which, however, can lay no claim to completeness.

The first originated with Pyrard, 1602–1607, and appeared in the Second and Third Editions of his *Voyage aux Indes Orientales*.†

The second Vocabulary was compiled by Christopher during his stay in Málé in the year 1834, and in 1841 was printed in the *Journal of the Royal Asiatic Society*. ‡

Pyrard's Vocabulary was subsequently published again by Gray, and compared with that of Christopher. §

Gray's Paper is the first attempt to discover the connection between the Máldivian and Siṇhalese languages.

A number of Máldivian words are found in Bell's book, || already mentioned; a few, too, which show the identity of

---

* See Appendix A.—B., *Ed.*

† A mistake. Pyrard's Máldivian Vocabulary appeared in no edition of his *Voyage*, save the third of 1619.—B., *Ed.*

‡ *Vocabulary of the Maldivian Language.* Compiled by Lieutenant W. Christopher, I.N.: communicated to the Bombay Branch of the R.A.S. by J. Wilson, D.D. *Journal, R.A.S.*, 1841, VI., pp. 42–76.

§ Gray, *The Máldive Islands: with a Vocabulary taken from François Pyrard de Laval*, 1602–1607. *Journal, R.A.S.*, 1878, new series, X., pp. 173–209.

A series of isolated remarks is also found in E. Kuhn, *Ueber den ältesten arischen Bestandteil des Singahalesischen Wortschatzes: Sitzungsber. der K. Bayer*, Akademie d. W., Philos.-Philol. und Hist., Cl. II., 1879, p. 199 *seq.*

|| Bell, *The Máldive Islands*, 1883.

the language which is spoken on Minikoi with that of the Máldivian Islands, occur in the communication of Rosset previously mentioned.

Texts.

As regards the text of the Máldivian Language, we possess (in print), up to the present time, only three Letters: one was lithographed in *facsimile* and translated by Christopher;* another by Bell; † a third is given in Bennett's *Ceylon and its Capabilities*, London, 1843, along with an official translation.‡ The last-mentioned Letter, however, is unknown to me. §

I myself began my Máldive collection (of words, phrases, &c.) in the winter of 1895–1896, during my stay in Ceylon.

As related in the Account of my Journey, I had the opportunity of meeting a Máldivian of high rank, Ibráhim Dídí,|| in Colombo, and, from his information, putting together a vocabulary, as well as a number of Máldivian paradigms and sentences.

My material has convinced me that only by a collection of new texts can we expect to further our Máldive linguistic studies.

Since my return (to Germany) I have kept up an unbroken correspondence with my excellent Sinhalese friend, A. Mendis Gunasékara, Mudaliyár; and it is to him especially that I owe the fact that I am now in a position to publish some contributions to the investigation of the Máldivian Language which I hope are not without value.

I sent sentences to Mudaliyár Gunasékara which I wished to have translated. He succeeded in discovering an Indian

---

* *Journal, R.A.S.*, 1841, VI., pp. 44–45, 73–74. [Plate III.—B., *Ed.*]

† Bell, *The Máldive Islands*, pp. 78–81. [Plate IV.—B., *Ed.*]

‡ Bennett, *Ceylon and its Capabilities*, London, 1843. See Bell, *loc. cit.*, p. 78, note 1, where the translation of a further Máldivian Letter, given in Campbell's *Excursions in Ceylon*, I., pp. 199–200, is mentioned.

§ *Sitzungsber. der K. Bayer*, Akademie d. W., 1896, pp. 213–215.

|| A. Ibráhim Dídí Effendi, Dorhiméná-kilagefánu, Prime Minister to His Highness the Sultán of the Máldives.—B., *Ed.*

merchant, named Sheik Ali, at the time residing in Colombo, but who had lived for many years in the Máldives, and spoke the language as his mother tongue.

Communicating with Sheik Ali (who neither wrote nor spoke English) through the medium of Siṉhalese and Tamiḷ, the Mudaliyár delivered the sentences written down by him to me for further elaboration.*

Vocabularies in Europe.

In conclusion, I have to mention the Máldivian materials which are found in *European Libraries.* They are certainly not very plentiful ; and, as far as I know, have not hitherto been adequately valued by any inquirer. †

"Copenhagen Vocabulary."

First, a short manuscript *Vocabulary of the Máldivian Language* is found in the Library of Copenhagen. ‡ By the kind mediation of Professor Fausböll, I received the manuscript at Erlangen, and was able to enter its contents into my list of Máldive words.

The Máldivian Writing § employed in this Vocabulary has a quite unique style, differing considerably from the Writing which I learnt, and which is used in the (two) Letters quoted below.

In the little manuscript I also discovered the original of a Máldivian missive which Sultán Muhammad Mu'ín-ud-dín

---

* It is with pleasure that I avail myself of this opportunity of publicly thanking my active helpers. I rejoice that in A. Mendis Gunasékara, Mudaliyár, I found a man specially fitted to act as an intermediary.

[It should be emphasized that the scholarly Mudaliyár must not, of course, be in any way held responsible for some doubtful renderings which have crept into the Professor's Siṉhalese transcripts here and there. See *infra.*—B., *Ed.*]

† See Appendix B.—B., *Ed.*

‡ I indicate the "Copenhagen Vocabulary" by K.V., the "London Vocabulary" by L.V.

§ Professor Geiger has not reproduced any of this L.V. writing (see *infra*, page 22, top), unless it may be the three words in the GABUḶI TÁNA alphabet given at bottom of his Table [Plate I.].—B., *Ed.*

Iskandar sent to the English Governor in Colombo (KOḶUBU RASGEFÁNU).* This is doubtless the Sultán of that name who in 1799 succeeded to the throne of his father, Hasan Núr-ud-dín.

"London Vocabulary."

Secondly, in the Library of the London India Office is *A Vocabulary, Persian and Hindústání,* † printed in Calcutta, 1808, and formerly belonging to the *Bibliotheca Leydeniana.*

In this book the Máldivian translation of every word is entered, with a few exceptions, by a native of Himịtí (in Nilandú Atoll), named Hasan-bin-Adam.

Mr. Tawney was so kind as to send the book to me, and with it a bundle of letters; from which it appears that some years ago, according to Mr. Bell's wish, it had been sent to Colombo. He showed it to some native Máldivians, who were to examine the Vocabulary; but they came to the conclusion that it was full of mistakes and errors, and of little or no value. ‡

This correspondence was indeed discouraging to me; but I did not allow myself to be deterred from putting the Vocabulary to a test on my own account, and preparing a copy for myself.

The result at which I arrived is happily much more favourable. I regret to be obliged to say that the Máldivians whose aid Mr. Bell sought, clearly did not take much pains in the matter: perhaps they did not possess the necessary knowledge of Persian and Hindústání.

At any rate they were in error in calling in question Hasan-bin-Adam's knowledge of their mother tongue. ‡

---

* How and when did this *official record,* belonging to the *British Government,* stray to *Copenhagen*—a "far cry" from Ceylon? No particulars are afforded. The year of the missive must be between A.D. 1799–1835.—B., *Ed.*

† See footnote ‡ on page 11, *supra.*—B., *Ed.*

‡ See Appendix B. Professor Geiger has allowed himself—not wisely—to wander somewhat from the strict facts, which he had before him in the "bundle of letters" kindly sent to him by Mr. Tawney.—B., *Ed.*

The "London Vocabulary" (which I have now to deal with on the basis of my own observations) is, indeed, not free from errors, and a considerable number of words contained in it can be rejected at once as worthless. But the mistakes can be partly explained on the general ground that the Máldivian language does not possess an absolutely fixed orthography.

The words which I characterize as worthless are not to be set down to the ignorance of the translator, but are explained by the praiseworthy, though naturally impracticable, endeavour to give, wherever possible, a translation for every Persian and Hindústání word.

Thus, there are in this Vocabulary numerous words (*e.g.*, technical terms, &c.) for which there neither are, nor can be found, equivalents in Máldivian.

In such cases, Hasan-bin-Adam got over the difficulty in two ways: either he gave instead of the translation an explanatory paraphrase, or he transliterated the Persian (or perhaps Arabic) or Hindústání word into the Máldivian alphabet.

Of the "paraphrases"—using this expression on account of its shortness—many are quite intelligible, and at least show us that the translator understood his task.*

Thus, for example, the grammatical terms "singular" and "plural" (p. 133) are written by him as EB-BAS, "one word," and GINA-BAS, "many words." Instead of "barren" (of a woman), he says (p. 176) DARI MAI NUVÉ, "she does not become mother of a child." The Persian *buz-i kúhí*, "wild goats," he translates (p. 39) closely by FARUBADA MATÍ BAKARI, "goats on the hills."

Many of the paraphrases may indeed be real terms; for the paraphrasing expressions do not seem at all strained to the Máldivians, and are also found in Christopher's Vocabulary. Thus, for instance, FINI-FEŃ-MAU, *i.e.*, "dew-flower," for "rose," the same expression being found in L.V., p. 67.

---

* See footnote ‡ on page 12, *supra*.—B., *Ed.*

The verb HUNU-KURÁN, "make hot" = "cook"; US-KURÁN, "make high," "raise"; LADU GANNAN, "be ashamed," and others which occur in L.V., do not differ, as regards their method of formation, from verbs like HUS-KURAŃ, "empty"; DÚ-KURAŃ, "lower"; BÍRUŃ GANNAŃ, "be afraid," in Christopher.

The expression MÍHUN MARÁ MÍHU, "the man who kills people" (p. 104), for "executioner," we shall meet below, in the story of "The Wise Judge." Consequently, others, such as DAḌU KOṚÁ MÍHU, "the man who tills the fields" = "countryman"; or ROṚI VIKKÁ MÍHU, "the man who sells bread" = "baker," may really be Máldivian and constantly used. We find also in Christopher expressions like DAGAḌU TAḶÁ MÍHUŃ, for "smith."

A really pretty and well-considered paraphrase is, for example, MAU-KOṚI, "flower enclosure," for "garden." The word, which might perhaps have been apt, GÓTÍ, is well known to our author: it occurs in several places; but here he evidently avoids it designedly, because it has the more general significance of "yard," corresponding to the Anglo-Indian "compound." *

Further, as regards the Arabic, Persian, and Hindústání words which occur in Máldivian guise in L.V., these are not very numerous.

As examples, I mention (*a*) the names of the Signs of the Zodiac (p. 4), like HAMALU, "Aries" = Ar. *hamal;* ASADU, "Leo" = Ar. *asad;* (*b*) expressions from the Islámic faith, like NABÍ, "prophet"; VALÍ, "saint"; IMÁMU, "religious leader" (p. 116); as well as (*c*) words like IRÁDÁ, "will," "resolution"; KABÚLU, "agreement"; MASALATU, "goods" (p. 94); FAIDÁ KURÁN, "explain" (p. 196; Persian *paidá*); FIKURU KURÁN, "consider" (p. 98); and many others.

* For "garden" two words are recognized at Málé: BAGÍCHA; GÓTÍ. With MAU-KOṚI as a "well-considered" paraphrase, compare the Málé term for a "beggar": E SALÁN DÉ MÍHÁ DURA(N)LÁṚÉ, "drive that beggar (*lit.*, the man-who-saláms) away"—the very acme of "pretty" and euphemistic politeness. *Cf.* the former use in France of "*les bons hommes*" for "lepers." Other cases will readily occur to mind.—B., *Ed.*

I have already said that these words can be eliminated as worthless—at least for our scientific purposes. But it must be mentioned emphatically that many of them, as a matter of fact, may belong to the Máldivian vocabulary, which has borrowed a good deal.

As regards doubt regarding the unreliability of the L.V., this is refuted by the fact that, without taking the Numerals into account, I have counted, in round numbers, five hundred Words which also occur, in like form and with the same meaning, in Christopher's list. By this its correctness is proved.

Further, it is not credible that all the remaining words which occur in the L.V., but are missing from Christopher, should be worthless.

Moreover, I am in a position to prove the correctness of a whole series of words (which have not been quoted otherwise), either by comparison with my own collection (Geiger), or by etymology.

Some Maldivian Words in the "London Vocabulary."

I subjoin the list here, with the observation that it is by no means exhaustive. But it is natural that I (in Germany), so many thousand miles away from the land of origin, was not in a position to verify all the new words of the L.V.; and for this reason especially deplore the fact that this could not be done at the time that the L.V. was in Bell's hands, and his Máldivian helpers were there.* I do not doubt that among the words whose correctness I cannot confirm—preliminarily, at least—there are many true Máldivian words.

1. ADUN, "ointment for the eyes" (p. 34) = Geiger, ANDUN; S. *aṇdun*; P. *añjana*. Forms with, and without, the ante-consonantic nasal are very frequently found close together. I heard HANDU, "moon"; L.V. (p. 3), HADU: Christopher has HAḌU, but the cerebral is certainly incorrect.

* See footnote ‡ on page 12, *supra*.—B., *Ed.*

I wrote KANḌU, "ocean": Christopher and L.V. (p. 8) have KAḌU. *Cf.* also Nos. 21, 31, 60, following. In these cases, it appears to me that there is a difference of dialect.*

2. AGU, "price," "value" (p. 74) = Geiger; S. *aga*; P. *aggha*; L.V. (p. 186), AGU-VÁN, "be worth," "to cost."

3. ARIKAṚI, "side" (p. 19) = Geiger; K.V., "rib."

4. ASEI MIRUS, "black pepper" (p. 55) = Geiger, ASÉ MIRUS.

5. AVI, "sunshine" (p. 2) = Geiger; K.V.; S. *avu*; P. *átapa*.

6. BANIÁDA', "pious man," "believer" (p. 178) = Geiger, BANIYÁDAŃ MÍHE', "man of good habits"; opposed to KÁLU MÍHE'.

7. BURIKAṚI, "back" (p. 18) = Geiger; K.V.: Christopher has only BURI.

8. BURUGAḌU, "wheel of a cart" (p. 78) = Geiger.

9. DAḶU, "horn" (p. 41) = Geiger; S. *daḷa*; P. *dáṭhá*, "tooth." The meaning "horn" was also confirmed by me. Christopher has only EDDAḶU, "ivory," *e.g.*, "elephant's tooth."

10. DELI, "charcoal" (p. 9) = S. *dẹli*; Christopher, DELI, "ink" = L.V. (p. 127).

11. DEVI, "demon" (p. 2) = S. *dev*, "good deity"; P. *deva*.

12. ENNÁN, "to come" (p. 182) = S. *enu*. I have recorded ANNÁN.

---

* If perchance *sounded*, the N is never *written*, in HADU and KAḌU, according to the Málé standard.

Such forms, in the "London Vocabulary," as, *inter alia*, ENNÁN for ANNÁN, FEFAḶI (older, FUFUḶA) for FOFAḶI, FUHÉN for AHAN, TELI for BAḌIYA, UGEN for DASKULAIN, sufficiently attest "a difference of *dialect*," well known to exist even at the present day, and quite to be expected, between the central Málé Atoll type and that of Atolls to the south, including, doubtless, a century or more ago, Nilandú Atoll, where the author of the "London Vocabulary" (Máldivian) lived.—B., *Ed.*

13. FAṚÁN, "to begin" (p. 186) = Geiger. *Cf.* S. *paṭan*, "beginning"; *paṭan gannu*, "to begin"; P. *paṭṭhána*, *paṭṭhápeti*. With respect to the equivalence of Máldivian Ṛ and Siṃhalese *ṭ*, see Geiger, *Litteratur und Sprache der Singhalesen* (*Ind. Grdr.*, 1, 10), p. 88.

14. FATAS, "ditch" (p. 92) = S. *patas*, "deep pit," "well."

15. FATURÁN, "spread out" (p. 190) = Geiger; S. *paturuvanu*; P. *pattharati*.

16. FAUḶU, "clear," "open" (p. 158) = S. *pahaḷa*; P. *pákaṭa*.

17. FÁLAN, "bridge" (p. 7) = Geiger; S. *pálam*.

18. FEFAḶI, "red coral" (p. 49) = Geiger, FOFALI. I conjecture that in L.V. there is a slight clerical error, and FOFAḶI is to be read.

19. FENIJJA, "to occur" (p. 185) = S. *peṇenu*; P. *paññáyati*.

20. FIDDIYA, "gall" (p. 22) = S. *pit*; P. *pitta*, "gall" + *diya*, "water."

21. FIDU, "buttocks" (p. 44) = Geiger, FÍNDU, "hips."

22. FORUVÁN, "to cover," "clothe" (p. 184) = Geiger. *Cf.* below, III. 1: 17. S. *poruvanu*; P. *párúpati*.

23. FUHÉN, "to ask" (p. 189) = P. *pucchati*. The word is of especial interest, because a Siṃhalese equivalent is no longer preserved.

24. FURÁN, "to fill" (p. 192) = S. *puraṇu*; P. *púreti*.

25. GÁḌIYA, "cart" (pp. 62, 78) = Geiger; Sheik Ali, GÁḌI-DAḌI, "yoke."

26. GOMAI, GUMAFUḶU, "prince" (p. 108) = Geiger, GOMA, "princess."

27. GUI, "excrement" (p. 23) = S. *gú*; P. *gútha*.

28. HAFÁN, "to chew" (p. 181) = S. *hapanu*.

29. HAḶÉḶÁN, "to make a noise" (pp. 26, 182) = Geiger, "to bark": *e.g.*, KUTTE' HAḶÉLANÍYÉ, "a barking dog."

30. HARU, "hard" (p. 25) = Geiger. See below, III. 1: 16.

31. HAṚIGAḌU, "body" (p. 15) = Geiger, HAṚIGANḌU.

32. HATURU, "enemy" (p. 99) = S. *haturu.*

33. HÁSFAT, "millepede" (p. 46) = HÁS, L.V. (p. 150); HÁHE', Geiger, "thousand" + FAT, FAI, L.V. (p. 20); FÁI, K.V.; FÁ, Christopher, "foot."

34. HEILAN, "awake" (p. 183) = Geiger, HÉLUŃ, "be awake."

35. HITU, "thoughts" (pp. 93, 135) = Geiger, HITUŃ; S. *hitu; P. citta.*

36. HUGU, "asafœtida" (p. 33) = Sans. *hińgu.*

37. INNÁN, "to sit" (p. 183) = S. *iṇdinu; P. sídati.*

38. IRÍNA, "to sit" (pp. 183, 190) = Geiger, IṚINNA; S. *hiṭinu;* Prákṛit *ciṭṭhai.* The R in IRÍNA is perhaps simply written by mistake; but the K.V. likewise has IRIDÉ. In just the same way HURI, "is," "exists," and HUṚI are also interchangeable.

39. ÍṬU, "tile" (p. 57) = Geiger. *Cf.* L.V. (p. 81), ÍṬU ANDÁ MÍHU, "man who bakes tiles." The word is interesting: it corresponds to the Sanskṛit *iṣṭaká* or *iṣṭiká;* in Siṇhalese it is wanting.

40. KANU, "blind" (p. 23) = Geiger; S. *kaṇa; P. káṇa.*

41. KEKURI, "cucumber" (p. 69) = S. *kękiri; P. kakkárí.*

42. KIBÚ, "crocodile" (p. 45) = S. *kiṁbul; P. kumbhíla.* The disappearance of the final L is purely Máldivian. *Cf.* MÚ, "root," but MULE', "a root"; MÁ, "flower" (Geiger), but MALE', "a flower."

43. KIRÁN, "to weigh" (p. 205) = S. *kiraṇu.*

44. KIRI-MAI, "nurse" (p. 11) = S. *kiri-mav; P. khíra + mátu.*

45. KOLU, "cheek" (p. 17) = Geiger, KÓ (*cf.* 42); P. *cos.* Perhaps = S. *kopul.*

46. KORU, "lame" (p. 24) = S. *kora; P. khoṇḍa.*

47. KOTABIRI, "coriander" (pp. 37, 69) = S. *kotaṁburu.*

48. KUJJÁ, "child," "son" (pp. 10, 175) = Geiger.

49. KUḶEN, "to play" (p. 191) = S. *kelinu;* Sans. *keláyati, kheláyati.*

50. KURUBAI, "young coconut" (p. 66) = Geiger, KURUMBA ; S *kurum̆bá*.

51. LAKUNU, "spot," "time" (p. 28) = S. *lakuṇu* ; P. *lakkhaṇa*.

52. MADOṚI, "a weight" (p. 120) = S. *madaṭa* ; P. *mañjiṭṭhá*.

53. MÉVA, "fruit" (p. 64) = Geiger; Persian; L.V.

54. MUGOṚI, "ichneumon" (p. 41) = S. *mugaṭi*.

55. MUḶÓ, "axe," "hatchet" (p. 84) = Geiger.

56. NAṚÁN, "to dance" (p. 183) = S. *naṭanu* ; P. *naṭṭa*.

57. NIANETI, "insight," "understanding" (p. 135) ; better "intelligent" = S. *nuvaṇeti*.

58. SIṬÍ, "letter" = Geiger. *Cf.* below, III. 1 : 21.

59. SUNGAN, "tax," "toll" (p. 112) = S. *suṇgam*.

60. TABU, "arrows" (p. 56) = Geiger, TAMBU ; S. *ṭem̆ba* ; P. *thambha*.

61. TABURU-MAU, "lotus flower" (p. 68) = S. *tam̆buru* ; P. *támarasa*.

62. TALA, "palate" (p. 18) = S. *talla*.

63. TELI, "pot" (p. 60) = S. *ṭeli* ; P. *tháli* ; Sansḱ. *stháli*.

64. UDUN, "oven," "hearth," "fireplace" (p. 60 ; on p. 9 incorrectly written ADUN) = Geiger, UDUN, UNDU ; S. *udun* ; P. *uddhana*.

65. UFI, "twig" (p. 65) = Geiger, OFI.

66. UGEN, "to learn" (p. 185) = S. *ugannu* ; P. *uggaṇháti*.

67. UKÚLU, "privy parts" (p. 19) = S. *ukul*, "hip."

68. UMAGU, "hollow," "hole" (p. 153) = S. *umaṇ* (*kaninu*).

69. VÁDA KURÁN, "take revenge" (p. 99) = S. *váda*, "rage," "fury."

70. VEHENÍ, "it rains" (p. 185) = S. *vahinu* ; P. *vassati*.

71. VIYÁFÁRI-VERI, "merchant" (p. 73) = Geiger. See III. 1 : 22.

II.—THE MALDIVIAN WRITING.

In the *Memoir on the Inhabitants of the Maldiva Islands* by Lieutenants Young and Christopher there is the following remark on the Máldivian Alphabet :—

" The different written characters found on tombstones on the Maldiva Islands are of three kinds. The most ancient are called by the natives DEWEHI HAKURA, which in all likelihood were used by the first inhabitants, but now the knowledge of them is nearly lost, being confined to a few individuals. In the Southern Atolls a knowledge of this writing appears to have been retained longest, for it is not remembered in the Northern ones at all, whereas orders are now written at MALÉ in this character for the inhabitants of the Southern Atolls. No old manuscripts with this character are preserved. One peculiarity in the alphabet is, that some of the consonants change their form according to the various vowel-sounds with which they are united, the construction of the letter being altogether different. This character is written from the left hand.

" The next is the *Arabic*, which is written in two different ways, the old and new ; but the old method of forming the letters is now discontinued. From the appearance of the tombstones it is evident that the DEWEHI character was in use prior to this, for the freshest inscription in that character bore more signs of age than any we have seen in the Arabic. The multitude of inscriptions in the latter character is an evidence that it was very extensively spread and known throughout the islands Both of these characters were invariably carved in relief. The modern *Arabic* character was apparently introduced about the same time as the present native writing.

" The modern alphabet contains eighteen letters, and is called by the natives GABAḶI-TÁNA. There are some auxiliary letters in it, derived from the *Arabic* and *Persian*, in common use, but not included in the alphabet. It is written from the right hand, and was introduced when the Portuguese garrison were overcome, and Muhammadanism re-established by a Chief and men from the Northern Atolls, and is now used throughout the Islands. . . . . . .

"There are several kinds of TÁNA writing; and we are inclined to think that the one at present used was not so generally adopted until within the last fifty years, as many tombstones are evidently inscribed in a character differing from the GABAḶI-TÁNA: the letters, at least, have a different sound, and the signs used for vowels are different.

"Letters of the alphabet are used as numerals, and they reckon by twelves, as we do by tens." *

Alphabets.

In the Table † which I have added to these Studies all four Alphabets are given completely.

The first two, (reproduced) in Columns I. and II., originate from the "London Vocabulary," in which they are entered at the end, with the remark that the first is called the DIVEHI AKURU Alphabet. ‡

The Alphabet in Column III. is (copied from) the one which Christopher gives as the "Ancient Form" of the Máldivian Alphabet. §

---

* *Transactions of the Geographical Society, Bombay*, I., pp. 68–69.

† See Plate I.—B., *Ed.*

‡ Photographic reproduction of "THE DIVAS ALPHABET" as given in the "London Vocabulary," and faithfully traced therefrom by Mr. D. A. L. Perera, Muhandiram, Head Draughtsman (and later Native Assistant), Archæological Survey, during the short time the book was in Mr. Bell's hands at Anurádhapura, appears in Plate V. 1.

As will be seen, the characters are more carefully delineated (dots and dashes, where given, being shown) than in Geiger's Table, Columns I., II. [Plate I.]; which, moreover, *reverses* the proper order of the columns in the "London Vocabulary"; and starts with H instead of M. —B., *Ed.*

§ See Plate II. for the Plate of Comparative Alphabets given by Gray (*Journal, R.A.S.*, 1878, new series, X.).

Christopher's copies of the *Ancient Máldive* (EVÉLA) and *Modern Máldive* (GABUḶI TÁNA) *Alphabets* were reproduced correctly by Gray; except that Christopher, on the one hand, began his Alphabets from H to V, followed by M to Ḍ, whilst Gray, for his part, reversed this order. Both group the eight (8) letters, extra to the ordinary eighteen (18), thus: Persian *ch*, *p*, *ṭ*; Arabic *z*, *y*, *j*, *gh*, *th* or *dh*.

Geiger, in his Table [Plate I.], has altered Christopher's letter transcripts RH, CH, J, GH, and TH or DH, to R, C, J (headed by small V), Greek G, and T (underlined), besides substituting the sign ' for Christopher's AVIENI transliteration. He adds the Ñ.—B., *Ed.*

In Column IV., finally, I give the Modern Writing as I myself have learnt it, and as it is used in the Letters hitherto published.*

I intend, next, to detail the material, as far as it is accessible, and make a series of observations on it.

Maldivian Writing.

We are still far from a history of the Script, and any far-reaching conclusion we make respecting the character of the Máldivian Writing must be considered rash and uncertain, until we have reliable copies—photographs, where this is possible—of the inscriptions still existing.

In regard to the "Ancient Form" of the Máldivian Writing in Column III., Gray has already written.

He shows its resemblance to the Ancient Sinhalese Alphabet of Twelfth Century Inscriptions, by simply placing the respective signs side by side.†

In single characters the agreement is, in fact, immediately perceptible. The sign for F (11) resembles the Sinhalese *p*, being only somewhat inclined to the right: the same is the case with the signs for N (3) and T (13): in the signs for K (7) and G (15) the connection is unmistakable: in others it seems more obscure; but it always appears quite probable.

The question is, whether Christopher's "Old" Writing really

---

* The form of GABUḶI TÁNA recorded by Christopher (see Plate II., Gray's reproduction) is that employed at *Málé Island* (the Sultán's Capital) about 1835, or more than three-quarters of a century ago. The present-day writing has naturally suffered some evolution.

This standard type, and, as such, that invariably used by A. Ibráhim Dídí Effendi, Dorhiméná-kilagefánu, Prime Minister, and other educated Málé officials, appears in a number of letters written—in beautiful caligraphy—to Mr. Bell some years ago, and still carefully preserved. This style differs from the somewhat stilted form of the alphabet noticeable in Geiger's Table, Column IV. [Plate I.].—B., *Ed.*

† *Journal, R.A.S.*, 1878, new series, X., p. 183, with Table.

represents *the oldest form* of Máldivian Writing—whether it corresponds to the DIVEHI AKURU.*

If this be the case—and I must remind the reader of what I have said about the uncertainty of our conclusions—a really remarkable result will follow.

The (Old) Máldivian Alphabet (given by Christopher) may especially be compared with the Siṃhalese signs which were used in the Inscriptions of the Twelfth Century (as has been done by Gray).

But we know that the period about the Ninth Century was of out-standing importance in the history of Siṃhalese Writing.† Before this, the universal Aṣóka Script, with extremely slight modifications, was in use (in Ceylon). Afterwards a Writing appears which in general is based on the Aṣóka Alphabet, but already shows traits of the Modern Siṃhalese Writing. The revolution is quite sudden and immediate.

This can only be explained by supposing that, in the preceding period, the Writing used among the *populace* had gradually deviated from that used in *Inscriptions*, so that the latter could no longer be understood. For monumental purposes, also, therefore, they gave up using the old Aṣóka Writing of the lapidaries, and employed the more cursive Alphabet used in general intercourse.

As regards the Máldivians, it would follow that they did not borrow their Writing from the Siṃhalese until the Ninth or Tenth Century; or that, if they brought their Writing with them, they did not settle in the Archipelago before this time. In itself it would be quite conceivable, either that (*a*) the Áryans coming from Ceylon were the first colonists of the Máldives, or that (*b*) they met with an older aboriginal population on the Islands.

But we must first see whether still older specimens of Máldivian Writing do not turn up.

---

* See Appendix C.

† Geiger, *Litteratur und Sprache der Singhalesen*, Section 19–20.

"London Vocabulary" Alphabets.

I come now to the two Alphabets of the L.V., of which the first is said to correspond to the DIVEHI AKURU.*

The Modern Máldivian Alphabet, as is well known, runs from *right to left*; the Old Alphabet is said to have had the *reverse* direction.

This agrees quite strikingly with the Alphabets in the L.V.

The more recent (of those given in Columns I. and II., Table) is clearly the direct source of the Modern Alphabet, and like this, also, has the *right to left* direction. We can without difficulty derive one from the other, by changing, in each letter, the vertical and horizontal stroke (which in the older form constituted the end of the letter) into a diagonal line, or, as—for example—in K, ', V (7, 8, 9), by entirely omitting it.

On the other hand, the Writing in Column II. is clearly a *reversal* † of the Writing in Column I., which doubtless ran from *left to right*, like the Siṃhalese. Only the signs for Ṇ (16) and Ḍ (18) offer any difficulty. The former appears in Column II. not as the reversal, but only as a slight variation of the (equivalent) sign in Column I.; and in the case of Ḍ (18)—if the modern form of the letter did not contradict it—one might easily believe in a simple interchange of the forms in Columns I. and II.

We have now, on the whole, got a complete history of the development of the Máldivian Writing, as (far as) shown in Columns I., II., and IV.

---

* To prevent confusion, it should be noted again that Geiger has *transposed*, and otherwise altered, Columns I. and II., as they actually appear in the "London Vocabulary." They are shown in their *true order* in Plate V. 1. Therefore, when Geiger speaks of Column I., the second column in the "London Vocabulary" must be understood, and, *vice versâ*, Column II. for the first column.—B., *Ed.*

† To bring out this "reversal" of the writing clearly, the Editor has added (Plate V. 2) a *third* column to those reproduced from the "London Vocabulary," by printing through the back of the negative in the case of the second column.—B., *Ed.*

Yet I cannot believe that the Alphabet in Column I. is the DIVEHI AKURU : the latter must, I think. be much further removed from the Modern Writing. Gray, however, has pointed out, correctly, that the modern signs for the nine letters H, Ṛ, N, R, B, Ḷ, K, A, V are nothing but the *Arabic Numerals* 1, 2, 3, 4, 5, 6, 7, 8, 9.

I should like to call attention to the statement in the *Memoir* quoted above, in which it is asserted as a characteristic phenomenon of the Ancient Máldivian Alphabet, that the separate letters appear in a different form, according to the vowel to which they are joined.* This points towards a Writing which is very closely related to the Aṣóka Alphabet.

It seems to me that both the Alphabets in Columns I. and II. are only *archaic variations of the Modern Alphabet*, but are *widely different from the* DIVEHI AKURU.†

I shall not lay too much stress on the *left to right* direction of the Writing in Column I. The Writing from *right to left* was certainly first introduced in Muhammadan times. It may indeed have been prevalent for a longer time, with fluctuations in its use. The Sinhalese Writing was always *from the left*, and yet inscriptions are occasionally found in Ceylon which have to be read in the reverse direction. ‡

---

* See Appendix C.

† The Alphabets exhibited in Columns I. and II. of Geiger's Table [Plate I.] may quite possibly—indeed not improbably—be, as the Professor surmises, "archaic variations of the Modern Alphabet" (GABUḶI TÁNA) once in use on the Máldives.

So far, however, no writings in either form have come to light.

On the other hand, the true DIVEHI AKURU, or DIVES AKURU, the Ancient Máldivian Alphabet, is occasionally employed on the Southern Atolls to this day. The Editor obtained two copies of *the full syllabary* (one from Málé, central; the other from Fua Mulaku, almost at the Southern limit of the group) some years ago. See Appendix C.—B., *Ed.*

‡ *Exceptio probat regulam.* The comparatively few lithic Inscriptions found in Ceylon which read from *right to left*, styled *pratilóma*, occur only at *caves*, and are probably due to "masons' freaks." Cave records show occasionally further deviations from the normal, in the letters being cut upside down, and sideways: these aberrations are known as *peraḷi-basa*.

Maldivian Orthography.

I should like to draw attention here to a few peculiarities of Máldivian orthography, which must be kept in sight all the more, as a fixed system apparently does not exist, and in the writing of single words variations are observed.

We deal, first of all, with the use of the two signs (transliterated in the Table as) Ṛ (2)* and ' (8).

(i.) The first sign, Ṛ, expresses a sound peculiar to the Máldivians, to which the (cerebral) ṭ in Siṇhalese is most closely allied. The sound is very difficult to describe and to imitate. It varies between R, H, and Ṣ; is rather soft; and is, so far as I could observe, uttered by putting the tip of the tongue in the highest part of the palate, and letting the breath escape sideways between the teeth.

(ii.) As a sound value for the Máldivian sign (transcribed here as) ' (8), Gray (following Christopher) gives A, because it is called by the Máldivians AVIENI; just as the other letters of the Alphabet (from the first letter onwards) are called HAVIENI, ṚAVIENI, NAVIENI, RAVIENI, BAVIENI, &c.†

But that is quite wrong. The sign corresponds (*a*) more completely with the Arabic *aleph* and *hamza*.

It also acts (*b*) as a support for a vowel at the *beginning* of a word, as well as *within* a word when a vowel precedes. In this case it is, of course, not taken into account at all in the transcription of words. The Máldivians write $^{U}D^{U}N$, "stove"; $F^{O}I$, "book"; we write simply UDUN, FOI.‡

---

* Written RH by Christopher and Gray.

† The sign for L has the name LÁMU.

‡ Geiger, in trying to represent the words, *pronounced* UDUN and FOI, as they are *written* by Máldivians, uses forms in which the vowel signs for U and O are added above, and that for I below. These entirely ignore the AVIENI *base-sign* (the evolution of the *Arabic* numeral Λ = "8"); and, further, make the representations read wrongly from left to right.

A far closer (though equally ugly) approximation to the Máldive forms would be N̊^{U}D^{U}Λ, (T̊)^{O}F, the sign Λ (inverted V) being used to represent the "semi-consonant" AVIENI, and (T) with *sukun* above, within parentheses, the consonant, in English *transcribed* T, but *pronounced* by Máldivians as a soft I.—B., *Ed.*

But the sign has also (*c*) another significance. Consonants like T, Ṭ, Ṛ, N, K often disappear at the end (of words), and in their stead (the Máldivian AVIENI sign here represented by) ' appears in the writing. The sign is intended, I believe, to denote a closing of the top of the wind-pipe.

This may be brought into agreement with what Christopher says of (the letter sign) AVIENI, that, with the "SOKUN" (*i.e.*, *without vowel*), it sounds like G.* In what Gunasékara wrote I also find G in such a place.

I always write (this AVIENI sign as) ', and am certain that this (mode) is correct.

My transliteration is, therefore, RA', "land" (S. *raṭa*; P. *raṭṭha*) = Christopher, RAG (L.V., RA', p. 111); FUA', "betel" = Christopher, FUVAG; ó', "camel" (S. *oṭu*; P. *oṭṭha*) = Christopher, óG; O', "stone (or kernel) of a fruit" = Christopher, óG; KO', "having power" = Christopher, KOG, Gunasékara, KOG; FOTE', "a book" = S. *potak*; E', "elephant" (S. *ęt*) = Christopher, EG.

The sign serves (*d*) yet another purpose: it indicates the *doubling of a consonant*. Thus: KU'TÁ', "dog," is written for KUTTÁ; KA'TIRI, "warrior," for KATTIRI; RASRASKALU'NÁI, "to the king," for RASRASKALUNNÁI; RÁ'JÉ-GAI, "in the kingdom," for RÁJJÉ-GAI.†

In both these cases, too, the sign (i.), which is expressed by Ṛ, may appear (in lieu of the AVIENI sign). In double

* His original manuscript shows that Christopher himself wrote words like the Máldive MUḶI(Ṛ), "all," KÁETIWÁ(Ṛ), "musket," as MUḶI and KÁETIWÁ, paying no attention to the final Ṛ, it being *silent*.

Further, he wrote the Máldive RA(Å), E(Å), O(Å), and the like, as RAG, EG, OG (the G being *silent* at the end of words); and NEFA(T), "nose," FO(T), "book," as NEFAI, FOI (the T at end having sound of soft I).

It was his *editor*, Dr. J. Wilson, who first *printed* these (and similarly-terminated) words as MULI', KÁETIWÁ; RAG, EG, OG; and NEFAĬ, FOĬ.—B., *Ed.*

† The sign, "called by the Máldivians AVIENI," is most nearly represented by the Arabic numeral ٨ ("8")—an inverted V.

Being a base-letter sign, Gray rightly styles it a "consonant," or "semi-consonant." "The initial vowels are formed by the *quasi*-consonant A" (*i.e.*, the Máldive adaptation of Arabic ٨) "with the appropriate vowel sign; and the second of two vowels following a consonants, in fact, it is used in the L.V.: for example, KUJJÁ, "child" (p. 10); RAJJEHI, "in the kingdom" (p. 112); SIKKA, "seal" (p. 71), are written KUṚJÁ, RAṚJEHI, SIṚKA.

It must be understood that we cannot speak at all here of the *sound-value* of Ṛ. But the fact that the *sign* for Ṛ has been confused with the sign ' (adopted here for AVIENI) can be explained in two ways.

In *speaking*, as we have already mentioned, Ṛ is mute, or nearly so: it is formed by closing the top of the wind-pipe. Also it can now be assumed that in many cases the old writing was preserved as historic; so that one used OṚ, "stone of a fruit," in *writing*, but *spoke* it as O'. This might lead to considering Ṛ as an equivalent sign for ' (AVIENI), and using it as equivalent.

Historical writing is found in the same way, with (final) T originally *pronounced*. The L.V. has ET, "elephant"; FAT, "leaf"; DAT, "tooth." I myself only heard (these words pronounced) E', FAĬ', DAĬ'; and Christopher also writes in this way, adopting the modern pronunciation.

In point of fact the sign for Ṛ—considering its resemblance in form to the sign for N—in *utterance* apparently represents a nasal sound; and in this case would be written Ń.* This

---

consonant is expressed in the same way; thus: GAI is written G with the vowel sign 'A' (ʹ above), followed by the *quasi*-consonant A with the vowel sign 'I' (͵ below)."

In the Modern Máldivian Alphabet (GABULI TÁNA)—as contrasted with the Old Alphabet (DIVES AKURU) and the Sinhalese Alphabet—"there is no inherent vowel: accordingly every consonant has either a *vowel sign* or the *sokun* (° above = Sinhalese ් *al* sign) .. in the latter case, if the consonant (be one that) cannot take the *sokun*, it is changed to one (of the six, viz., A, N, Ṇ, Ṛ, S, T) which can."

For *transliteration* (as distinct from *pronunciation*) it might be well to adopt in every case the particular *sukun*-marked letter employed, placing it *within parentheses*, either at the *end* of a word as mute, or in the *middle*, when used to *double the preceding consonant*. This would avoid the indistinctly-marked sign ', so liable to pass unnoticed.

In his footnotes the present Editor has followed this plan.—B., *Ed.*

* Christopher uses Ṛ in transcribing some words (*e.g.*, DEṚNANG, KAṚNÁDI), where the Ṛ clearly has the nasal sound of the consonant following. He does not seem ever to write it as the *final* letter having the sound of N.—B., *Ed.*

nasal sound is found occasionally, instead of the complete vanishing of the consonant, perhaps instead of the closing of the top of the throat; and was clearly heard by me. *Cf.* Notes to III. 1: 3. It represents a transitional stage, the retention of which was apparently rendered possible by the rhythm of the sentence.

Even N, when final, shows a tendency to be pronounced as a velar, and can then be expressed by that symbol; and here again the closing of the top of the throat is a further stage of development.

The forms MÍHUN, MÍHUṄ, MÍHU', and MÍHU, "human being," are found, with no distinction between them.

Maldivian Alphabet Signs.

In conclusion, two more remarks.

Originally the Máldivian Alphabet is said to have possessed only the (eighteen consonant) signs (numbered) 1 to 18 (see Table). For the signs (in the same Table, running from) 19 to 27 Christopher gives no older forms; and the signs 25 to 27—sounds which generally occur only in foreign words—are also wanting from the Alphabets found in the L.V.

As regards the signs 19 to 24, and the sounds which they are said to express, that for Z occurs only in borrowed words; whilst Ñ and Ṭ are very rare, the latter being regularly represented by Ṛ. On the other hand, Y, C, J are found in real Máldivian words; although the last two, as in Siṇhalese, may be more recent developments.

The strongest argument against the connection of the Modern Alphabet—and consequently the two Older Alphabets given (Columns I., II., Table) in L.V.—with the Ancient Siṇhalese, is *the form of writing the vowels.*

This has been borrowed directly from the *Arabic* writing. The vowel signs for A, I, U are identical with the Arabic *fatha*, *kasra*, and *damma;* their long equivalents being shown by doubling the simple signs: for E, É, O, Ó the vowel symbols are new formations from the borrowed material, easily explicable.

III.—AIDS TO KNOWLEDGE OF THE MALDIVIAN LANGUAGE.

1.—Sentences in Maldivian, with literal line-for-line English version.

1. I asked (you) something: (you) answer give
MA EHÍ ECCEKÉ: SUVÁBU DÉŃ
must.
VÁNÉ.

2. I need a book; the book to me give.
MAṚA BÉNUME FOTE'; FOI MAṚA BADI (or DI).

3. To that boy's father I it gave.
E SORU-GE BAFÁYAŃ TIMAŃ ETI DÍNÍM.

4. I gave the book to your brother.
MA DENI FOI KALÉ BÉBÉ ATA'.

5. On this tree the branches long (are).
MI GAHU-GA' OFI DIGÉ.

6. In our garden are fifty-four
AHARAMEŃ-GE GÓTÍ-GA' HURI FANSÁS HATARU
coconut palms.
RUKÉ.

7. We three persons (are).
AHARAMEŃ TÍM-MÍHU'.

8. How many children are to you?
KITA KUDIŃ EBA-TIBÚHÉ KALÉ-GE?
I have (Of me are) five children.
MA-GE TIBÍ FAS KUDIŃ.

9. (Is) this a poisonous snake?
MI VIHA-HARUFAYET-TA?
This snake a poisonous one (snake) is.
MI HARUFAYÍ VIHA-HARUFAYEKÉ.

10. Honey very sweet thing (is).
MÁMUI VARA' FONI ECCEKÉ.

11. Of this fruit the taste sweet (is).
MI MÉVA RAHA FONYÉ.

12. My daughter younger (is)
MA-GE AŃHEŃ-DARI-FUḶU HAGÉ
my son than.
FIRIHEŃ-DARI-FULA' VUREŃ.

13. This tree very large tree (is).
MI GAHÍ VARA' BOḌU GAHE'.

14. This tree higher that tree than (is).
MI GAS UHÉ E GAHA' VUREŃ.

15. My house smaller your house than (is).
MA-GE GÉ KUḌAYÉ KALÉ-GE GEYA' VUREŃ.

16. The coconut shell very hard (is).
NÁṚI VARAŃ HARÉ.

17. Yesterday very the wind strong (was);
ÍYA VARA' VÁE GADÉ;
clouds covered the sky.
VILÁ FORUVAIPPÉ UḌU.

18. The elephant stronger the horse than (is).
E' GADAFADAYÉ AHA' VUREŃ.

19. The sun rises; the sun rose;
IRU ARANI; IRU ARÁDÁNÉ;
the sun will rise.
IRU ARÁNÉ.

20. The sun sets; the sun set;
IRU OSSIJJÉ; IRU OSSIDÁNÉ;
the sun will set.
IRU OSSÉNÉ.

21. That servant to me brought a letter yesterday
E NÓKIRU MAṚA GENÁÍ SIṬIYE' ÍYA
evening.
HAVÍRU.

22. From the town a messenger came: he (that man)
RAṚUŃ BALÁMÍHAKU ÁI: E MÍHÁ
a merchant by was (the man) sent.
VIYÁFÁRI-VERIYAKU FURUŃ FONUVENI MÍHEKA.

23. I wrote a letter to you here
MA LIYUNÍME SIṬIYE' KALÉ MI-TANAŃ
to come.
ANNÁŃ.

24. Whence (do) you come?
KOŃTAKUŃHE TIYA ANNANI?

25. All (men) die must.
ENMEŃ VES MARUVÁŃ VÁNÉ.

26. Do not strike that dog:
NU-TALAHAṚE E BALU-GA':
it will bite you.
ETI DÁE-GEŃFÁNÉ KALÉ-GÁE-GA'.

27. Sleep well! Are you well?
GADA NIDI! KALÉ GADA-TA?
This child weeps why?
MI KUJJÁ RONI KÍ-VEGEŃ?

28. That fruit falls from the tree on to the ground.
E MÉVA VETUNI GAHUŃ BIMAṚÉ.

29. Of the tree the leaves green (are). Green leaves.
GAS-GAHU-GE FAI FESÉ. FEHI FAI.

30. This dress white (is). This sand yellow (is).
MI HEDUŃ HUDU. MI VELI RÍNDU.
Blood red (is). The sky blue (is).
LÉ RAI. UḌU NULÉ.

Notes to III. 1.

1. ECCEKÉ. The word ECCE, or, more correctly, ECCE', means "thing," "affair," "fact." *Cf.* ECCEŃ (for ECCE') NU-KÁTI, "he eats nothing," L.V., p. 32, translation of Persian *parhíz*, "abstinence"; Sheik Ali, KOŃ-ECCE', "what?" literally, "what sort of thing?"

2. BÉNUME. *Cf.* Christopher, BÉNAŃ, "to want," "to desire." * The -ME seems to be an Emphatic Particle, corresponding to the Siṇhalese *-ma*.

3. SORU-GE BAFÁYAŃ, or SORU-BAFÁYAŃ. According to Ibráhim Dídí, BAFÁ and BAPÁ are used for "father"; the former belongs to lower class, the latter to higher class, speech. BAFÁYAŃ is, I think, the Dative.

The Ń (as I heard it) here expresses the sound of a disappearing consonant, which in this case was Ṛ. *Cf.* Siṇhalese *-ṭa*. The nasal sound appears to be due to the *sandhi* of the context. In most cases there is a complete disappearance, or rather a closing of the top of the throat; thus, ATA' (4), FUḶA' (12), GAHA' (14), GEYA' (15), AHA' (18), is in every case the correct way of writing; not GEYA, FUḶA, &c. TIMAŃ is the Reflective Pronoun; ETI a Demonstrative Pronoun.

4. Literally, "I gave the book to your brother's hand." According to Ibráhim Dídí, MA DINI, "I give"; MA DENI, or MA DINI, "I gave."

5. -GA' or -GAI. Suffix, which indicates place. *Cf.* MI RAṚU-GAI, "in this town"; RAṚU-GAI HUNNA MÍHÁ (L.V., p. 110), "the in-the-town-dwelling man," "townsman." To -GA' belongs, as dative, -GÁTAŃ, -GÁTA', "towards" = S. *laṇga-ṭa* (III. 3: B 1). The -É at the end of the sentence appears to correspond to the S. *-ya*. *Cf.* III. 1: 6, 9, 12, 13, &c.

6. HURI. "Exists," "is," "there is" = Christopher, HUṚI. *Cf.* III. 2: 4, 7, &c.

---

* Christopher writes BENANG. I throughout replace his NG by Ń.

7. TIM-MÍHU'. Assimilation for TIN-MÍHU'. Such assimilations are frequent everywhere in Máldivian. *Cf.*, for example, HARUFAYET-TA in 9 (= HARUFAYEK-TA); EBBAI, in III. 3 : A 3 (for EK-BAI), &c.

8. EBA-. Particle, I was informed, of the Present Tense.

9. -TA. Interrogative Particle. The termination -Í, in MI HARUFAYÍ, is used emphatically. *Cf.* also MI GAHÍ, III. 1: 13; but MI GAS, III. 1: 14.

12. HAGU. "Young," speaking of length of life. In a general sense ḶA is used for "young," "fresh," "new" = S. *lẹ*. DARI-FUḶU means "son" or "daughter"; FUḶU is a so-called honorific. When required, FIRIHEŃ, "male," and AŃHEŃ, "female," can be prefixed. For the use of VUREŃ. *cf.* the following sentences, III. 1: 14, 15, 18.

20. The Tenses were told to me most exactly in the series quoted; but it still appears to me doubtful whether ARÁDÁNÉ and OSSIDÁNÉ are Preterites. *Cf.* also III. 2: 20, the synonym IRU TIRIVIDÁNÉ, as Future, "the sun will set"; TIRI means "down," "low."

21. GENÁÍ. Literally, "having taken came he" = S. *geṇá-váya*. *Cf.* Máldivian ÁÍ = S. *áváya*, in III. 1: 22. ÍYA HEN-DUŃ, "yesterday morning."

22. VIYÁFÁRI. "Gain" (L.V., p. 73). In the sense of "owner," "master" (L.V., pp. 75, 115), -VERI, or -VERIŃ, often occurs at the end of a compound word. Christopher, MAS-VERIŃ, "fisherman"; ATOḶU-VERI (L.V., p. 109), "master of an Atoll"; Christopher, DAḌU-VERI, "countryman."

23. MI-TANAŃ. Dative, "to this place," "here" = S. *metana-ṭa*.

24. TIYA, or KALÉ-TIYA. The latter is the more respectful Pronoun of the Second Person.

25. VES. According to Christopher = "also": VÁNÉ appears to be equivalent to the S. *óné*.

26. ETI. Used of animals and things; ÉNÁ of persons, Pronoun, Third Person. -GÁE signifies "person." *Cf.* SIŃGA-GÁTAK, "the lion," III. 3: C 4; HIYAL-GÁTU-GA', "to the donkey," III. 3: C 5.

27. KALÉ GADA-TA. According to Ibráhim Dídí, GADA VEVULÉI.

28. Ibráhim Dídí gives MÉVA VEṬENI, "the fruit fell"; MA VETIJJÉ, "I fell."

2.—Sentences in Sinhalese and Maldivian, with literal line-for-line English version.

1.

Your mother,	where (is she)?
Uṁbé ammá,	*kó?*
UMBA AMÁ,	KOBÁHE?

My	mother	and father	in the house (are).
Magé	*ammat*	*táttat*	*gedaraya.*
MAGE	AMÁ-YÁ	BAFÁ-YÁ	GEDARA-GAI.

2.

Our	sister	in the kitchen	being,
Apé	*sahodarí*	*kussiyé*	*iṇdageṇa,*
AHARAMEŃ-GE	KOKKÁ	BADGÉ-GAI	HURIŃGE',

rice	cooks.
bat	*uyayi.*
BAI	KAKKANI.

3.

On the Máldives	what	kinds of fruits
Máladivayiné	*mona*	*geḍi varga*
DIVẸHI-RÁJJÉ-GAI	KOŃ	KAHALA FAF-FALÓ-TAŃ

are cultivated?
vẹvé-da?
HEDENI?

4.

In our	island	many	coconut palms
Apé	*divayiné*	*bohoma*	*polgas*
AHARAMEŃ-GE	RAṚU-GAI	BÁVAR	DIVEHI-RUT-TAŃ

are.
tibet.
HURI.

5. Of nuts fifty, the price how great (is it)?
Geḍi paṇahaka, mila kopamaṇa-da?
FANSÁS KÁṚI-GE, AGA KÍHÁVARU?

6. We of coconut-palm wood our houses
Api pol-lí-valin apé gé
AHARAMEŃ DIVEHI-RUKAŃ GÉ-TAŃ
build.
sádamuva.
AḶAMEVÉ.

7. On those islands rats very numerous are.
É divayinvala miyó itá bohóya.
E RATTAKU-GAI MÍDA-TAŃ VARA' GINA-KO' HURI.
They (rats) to the coconut palms
Ovhu pol-gas-vala-ṭa
E MÍDA-TA' RUT-TA'
harmful are.
antaráya karati.
HALÁK-KURÁ TAKACCA EVÉ.

8. Of this country (the) climate healthy
Mé déṣa guṇaya sanípa
MI RÁJJÉ-GE GOI FASÉHAKAMU-GE
is not; to us coming
neṭa; apa veta-ṭa ena
NÚNÉ; AHARAMEŃ GÁTAŃ ANNA
strangers from dysentery very much
paradéṣikayó pácana-rógayen boho-sé
FURUDDEHI MÍS-MÍHUŃ BÉRUHIGÁ-BALIYIN GINA-KO'
suffer.
peḷeti.
ÁDATA-VÉ.

9. Yesterday my brother together with
Iyé magé sahódarayá samaga
ÍYA MAṚA BÉBÉ EKU
to the jungle I went.
keḷéṭa mama giyemi.
VALAŃ DIYÁME.

10. You there did what?
Umba ehedí kaḷé mokada?
KALÉMEŃ ETA-GAI KÍŃHÉ KOḶEFÍM?

11. We firewood gathered:
Api dara ekatu-keḷemuva:
AHARAMEŃ DARU EKU-KOFFÍM:

we it to our house brought;
api eya apé gé-ṭa geṇávemuva;
TIMAŃMEŃ EYITI TIMAŃMEŃ-GE GEYA' GEŃGOSFÍM;

we fire kindled; (and)
api gini pattu-keḷemuva;
AHARAMEŃ ALIFÁNU RÓ-KOFFÍM;

our food we cooked.
apé kẹma api ivvemuva.
AHARAMEŃ-GE BAI KAKKÁFIM.

12. You to-morrow what will (you) do?
Umba heṭa karanné mokada?
KALÉMEŃ MÁDAM KOŃ-ECCE HADÁŃ ULUVANI?

13. We to the shore going
Api múdu-varaḷaṭa gos
AHARAMEŃ GONḌUDORA' GOS

for fishing in the boat will embark.
masun allaṇ-ṭa oruvakin yannemu.
KEVIḶUKAMAD DAHAṚE DÓNIYAKA' ARÁNUME.

14. My father since he died now one year
Magé piyá mẹri dẹn avuruddak
MA-GE BAPPÁ NIYÁ-VEGEŃ MIHÁRU EŃ AHARU

(it) was.
viya.
VEJJEVÉ.

15. My mother still in life is;
Magé mẹniyó tava-ma jívatva siṭi;
MA-GE MAMMÁ ADIVEI FURÁṆA-EKA ULANI;
but she very old become,
ehet ẹ bohoma nákiyi,
EKAMAKU ÉNÁ VARA' MUSKULI VEFAYE',
very weak become, is.
durbalayi.
VARA' DERA VEFAYE', ULANI.

16. This woman four children has borne;
Mé am̆buva daru hatara denek vadá-siṭi;
MI AMBI HATARU DARI VIHAYEPPEVÉ;
of my friends, one, her
magé mitrayek, ẹ-gé
MA-GE RAHUMAITTERÍN KUREŃ, EKAKU, ÉNÁ-GE
youngest daughter, has married.
bálama duva, kárabẹn̆da-gẹna-siṭi.
HAGU AŃHEŃ-DARIYA', INÍ.

17. This man blind (is).
Mé minihá kaṇayi.
MI MÍHÁ KAṆU.

18. Of this man the wife deaf (is); to her
Mé miniha-gé am̆buva bihiriyi; ẹ-ṭa
MI MÍHÁ-GÉ AMBI BÍRU; ÉNÁYA
our words heard are not.
apé vacana ẹsenné nẹ.
AHARAMEŃ-GE BAS-TAŃ NU-IVÉTE.

19. I this night well have slept.
Mama mé rẹ hon̆da-ṭa nidá-gatimi.
MA MI RÉ RAŃGALA NIDAIFÍME.
I very early have risen.
Mama itá udayen nẹgiṭṭemi.
MA VARA' HENDUNU TEDU-VEJJÍME.

20.

Haste	make! (Make haste!)
Ikman	*karapan!*
AVAHA'	HADA!

The sun	in a short time	will set.
Ira	*ikmana-ṭa*	*basinnéya.*
IRU	AVAHA'	TIRIVIDÁNÉ.

21.

To us	the road	invisible somewhat (is);
Apa-ṭa	*maga*	*no-peṇena tarama-ṭa;*
AHARAMENNA'	MAGU	NU-BELÉNÉ;

very	dark	it will become.
bohoma	*andhakára*	*vévi.*
VARAKA'	ADIRI BOḌU	VIDÁNÉ.

22.

To us	moonlight	will it fall?
Apa-ṭa	*haṇda-pána*	*lẹbé-da?*
AHARAMENNA'	HANDU-VARU	DÉNEBÁ?

23.

I	do not know.	I	so	think.
Mama	*no-danimi.*	*Mama*	*esé*	*sitimi.*
MAṚA	NÉNGE.	MAṚA	EHEŃ	HÍVANI.

I	in my mind	accept (the idea).
Mama	*kalpaná*	*karami.*
MA	HITU-GAI	GANNANI.

24.

In the jungle	many	snakes	are found;
Kẹlé	*bohó*	*sarpayó*	*iṇditi;*
VALU-GAI	LAKKA	HARUFÁ-TAŃ	HUNNATI;

a snake	us	if it bite,	we	die
sarpayek	*apa*	*daṣṭakaḷot,*	*apa*	*nasiṇ-ṭa*
HARUFÁ		DÁ-GATIYÁ,	AHAREŃ	MARUVÁŃ

must.
ónẹya.
VÁNÉ.

25.

Fear	not!
Bayaveṇ-ṭa	*epá!*
BIRU	NU-GANÉ!

26. I the letter to you will send;
Mama liyuma uṁba-ṭa evannemi;
TIMANNÁ E SIṬI KALÉYA' FONUVÁNAME;
you writing (and) reading understand?
uṁba-ṭa liyaṇ-ṭa kiyavaṇ-ṭa puḷuvan-da?
KALÉ LIYÁKA KIYAVÁKA DANNUM-HÉ?

27. In last year the monsoon (it) broke
Giya avuruddé ṛitu-sulaṅ bahiṇ-ṭa paṭangatté
DIYA AHARU MÓSAMU-VÁI JEHUNI
when?
kavadáda?
KOṄ-IRU?

28. From your country to Ceylon you
Uṁbé divayiné siṭa Laṅkáva-ṭa
KALÉ-GE RAṚUṄ OLUDUKARÁYA' KALÉ
having sailed how many days (were spent)?
nęven íma-ṭa kopamaṇa kal gatavi-da?
OḌI-GOS-LEFÍ KIHÁ DUVAHUṄ?

29. Of the king the house in what town (is it)?
Aga nuvara kóka-da?
RASKAMU-GE GÉ KOṄ RAṚEN-HÉ?

30. Of the there dwelling inhabitants the number
Ehi kopamaṇa janayá vásaya-karad-da?
ETÁ-GAI HUNNA RAYYATUṄ-GE ADADÁ
(is) how large?
KIHÁVARU?

Notes to III. 2.

1. IMBA = S. *uṁba*. Also used KALÁ-GE, or KALÉGEFÁNU-GE, according as the person spoken to is of higher or lower rank. MAMMÁ, "mother," is more respectful than AMÁ. The form -YÁ occurs after vowels; -Á, -ÁI after consonants. *Cf.* III. 3: A 1; III. 3: B 1.

2. KOKKÁ. "Brother" or "sister"; may be more clearly indicated by FIRIHEŃ and AŃHEŃ. See III. 1: 12, Note. HURIŃGE' = S. iṇdageṇa.

3. HEDEŃ. Passive of HADAŃ, "to make"; in Siṇhalese also, according to Gunasékara, hẹdé, in the sense of "it is produced," "it grows," is used. The sign of the plural is represented by -TAŃ or -TA, perhaps more correctly -TA'.

7. KO'. Gunasékara writes KOG. *Cf.* p. 27. It serves here, like the S. *koṭa*, to form Adverbs. So in the following sentences.

8. FASÉHA. In L.V., p. 139 = Persian *árám*, "rest," "peace." According to Sheik Ali, FASÉHAKAM means "health."

10. ETA-GAI. "Within." *Cf.* ETI, III. 1: 26, and ETÁ-GAI, III. 2: 30.

11. I recorded EKU-KOFFÍM, RÓ-KOFFÍM, &c. KOFFÍM = KO'FÍM, in Máldivian writing.

The forms are constructed in the same way as GEŃGOS-FÍM, "we brought"; KAKKÁ-FÍM, "we cooked"; HIFAI-FÍMU, "we caught." The Auxiliary Verb included in -FÍM I compare with the S. *piyanu*. As regards this use, see Geiger, *Litteratur und Sprache der Singhalesen*, p. 83.

12. ULUVANI. Plural; the Singular would be ULANI. See III. 2: 15.

13. DÓNIYAKA. DÓNI, according to Ibráhim Dídí, is employed on many islands instead of ORU; GONḌUDORA' = GONḌUDO', Geiger; GOḌUDAN, L.V., p. 7.

14. VEJJEVÉ. Gunasékara states that in colloquial Siṇhalese *vecca* or *vejja* is frequently used in the sense of "was," "became." NIYÁ-VEGEŃ: the meaning is not clear to me. MIHÁRU, MÍHÁR (MIHAIRU), "present (time)."

16. VIHAYEPPEVÉ. Gunasékara has VEHAYEPPEVÉ. I find VIHÁN, L.V., p. 186 = Persian *zádan*: KUREŃ = S. *keren*, "out," "of," "under."

18. ENÁYA', &c. Passive construction, which at times is preferred in Máldivian: "to her our words are not heard." Christopher, IVEŃ, "to hear," "to mind."

22. DÉNEBÁ, or DÉNEHÉ. Future, with an Interrogative Particle: "will be given?" See III. 2: 24 and 29.

23. NÉŃGÉ. Christopher, ENGEDÁŃ, "to learn," "acquire" = S. *hęngenu.*

24. DÁ-GATIYÁ. Conditional; *cf.* VÍYÁ, III. 3: B 5.

26. DANNUMHÉ. See Note 22 above. HÉ is an Interrogative Particle.

27. DIYA, HINGI, FÉBI. Synonyms, meaning "past." AHARU (older form, AVARADU) = S. *avurudu.* MÓSAMU-VÁI, *cf.* Arabic *mausim.*

3.—Stories * in Sinhalese and Maldivian, with literal line-for-line English version.

A.—The Horse and the Donkey.

1.	A horse	and a donkey
	Aṣvayek	*saha búruvek*
	AHAK-ÁI	HIMÁRAK-ÁI

together	on the road		were going.
eka	*maga*		*giyóya.*
EM-MAGUŃ		EKKULAVAYE'	HINGI-EVÉ.

---

* The Professor does not say where, when, or how he acquired these three "Stories," the originals of which he admits (*infra*, Section II.) are in "English."

The following explanation is possible:—

The tales occur (with several other like fables) in a small book entitled *Pleasant Stories*, formerly in the possession of the present Editor. When attached to His Majesty's Customs at Colombo in the Eighties, and able to give some little attention to the Máldive language, he got, by *vivâ voce* questioning, from chance Máldivians visiting the Port, rough summarized translations of some of these "Stories."

Subsequently his good friend, I. Ahmad Dídí, elder son of A. Ibráhim Dídí (who was returning to Málé, on the completion of a sound English education at the Richmond College, Galle), kindly undertook

2.	That	donkey's	back	upon	great	load
		Búruvá-gé	*piṭa*	*uḍa*	*loku*	*barak*
	E	HIMÁRU	BURIKAṚI	MACCA	LAKKA	BARU

because there was,	he	very	weary	became.
tibuna-nisá,	*úṭa*	*bohoma*	*vehesa*	*viya.*
HURI-NI,		VARA'	BALI	VEJJEVÉ.

3.	The donkey,	the horse	begged,	from	my	load
	E-tema				*magé*	*barin*
	HIMÁRU	AHU-GÁTA'	AHEPPEVÉ		MA-GE	BARUŃ

something	do thou	take away;	I	to thee
koṭasak		*ara-ganin;*	*mama*	*um̆ba-ṭa*
EBBAI	KALÉ	NAGAHAṚE;	MA	KALÉ-GE

blessing wishing shall be.
stutivantava siṭinnemi-yi kíya.
HÉUKAŃ GOVÁ VERIYAKA VANÁME.

4.	But	the horse,	this	word	not hearing,
	Ehet	*aşvayá,*	*í-ṭa*		*kan-no-dí,*
	EKAMAKU	AS,	MI	BAS	NÁHÁ,

went on.
giyéya.
HINGI-EVÉ.

---

to translate the book fully into Máldivian for his benefit. This was in 1890 (Letter, June 16: "I shall try my best to translate the *Stories* as soon as possible, with the greatest pleasure"); but, owing to Ahmad Dídí's repeated serious illnesses at Málé from Máldive "gift fever," as it is called, no progress could be made.

Five years later, Ahmad Dídí wrote (Letter, December 7, 1895): "The book of *Pleasant Stories* sent to me for translation into the Máldivian language will be sent to you now very soon, with its translation."

Doubtless the book came back to Ceylon shortly afterwards; ***but it never reached the Editor.***

If, mayhap, it fortunately fell into the hands of Professor Geiger (who was in Ceylon from December 8, 1895, to March 15, 1896), and is the source from which he drew the three "Stories" he gives, every satisfaction must be felt that Ahmad Dídí's generous, though belated and unintentionally deflected, aid has borne such valuable fruit by appearing in the present publication.—B., *Ed.*

5. A short time afterwards the donkey
Madu vélávaka-ṭa pasu búruvá
KUḌA IRU-KOLU FAHUŃ HIMÁRU

to the earth falling, died.
bima veṭi, muḷéya.
BIM MACCE VEṬṬIGEŃ, MARUVEJJEVÉ.

6. The donkey's master the horse's back upon
Búruvá himiyá ahu piṭa
HIMÁRU VERI-MÍHÁ AHU MACCA

the whole load laid.
muḷu bara peṭevvéya.
HURIHÁ BARU-TA' LÁJPPEVÉ.

7. Towards the in-misfortune
Vipattiya-ṭa
TADUKAMU-GAI-YÁI

and-sorrow-being people,
saha duka-ṭa pemiṇiyaṇ-ṭa,
DATI-GAI-YÁI ULÉ MÍS-MÍHUŃ MACCA,

merciful be!
karuṇá-karapan!
KUḶUVERIYAKA HURÉ!

Notes to III. 3: A.

2. HURI-NI. Terminatioṇ -NI = S. *-niyá.* MACCA = S. *matu, mallé*

3. NAGAHAṚÉ. Imperative: NAGAŃ, "lift up," "take."

5. KUḌA; KOLU. Both = "small." The former could be dispensed with.

6. BARU-TA'. Gunasékara, again, has BARU-TAG. *Cf.* p. 27.

B.—The Wise Judge.

1.

Two women,	a child	on account of,
Strívaru ḍe-ḍenek,	*daruvek*	*gẹṇa,*
DE AŃHENUŃ,	EMME KUJJAYAṬ	-ṬAKÁI,

the one with the other	quarrelling,
ekí anikí-ṭa	*dos pavaramin,*
EKAKU MACCA ANEKAKU	KUŃ ARUVÁIGEŃ,

a Judge	to	came.
viniṣcaya-kárayek	*laṇga-ṭa*	*áváhuya.*
EMME NIYÁYAVERI	GÁTAŃ	ATUVEJJEVÉ.

2.

The two women	said,	from me	that child
Ohu de-dena-ma	*kívóya,*	*mama*	*daruvá*
E DE AŃHENUŃ	BUNI BAHAKÍ,	TIMANNÁ	E KUJJÉ

is born,	that child	to me belongs.
vẹduvemi,	*daruvá*	*magéya-yi.*
VIHAIFÍMEVÉ,	E KUJJÁ	TIMANNÁGA' EVÉ.

3.

The Judge	the executioner	calling,
Viniṣcaya-kárayá	*vadakaruvá-ṭa*	*aṇḍagasá,*
NIYÁVERI	MINI-MARÁ-MÍHÁ	GOVÁGEŃ,

the child	in two parts	cutting	it,
daruvá	*deka-ṭa*	*kapá*	*eya,*
E KUJJÁYA'	DEFALIYAKA'	FALÁGEN	EYITI,

to the two women	give,	he directed.
striṇ-ṭa	*deva-yi,*	*aṇa-kaḷéya.*
E DE AŃHENUNNA'	DEHEṚE,	BUNI.

4.

This	word	hearing,	of the two women,	one
Mé	*vacanaya*	*asá,*	*é striṅ-gen,*	*ekiyak*
MI	BAS	EHI,	AŃHENUŃ KUREŃ,	EKAKU

silent	remained.
niṣṣabdava	*siṭiyáya.*
AŃGAYIŃ	NUBUNE HURI.

5. The other woman to weep beginning, my
Anik strí aṇdaṇ-ṭa paṭan-geṇa, magé
ANEŃ AMBI ROŃ-FAṚÁIGEŃ BUNI, MA-GE

child do not kill! said: This Your (Honour's)
daruvá no-marava-yí! kíváya: Mé obavahansé-gé
DARI NU-MARÁṚE! MIÍ KALÉ-GE

decision if it be, by me the child is not taken.
viniṣcaya-nam, mama daruvá no-gaṇimi.
NIYÁKAŃ VÍYÁ, TIMANNAYA' DARI NU-LIBÉNÉ.

6. The Judge that woman the child's mother
Viniṣcaya-kárayá ẹ mava
NIYÁVERI-MÍHÁ E KABULÉGE DARI-GE AMÁ

to be recognising, the child to her
bava dẹna, daruvá ẹ-ṭa
KAŃ KAṚAVARA DENIGEŃ, DARI E KABULÉGEYA'

giving, the other woman to prison he sent.
dí, anik hiragé-ṭa yẹvvéya.
DÍFAYA', ANEK-KABULÉGE JELA' FONOVÁFÍYEVÉ.

Notes to III. 3: B.

1. Suffix -ṬAKÁI', -ṬAKA. "With reference to": NIYÁYA-VERI, or NIYÁ-VERI.

3. DEFALIYAKA'. *Cf.* with S. *depaḷu-karaṇu*, and FALÁGEŃ with S. *paḷanu.*

5. Gunasékara writes FARÁIGEŃ and MARÁRÉ; as also, in III. 3: A 3, NAGAHARÉ, and in III. 3: B 3, DEHERÉ, not DEHEṚÉ.

6. KABULÉGE. The more respectful expression for "woman": ABI-KABULÉGE (for AMBI-KABULÉGE), "spouse" (Feminine); FIRI-KALÉGE, "spouse" (Masculine), L.V., p. 13. KAŃ = S. *kiyá*: KAṚAVARA = S. *niṣcaya-koṭa.*

C.—The Lion, the Ass, and the Jackal.

1. A jackal | and a lion | and an ass | hunting
Hivalek-ut | *siṇhayek-ut* | *koṭaluvek-ut* | *daḍayam karaṇ-ṭa*
HIYALAK-Á | VAGAK-Á* | HIMÁRAK-Á | SIKÁRU KURÁŃ

on account of, | into the forest | went.
onẹ́va, | *vala-ṭa* | *giyáhuya.*
VEGEŃ, | VALA' | VEDÉ.

2. Hunting | having finished, | the booty gained
Daḍayam | *koṭa nimavú,* | *vigaha lẹbunávú*
SIKÁRU | KO' AVADI VEGEŃ, | LIBUNUHÁ

meat | in a heap | collecting, | the ass
mas | *goḍaka-ṭa* | *ek-koṭa,* | *koṭaluvá-ṭa*
MAS-TÁ | FUÑÑAKA' | EK-KOFFÁ, | HIMÁRA'

in three parts | to divide, | the lion
tun-bhágayaka-ṭa | *bedan-ṭa,* | *siṇha-tema*
TIM-BAYA' | BAHÁŃ, | SIŃGÁ

commanded.
aṇa-kaḷéya.
AMRU-KOFFIYAVÉ.

3. The ass | the whole thing | collecting, | three parts
Koṭaluvá | *é siyalu dé* | *ek-koṭa,* | *tun-bhágayak*
HIMÁRU | E HURIHÁ TAKATI | EK-KO', | TIM-BAI

making, | to each one | (the) desired | share
koṭa, | *é é aya* | *kẹmati* | *bhágaya*
KOFFÁ, | EBEKALAKU | HITÁVÁ | BAYE'

to take | he told.
ganna-lesa | *kívéya.*
NAGAŃ | BUNEPPÉ.

---

* SINGÁ, S. *siṇha,* "lion," is used elsewhere in the Story correctly. The word here given, VAGAK, really means "tiger" (Sans. *vyágra*): MINI-KÁ VAGU, "man (or flesh) eating tiger."—B., *Ed.*

4. Thereupon the lion, greatly angered,
É saṉda siṉhayá, bohoma kópavi-geṇa,
E-HINDU SIŃGÁ-GÁTAK, VARA' RULIYÁS-GEŃ,
that donkey killed.
é koṭaluvá mará-dẹmméya.
E HIMÁRA' MARÁ-LEYJPPÉ.

5. Then the jackal to divide, he told.
Pasuva hivalá-ṭa bedaṇ-ṭa, kívéya.
DEN HIYAL-GÁTU-GA' BAHAŃ, BUNEPPÉ.

6. The jackal for himself a small part
Hivalá tamá-ṭa svalpa koṭasak
HIYALU TIMANNAYA' KUḌA ETIKOLEI
taking, the rest all the lion
ara-geṇa, itaru siyalu déval siṉhayá-ṭa
NAGÁFAYE', ITURU HURIHÁ TAKACCE SIŃGÁ
to take he told.
ganna-lesa kívéya.
NAGAŃ BUNEPPÉ.

7. The lion thereupon, greatly pleased,
Siṉhayá é-saṉda, bohó santóshayen,
SIŃGÁ E-HINDU, VARA' UFÁVEGEŃ,
the jackal asked: "Thus to divide,
hivalá-gen ẹsuvá: "Mesé bedíma-ṭa,
HIYAL-KUREŃ EHI: "TIYAHEŃ BEHI,
the reason what is (it)?"
karuṇu kavaréda?"
KAMAKI KOBÁHÉ?"

Notes to III. 3: C.

3. EBEKALAKU. *Cf.* KALÓ, "person." Originally it signifies "small," and indicates the common people. (Bell, *The Máldive Islands*, p. 63.)

4. SIŃGA-GÁTAK. See Notes to III. 1: 26.

IV.—MALDIVIAN LETTERS.*

1.—Maldivian Malim's Letter: † A.D. 1837.

(Christopher: *Journal, R.A.S., 1841, VI., pp. 73, 74.*)

In Galle being, of the Máldives to all people
GÁLI-GAI TIBI, DIVEHÍN-GE EMME KALUNNA'

of the Arab boats, ‡ of the Captain greetings
ARABU OḌI, MÁLIMÍ-KALÉGEFÁNU [1] *SALÁM*

at this time. At this town being boats,
MI FAHARA'. MI RAṚU-GAI HUṚI OḌI FAHAṚI,[2]

the Arab boats, Finladu § boats. the tribute boats,
ARAB OḌI, FINLADU OḌI, VEDUN OḌI,[2]

---

* In these Máldivian Letters the words printed in *italic capitals* appear in the original in *Arabic* characters.—B., *Ed.*

† See Plate III. Geiger's line-for-line *transcript* of the Máldivian text follows Wilson's adaptation of Christopher's original manuscript, with some alterations in the transliteration only.

Christopher wrote out the Máldive (GABUḶI TÁNA) characters as they appear in Plate III., placing his English transcript below the Máldivian text, under each word, *from left to right,* and interpolating a word-for-word translation between the two lines.

By relegating the Máldive Letter to a separate Plate, Dr. Wilson, his editor, was able to amend this obviously unsuitable arrangement. He transcribed the text—as, *mutatis mutandis,* reproduced by Professor Geiger—giving (with slight modification) Christopher's translation below it.

Geiger evidently preferred not to utilize the previous translations of 1837 and 1881 respectively, but to re-translate the text of both Letters direct, as there are differences in his German renderings (not due to conversion into English) from those of Christopher and Bell.

The *original translations* are, therefore, reprinted in Appendix D for comparison.—B., *Ed.*

‡ Geiger uses the plural, *die Boote* ("boats"), throughout. This is wrong: OḌI FAHAṚI (plural), "boats"; OḌI (singular), "boat."—B., *Ed.*

§ FINLADU. An island in Tiladummati Atoll, the penultimate Atoll of the group to the North.—B., *Ed.*

the (Chief) Judge's boats, Ahmad Dídí's boats,
FAḌIYÁRU ODI,[2] AHAMMÁ DÍDÍ ODI,[2]

of the Mándu House the boats, of the Hiti-gas-daṛu House
MÁNDU-GÉ ODI,[2] HITI-GAS-DAṚU-GÉ

the boats. At this time all the people
ODI.[2] MÍ FAHARA' EMMA KALUN

in health being are. At your
GADA-VE EBA-TIBÚVEVE.[3] TIYÁ

port occurring news you should send.
RAṚU-GAI HUṚI KABARUN FONUVÁTI.

At this port occurring news I send.
MI RAṚU-GAI HUṚI KABARU MI[4] FONUVÍE.

From England a new Governor is come.
VILÁTUN AU BOḌÁ-SÁHIBEN[5] ATUEVE.

England's King is dead.* Many million
VILÁTU RASGE MARUVEJJEVE. LAKKA GINA

strings (of) greetings. At this port fish we sold:
FAṚU' *SALÁM*. MI RAṚU MAS VIKKÍ:

fish from Himití (for) seventy-seven dollars,
HIMITÍ-MAS[6] HAN-DIHA HAT RIYÁLAYA',

fish of the Málé Atoll (for) sixty-seven,
MÁLE-ATOḶU MAS FAS-DOḶOS HATAKA',

fish of F.-f.-k. (for) forty-seven.
FÁDIN-FUḶU-KIRÁ-MAS † SÁḶIS HATAKA'.

---

* The date of the Letter (not given in it) is fixed very approximately by the double intimation sent from Colombo. William IV. died on June 20, 1837. The Right Hon. James Alexander Stewart Mackenzie assumed the Governorship of Ceylon on November 7 of the same year. Christopher sent the Máldive Letter, with his Vocabulary, to Dr. Wilson in April, 1838.—B., *Ed.*

† See footnote * on page 52, *infra*.—B., *Ed.*

Thus having sold occurring,
MI-HIDAN VIKKAIGEN TIBI AGÍMIVEVE,[7]

many million strings (of) greetings. I write,
LAKKA GINA FAṚUN *SALÁM.* MI LIYUNÍ,

here being on Thursday.
MI-TAN-VÍ BARUSFATI DUVAHUN.

God if He permits, fourteen days I
MÁT-KALÁGE RUSSEVÍYÁI, SAUDA DUVAHU AḶU-GAḌU

shall remain. My resolve stands firm.
FURÁNEMEVE.[8] * HITAI HUṚI-MEVE.

Translation.

The Captain of the Arabian ships (sends) greeting to all the Máldivians staying in Galle.

The boats which at present are in this harbour are the Arabian boats, Finladu boats, the boats with Presents, the (Chief) Judge's boats, Ahmad Dídí's boats, the boats of the Mándu House, and the boats of the Hiti-gas-daṛu House.

All the people are well at the present time.

You should send us the news which you have (learnt) at your port. I send the news which we have (heard) here.

A new Governor has come from England. The King of England is dead.

Many thousand greetings.

---

* FURÁNEMEVE here has nothing to do with FURÁN, "to fill": it = S. *piṭatvenavá*, "start." Both Christopher (*lit.*, "I shall have sailed") and his editor, Dr. Wilson (*lit.*, "sailed I shall be," "I shall sail"), were, therefore, quite right in their renderings.

The word is in use throughout the Máldives from North to South, in the sense of "starting (on a voyage)," "sailing." Thus: MA BUNBÁYA(N) DAHARÉ FURANÍ (Málé); MA BUNBÁRA E(Ṛ)NÁVE FURA(Ṛ)-NÉNÍ (Fua Mulaku), "I will sail for Bombay."—B., *Ed.*

In this place we sold fish, thus: from Himití for 77 dollars, from Málé Atoll for 67, from . . . . for 47. *

A thousand greetings.

I write this from here on Thursday. God willing, I shall remain † here fourteen days yet. That is my intention.

Notes.

1 The first sentence is wrongly understood by Christopher. KALÉGEFÁNU is the title of the particular MÁLIMÍ. ‡

2 FAHAṚI. Obscure. In Christopher it is not translated. §

In what follows, the persons or families (MÁNDU-GÉ, HITI-GAS-DAṚU-GÉ, the latter being translated by Christopher as "bitter-tree-corner-house") to whom the boats belong are named.

For FAḌIYÁRU, *cf.* L.V., p. 104; Bell, *The Máldive Islands,* p. 59.

---

* Geiger leaves FÁDIN-FUḶU-KIRÁ-MAS untranslated. Christopher (Wilson copying, with omission of "the") has "the FÁDING-FUḶU weighed fish." Both misunderstand KIRÁ in the particular connection. "Until recently the different pieces of dried *bonito*, or 'Máldive fish' (KAḶU-BILI-MAS, S. *um̆balạkaḍa*), had a relative value to one another. Thus, 4 MEDU MAS (the middle slices) = 2 GAḌU MAS (the pieces along back and belly; considered best) = 7 HIMITÍ MAS (whole fish divided into four pieces; at Himití, and other islands of Nilandú and adjoining Atolls) = their weight of KIRÁ MAS (pieces between head and MEDU and GAḌU pieces)." (Bell, *The Máldive Islands*, p. 94.)

The words, therefore, mean "KIRÁ pieces (of Máldive fish) from FÁDIFFOLU Atoll."—B., *Ed.*

† See footnote * on page 51, *supra;* also footnote ‡ on page 53, *infra.* —B., *Ed.*

‡ Dr. Wilson supplemented Christopher's word-for-word translation with a running version of his own, intended to do little more than give the "summarized meaning" of the Máldive letter.

Geiger, not aware of this, has turned his guns on Christopher, whom he here unconsciously wrongs. Christopher—not incorrectly—translated MÁLIMÍ-KALÉGEFÁNU SALÁM, "the *salám* of the Málim Chief." This Wilson spoilt by separating the first two words, and rendering thus: "the Málim. The Chief's *salám*."

KALÉGEFÁNU is about equivalent to the Siṇhalese *Rálahámi*; KILA-GEFÁNU to Siṇhalese *Nilamé*.—B., *Ed.*

§ See footnote ‡ on page 49, *supra.*—B., *Ed.*

VEDUN OḌI is the boat which has to bring the Yearly Tribute of the Sultán to the English Governor in Colombo.

3 Christopher, GADA VEEBA TIBÚVEVE. With EBA, *cf.* above, III. 1 : 8, with Note ; GADA-VE = GADA-VI.

4 MI. Here MI, I believe, stands for MA : similarly below, MI LIYUNÍ.

5 SÁHIBEN. Only another method of writing SÁHIBE'. *Cf.* above.

6 HIMITÍ. The island home of Hasan-bin-Adam, mentioned above. *

7 Obscure. Christopher translates AGÍMIVEVE by "for the price." †

8 AḶU-GAḌU FURÁNEMEVE. Translated by Christopher as "sailed I shall be," "I shall sail." I am in doubt with respect to the second word. ‡

AḶU is "slave," and GAḌU or GANḌU often appears pleonastically at the end of words: *e.g.*, FÁRU-GAḌU, "wound"; BURU-GAḌU, "wheel." AḶU-GAḌU is a deferential mode of expressing the Pronoun of the First Person; just as in the following Letter (*cf.* Note 13) for the Pronoun of the Third Person.

FURÁNEMEVE belongs to FURÁN, "to fill"; thus, literally, "I shall complete fourteen days." *Cf.* also Note 14 to the following Letter. ‡

---

* The fame of Himití Island, in Nilandú Atoll, rests on the particular class of "Máldive fish" it specializes in.—B., *Ed.*

† The meaning of the sentence MI-HIDAN VI(R)KAIGEN TIBI AGÍMIVEVE is: "This is the price at which we have sold just now" (or "for the present").—B., *Ed.*

‡ See footnote * on page 51, *supra*.

Geiger is all abroad in his rendering here.

Christopher partially misunderstood SAUDA DUVAHU, which he translated (Wilson copying) "in fourteen days."

The sentence means: "It is my intention (HITAI HUṚI-MEVE) to sail (*lit.*, start) on the fourteenth day, God willing."—B., *Ed.*

2.—Missive from the Sultan of the Maldives : * A.D. 1795.

(Bell, "*The Máldive Islands*," *Ceylon, 1883, pp. 78–81.*)

Hail! The glorious, great-fame-possessing,
SUVASTÍ, SIRÍMATA, MAHÁ-SIRÍ-BARI,

in wisdom pre-eminent, from noble race sprung,
KUSA-FURADÁNA,[1] † SIRÍ KULA,

to the moon and the sun comparable ruler,
SADA IRA SIÁKA[2] † SÁSTURA,

the excellent warrior Sultán Hasan Núr-ud-dín
AUDÁNA[3] † KATTIRI *AS-SULṬÁN HASAN NÚR-UD-DÍN*

Iskandar, the warrior of the world, the great King,
ISKANDAR, KATTIRI BOVANA, MAHÁ-RAḌUN,

to the Colombo Governor's King,
KOḶUBU GORUNU DÓREVE KIYÁ[4] RASGEFÁNA',

here a thousand million strings greetings.
MI-TA' LAKKA HÁS FAṚU' SALÁM.

Of Your Excellency in Colombo formerly existing
MANIKUFÁNUME'-GE KOḶUBU-GAI IHU UḶU'VI

Kings (and) in this Máldivian kingdom
RASRASKALUNNÁI MI DIVEHI-RÁJJÉ-GAI

formerly existing Kings friendship
IHU UḶU'VI RASRASKALUNNÁI RA*ḦMAT*RIKA'

---

* See Plate IV.

† KUSA-FURADÁNA ; SIÁKA ; AUDÁNA. Regarding these, and all the other epithets, see the full explanations (ignored by Geiger) suggested in the Notes which accompanied the previous translation of this Missive of Sultán Ḥasan Núr-ud-dín (Bell, *The Máldive Islands*, pp. 78–81). They will be found reproduced in Appendix D.—B., *Ed.*

had existed to Your Excellency
BEHEṬṬEVI FADAI' ME [5] MANIKUFÁNÁI

we in our hearts friendship
TIMA' MANIKUFÁNU HI'-FUḶU-GAI [6] *RAHMAT*

cherishing are on Your Excellency's part
BAHAṬṬAVAIGE' HUNNEVÍME MANIKUFÁNUME' KIBAI' [7]

wishing (it) are. Of this Máldivian kingdom
EDI TIBÍMÁVE. MI DIVEHI RÁJJEI'

a boat or vessel wrecked being to Your Excellency
OḌIE' DÓÑE' [8] BEHIGE' GOS MANIKUFÁNA'

a known place if it is, then you should send for,
XABARI-VÉ TANAKU TIBI-NAMA, E-BAYAKU [9] GE' DAVAI,

these people's welfare you should see to.
E MÍHU'-GE HAIHÚNU-KA' [10] BELLÁVUMÁI.

Against this kingdom an enemy
MI DIVEHI RÁJJEA' *ADÁ*VÁTTERIAKU

to Your Excellency if is known, to him
MANIKUFÁNA' EGIJJE-NAMA, E-BAYAKA'

Your Excellency should not lend countenance.
MANIKUFÁNUME' NU-RUSSEVUMEVE.

Of Your Excellency worthy though it be not, a little
MANIKUFÁNUMENNÁI ARAFÓDI GE' NUVÁ, KUḌA

present (by) Ahmad the Under Treasurer
HADIAYÁ-KOḶA-KÁI [11] *AḤMAD* KUḌA BAḌÉRI KÉVÍ [12]

to you we (have) sent. By him intimated a wish
TIÁ FANUVVÍMU. MI AḶÁ DENNEVI KAME'

you should fulfil. On his part a mistake
KURAVVAI. MI AḶU' [13] KIBAI *TAXSÍRE'*

if it happen	you should pardon.	By first monsoon
VIAS	*MU'AF* KURAVVAI.	AVVALU MÚSUMU-GAI

....	wishing	we are.
FURUVÁ KAMA'[14] *	EDI-VAḌAIGE'	HUNNEVÍME.

In the Hejira year 1210.
1210 *SANAT.*

Translation.

Hail! The glorious, renowned, most wise, nobly-born ruler, comparable to the moon and the sun, the heroic warrior *Sultán Hasan Núr-ud-dín Iskandar*, the warrior, the great King of the earth, to the King of the Governor in Colombo,† many thousand greetings from here.

As friendship has existed between the former Kings of Your Excellency in Colombo and the former Kings of the Máldivian kingdom, we also bear friendship to Your Excellency in our hearts, and desire the same on Your Excellency's part.

Should any kind of boat or vessel of this country be wrecked, if the place is known, Your Excellency should have the people brought away and care taken for their well-being.

If any one is known to Your Excellency who is inimicably disposed to this country, Your Excellency should not tolerate (such person).

Although it does not correspond to the dignity of Your Excellency, I have sent you a little present by the Under Treasurer, Ahmad. If he intimates any wish, you should (kindly) gratify it: if a mistake is made on his part, you should (kindly) pardon it.

I await his return by the first monsoon.

---

* FURUVÁ KAMA', "starting" (*i.e.*, sailing).—B., *Ed.*

† KIYÁ = S. *kiyá*, "called." GORUNU DÓREVE KIYÁ RASGEFÁNA(Å), "to the Ruler styled the Governor"; not "to the King of the Governor" (*an den Kōnig des Gouverneurs*), as Geiger has it.—B., *Ed.*

Notes.

1 FURADÁNA. Sans. *pradhána*. But what is KUSA ? *

2 A difficult word. I should think it is corrupted from Sans. *cháyá*, " shadow " ; here " image " = S. *sé*. *

3 AUDÁNA. I here take for Sans. *avadána*, in the significance of " heroic deed." *

4 Could the word, to which KIYÁ seems to point, be a proper name ? †

5 Not completely clear. BEHEṬṬEVI belongs to a Passive Verb, BAHAṬṬAŃ (*cf.* BAHAṬṬAVAIGE'). In Christopher it is = " to place," " to arrange." ‡

6 TIMA' MANIKUFÁNU. Literally, " My (Our) Excellency." HI' FUḶU = HIŃ-FUḶU ; HIŃ, " heart " ; FUḶU, a pleonastic epithet, as, for example, in DARI-FUḶU, and more frequently.

7 KIBAI'. *Cf.* QUIBAT, " side," in Pyrard.

8 As regards OḌI and DÓNI (here DÓÑE'), see Notes to III. 2 : 13.

9 My helper gave me forms of verbs like EBÁE-MÍHUŃ DIYA, " they go " ; EBÁE-MÍHUŃ RONI, " they weep," &c. This EBÁE is in each case put in for comparison.

10 Uncertain. HAIHÚNU-KA' appears to be related to HÉU, " good." § KA' (S. *kam ;* P. *kamma*) often forms abstract terms: *e.g.*, RAẔMATRIKA' above, which appears to be a corruption from RAẔMATTERIKA'.

11 For KUḌA and KOḶA, *cf.* Notes to III. 3 : A 5.

---

* See footnote † on page 54, *supra*.—B., *Ed.*

† See footnote † on page 56, *supra*.—B., *Ed.*

‡ BEHE(Å)ṬEVI FADAI(Å), " as existed before."—B., *Ed.*

§ HAIHÚNU-KA(Å), " wants," or " welfare."—B., *Ed.*

[12] BAḌÉRI. This, as Bell states, is a title, which originally only belonged to the Treasurer (Sans. *Bhánḍágárika*), but subsequently was also applied to other persons of rank. The word KÉVÍ is obscure. *

[13] For MI AḶÁ, MI AḶUN, *cf.* Note [8] to preceding Letter.

[14] The conclusion is not quite clear to me. According to Bell, the meaning is, "allow him (the Ambassador) to return in the (first) favourable monsoon." †

In Christopher, VAḌÁIGENNAVÁŃ, "to go," is found. To me the verb appears to be merely periphrastic; like the use of the S. *vadinu*.

In FURUVÁ KAMA' there must be included some idea like "return." ‡

---

* KÉVÍ. Perhaps = NÉVI, "tindal" (Bell, *The Máldive Islands*, pp. 63, 80).—B., *Ed.*

† A(Å)VALU MÚSUMU-GAI. More closely, "at the beginning of the monsoon" (or "season").—B., *Ed.*

‡ See footnote * on pages 51, 56, *supra*.—B., *Ed.*

SECTION II.

THE GRAMMAR OF THE MALDIVIAN LANGUAGE.*

The desire to study Sinhalese in connection with the dialects most closely allied to it caused me, during my stay in Ceylon,† to follow the study of the still very little known Máldivian Language, so far as time and opportunity were available.

My interest has not diminished with the great distance which now separates me from my beloved Ceylon. On the contrary, it has only increased; and extends not only to the language, but to the people of the Máldives, their civilization, and their history.

I think that each one of us, within the sphere of his studies, has a special, narrower province, in which he busies himself with particular predilection and inward zeal, and to which he always returns. Such a province to me, at this time, are the distant Máldive Islands, surrounded by the blue waves of the Indian Ocean.

At first it was the special attraction of the new and unknown which drew me. I must confess, even at the risk of being blamed by one or other of my fellow students, that I was always very susceptible to this charm. With each step forward in the Máldivian wilderness my wish became stronger, to perform, in a modest sphere, the work of the pioneer, and at least to break a little new ground here and there.

Our knowledge of the Máldive Language up to the present time has been indeed scanty.

Only the first narrow track was cut by the "Vocabularies" published by Pyrard and Christopher.‡ They gave scarcely

---

* *Cf. Sitzungsber. der K. Bayer,* Akademie d. W., 1900, p. 641 *seq.*

† From December 8, 1895, to March 15, 1896. (*Reise nach Ceylon in Winter, 1895-1896.*)—B., *Ed.*

‡ See Appendix A.—B., *Ed.*

any explanation of the Structure of the Language and the Grammar of the Máldivians. Of Máldivian Texts, only two incantations (given by Bell) are known,* as well as two short Letters, communicated by Christopher † and Bell. ‡

The results which these Texts afforded for the knowledge of Máldivian Grammar are, indeed, extremely scanty. Besides, there is much in the Letters, especially in the second, which is difficult and obscure.

I, therefore, at the beginning, directed my aim to recording simple Sentences, as well as connected Stories, in addition to isolated Grammatical Forms.

My helpers, when in Colombo, were Ibráhim Dídí; § and since (through the aid of my friend, A. Mendis Gunasékara, Mudaliyár) the Bengáli merchant Sheik Ali, who, having lived many years on the Máldives, was a past master in Máldivian.

---

* Published in the *Journal, R.A.S., Ceylon Branch,* 1881, VI., p. 121.

† *Journal, R.A.S.*, 1840, VI., p. 73.

‡ Bell, *The Máldive Islands*, Colombo, p. 78.

§ *Cf.* the Account of my Journey in the *Sitzungsber. der K. Bayer,* Akademie d. W., 1896, p. 214.

[Professor Geiger does the scantiest justice in these "Studies" to that very courteous gentleman, A. Ibráhim Dídí Effendi, Dorhiméná-kilagefánu, Prime Minister to His Highness the Sultán of the Máldive Islands, to whose kind consideration the Professor owed so much in the prosecution of his Máldivian research.

With infinite patience and condescension the Prime Minister seems to have allowed himself to be "bombarded" for three days on end by a continuous "fire" of wearying linguistic questions, until—the Professor is fain to admit—he, very naturally, "grew tired" (*ermüdet schien*).

The invaluable aid, ungrudgingly rendered, has been barely acknowledged here, or elsewhere (see *supra*, page 11, footnote *); though the Professor pays special and well-deserved compliments to A. Mendis Gunasékara, Mudaliyár, and the late Sheik Ali.

The following paragraph (kindly translated by Mr. C. H. Collins, Honorary Secretary of the Ceylon Branch of the Royal Asiatic Society) appears in Geiger's *Ceylon Tagebuchblätter und Reiseerinnerungen* (Wiesbaden, 1898) :—

"A favourable opportunity occurred, on which I had, indeed, not reckoned. My resourceful friend, Gunasékara Mudaliyár, came to know that the Prime Minister of the Sultán of the Máldives, Ibráhim Dídí Effendi, was staying in Colombo.

We must always count on double uncertainty—first, the possibility of verbal error having slipped into Sheik Ali's communications, and secondly, that I myself, in spite of all my pains, can hardly have completely escaped errors and misunderstandings.

The Texts which I have collected in Section I., and which are printed in the *Sitzungsber. der K. Bayer*, Akademie d. W., 1900, include :—

I.—Thirty Sentences in German and Máldivian.

II.—Thirty Sentences in German, Siṃhalese, and Máldivian.

III.—Three Fables in German, Siṃhalese, and Máldivian :—

A.—The Horse and the Donkey.

B.—The Wise Judge.

C.—The Lion, the Ass, and the Jackal.

IV.—Two Máldivian Letters (taken from Christopher and Bell).

I must state plainly, that the Fables, which have well-known titles, are not Máldivian originals, but have been translated, from English sources,* into Máldivian. In spite of this, I believe that with the publishing of the Texts a good step further forward has been taken.

I hope that, through the assistance of the British Government in Colombo (to whom I have applied), I shall succeed in

---

"I sought him in the house of his host, which was not far from my bungalow, and found him prepared to acquiesce in my desires. Not without a certain natural dignity, such as the more distinguished Muhammadans often possess, and at first not without a certain hesitancy, he met me in the verandah. His mistrust, if his hesitancy proceeded from that cause, quickly vanished, and we understood each other excellently.

"For three days a lively play of question and answer went on. When Dídí seemed tired, one of his companions took over the conversation in his place. He was an intelligent man, and, like Dídí himself, spoke tolerable English."

Small wonder—as the Professor himself adds ingenuously—that the "servants stood around, staring and amazed, and perhaps considered me, with my singular tastes, a trifle cracked!" (*hielt mich mit meinen absonderlichen neigungen vielleicht auch fur ein wenig verrücht!*).—B., *Ed.*]

* See *supra*, page 42, footnote *.—B., *Ed.*

getting more extensive Texts in the Máldivian Language; and especially copies of the Inscriptions which are still to be found on the Máldives. The knowledge of the Old Writing, in which these Inscriptions are cut,* seems, besides, to be confined to single persons.

I myself shall never again have an opportunity of a journey to Ceylon, however willing I may be to undertake it. The greatness of the distance gives rise to many difficulties.

Thus, the principal object of my "Máldivian Studies" must be, to put in motion an energetic beginning to *Scientific Investigation of the Máldivian Language on the very spot;* where alone it can really be carried out with satisfactory results.

In the following pages I intend to arrange, first, the Grammatical Materials contained in the Texts collected by me; then to complete it from the Forms and Paradigms which I wrote down in Colombo.

It need hardly be said that herein no claim is put forward to a completely finished account of the Máldivian Language.

---

* With the exception of tombstone records—of which Mr. Bell, when at Málé in 1879, copied three or four carved in the old characters (DIVES AKURU), as well as the new (GABUḶI TÁNA)—it is improbable that real inscriptions have survived on the Islands, save such Arabic epigraphs as that round the Tower of the Chief Mosque at Málé.—B., *Ed.*

I.—SUBSTANTIVES.

(a) Expression of the Numbers.

Definite Article Forms.

E',* "the elephant"; EMME ETE', "an elephant"; ETTA', "elephants."

MÍHÁ, "the human being"; EMME MÍHE', "a human being"; MÍHUŃ, "human beings."

MI GAS, "this tree"; EMME GAHE', "a tree"; GAS-TA', "trees."

FOI, "the book"; FOTE', "a book."

OFI, "the twig"; OFI-TA', "twigs."

MALE', "a flower"; MÁ, "flowers."

MULE', "a root"; MÚ, "roots."

Compare the Plural Forms in the Text, like FAS KUDIŃ, "five children" (III. 1 : 8); HATARU DARI, "four children" (III. 2 : 16); TÍM-MÍHU', "three people" (III. 1 : 7); KIHÁ DUVAHUŃ, "in how many days?" (III. 2 : 28); RAṚU-GAI HUṚI KABARUN, "the news at the port" (Málim's Letter).

Further, MÍDA-TA', "rats" (III. 2 : 7); HARUFÁ-TA', "snakes" (III. 2: 24); DIVEHI-RUT-TA', "coconut palms" (III. 2: 4).

---

* The mute sound (closing of the top of the throat) which appears in Máldivian at the end of a word in the place of different consonants—here, *e.g.*, for T—is regularly transcribed by me as (the sign) ' in the words which follow. The Máldivians themselves, who have no fixed orthography, write this sound variously as N or Ṛ. The symbol for Ṛ is very close to N and (AVIENI, shown as) ', and are interchangeable.

[See *supra*, pages 27–28, footnote †. The Máldive sign for Ṛ is easily differentiated from that for N by its having but one loop, instead of two, in the upper or horizontal part of the letter (*cf.* Máldivian Letters given in Section I., Plates III., IV.). The sign for AVIENI is quite unlike both Ṛ and N, resembling roughly the Arabic numeral ٨, "8." —B., *Ed.*]

Sometimes, in the formation of the Plural, the Substantive is doubled: FAFFALÓ-TA', "fruits" (from FAL-FALÓ); MÍS-MÍHUŃ, "human beings" (III. 3: A 7).

The Particle indicating the Plural is pronounced TA, or, more accurately, TA'. I also heard TAŃ.

In Máldivian letters we find TAN or TA' (*cf.* the Note).

In writing in Siṃhalese characters, as is sometimes done by my friend, A. Mendis Gunasékara, Mudaliyár, at times TAG appears. The G here is to express the closing of the top of the throat.*

Indefinite Article Forms.

Forms with the so-called Indefinite Article are SIṬIYE', "a letter" (III. 1: 23); BAYE', "a share" (III. 3: C 3); OḌIE', "a boat" (Sultán's Missive); BALÁ-MÍHAKU, "a messenger" (III. 1: 22; at the end of the sentence: MÍHEKA); EKAKU, "one," "the one," Masculine and Feminine (III. 2: 16; III. 3: B 1 and 5); EMME KUJJAYAṬ-ṬAKÁI (III. 3: B 1; from AK-ṬAKÁI); AHAK-ÁI HIMÁRAK-ÁI, "a horse and an ass" (III. 3: A 1); HIYALAK-Á, VAGAK-Á, HIMÁRAK-Á, "a jackal, a lion, and an ass" (III. 3: C 1).

(b) Expression of the Cases.

1.—Genitive.

MI MÍHÁ-GE AMBI, "this man's wife" (III. 2: 18); E SORU-GE BAFÁYA', "to the father of the boy" (III. 1: 3); FANSÁS KÁṚI-GE AGA, "the price of fifty coconuts" (III. 2: 5); RÁJJÉ-GE GOI, "the climate of the country" (III. 2: 8); DAṚI-GE AMÁ, "the child's mother" (III. 3: B 6). A Genitive Plural is GAS-GAHU-GE FAI, "the leaves of the trees" (III. 1: 29).

There is no need to remark that the Genitive formation (-GE) of the Máldivian Language is the same as the Siṃhalese *gé*. As regards this, see Geiger, *Litteratur und Sprache der Singhalesen* (*Ind. Grdr.*, I., 10, p. 62).

---

* *Cf. infra.*

I have written the Máldivian -GE (not -GÉ); but I note that the length of the final vowel, the E, is very uncertain. Not my own writing only, but that of the Máldivians also varies frequently (in this respect).

The Genitive relation can also be expressed by Compound Words.

Thus, E SORU BAFÁYA' is found, beside E SORU-GE BAFÁYA'. So also E HIMÁRU BURIKAṚI MACCA, "on the back of the donkey" (III. 3 : A 2); HIMÁRU VERI-MÍHÁ, "the owner of the donkey" (III. 3: A 6); KALÉ BÉBÉ ATA', "to your brother's hand" (III. 1 : 4).

2.—Instrumental.

EM-MAGUŃ (= EK-MAGUŃ), "by means of the straight road" = "on the straight road" (III. 3: A 1); DIVEHI-RUKAŃ, "with coconut wood" (III. 2 : 6); BALIYIŃ, "by illness" (III. 2 : 8); AŃGAYIŃ, "with the mouth" (III. 3 : B 4).

The first two admit of different meanings, but the last two show the same mode of formation as the Siṇhalese, with Inanimate Substantives.

3.—Dative.

BAFÁYA', "to the father" (III. 1 : 3); MI-TANA', "to this place" = "hither" (III. 1: 23); VALA', "to the jungle," "in the jungle" (III. 2: 9) = S. *kęlé-ṭa;* GEYA', "to the house," "in the house" (III. 2: 11) = S. *gé-ṭa;* GONḌUDORA', "to the sea coast," "on the shore (gone)" (III. 2: 13); JELA', "to prison" (III. 3 : B 6) = S. *hira-gé-ṭa;* TIM-BAYA', "in three parts (to divide)" (III. 3: C 2) = S. *tun-bhágayaka-ṭa;* FUÑÑNAKA' EK-KOFFÁ, "in a heap gathering" (III. 3: C 2) = S. *goḍaka-ṭa ek-koṭa;* DÓNIYAKA' ARÁNUME, "we will embark on the boat" (III. 2 : 13).

Compare, further, E DE AŃHENUNNA', "(give it) to the two women" (III. 3 : B 3) = S. *stríṇ-ṭa;* AHARAMENNA', "for us" (III. 2 : 22) = S. *apa-ṭa;* TIMANNAYA', "for himself" (III. 3 : C 6) = S. *tamá-ṭa;* KALÉYA', "to you (I shall send)" (III. 2 : 26) = S. *um̆ba-ṭa;* E-KABULÉGEYA', "to her (giving)" (III. 3 : B 6) = S. *ẹ-ṭa.*

Also -GÁTA, "to," "in the neighbourhood of": *e.g.*, AHARA-MEŃ-GÁTA', "to us" (III. 2: 8) = S. *apa vetaṭa ;* NIYÁYAVERI-GÁTA', "to the Judge" (III. 3 : B 1) = S. *viniṣcaya-kárayek laṇga-ṭa*, Datives of the suffix -GAI.

The writing of the Dative varies between -AN', -A', -AṚ, -AG, -A. I heard -A' or -AŃ (see the Text); but have here used the spelling -A'.

I think that the Máldivian Dative formation corresponds to the Siṇhalese *-ṭa*, the sound of which is very close to -ṚA ; and that instead of Ṛ being suppressed after the disappearance of the short final vowel, the closing of the top of the throat has been introduced.

In just the same way, from the Siṇhalese *koṭa* we get the Máldivian KO', "having done"; from the Siṇhalese *oṭu*, "camel," the Máldivian ó'.

But MAṚA, "to me," has retained the original Dative ending (= S. *maṭa*): *e.g.*, FOI MAṚA BADI, "give me the book"; E NÓKIRU MAṚA GENÁI SIṬIYE', "the servant brought me a letter" (III. 1 : 2 and 21), &c.

The ending is preserved if there is a *lengthening of the word*, as, *e.g.*, in the Sentence (III. 1: 28) E MÉVA VETUNI GAHUŃ BIMAṚÉ, "the fruit fell from the tree (on to the ground)" = S. *bima-ṭa*. The É added at the end, which appears to correspond to the *-ya* ending sentences in Siṇhalese, has in this place prevented the Ṛ from becoming mute.*

As in Siṇhalese, the Dative appears in Máldivian in Sentences of Comparison.

Thus, *e.g.*, MI GAS UHÉ E GAHA' VUREŃ, † "this tree is higher than that tree" (III. 1 : 14).

---

* This is the general rule, but it is liable to occasional exceptions : *e.g.*, VILÁ(T) or VILÁ(Å), "Europe"; MALÁ(T), "Malay"; SÓḶIYÁ(T), "Moor"; also FENFÓ(Å)RU(Å), "arecanut tree"; and in Anglo-Máldivian words, such as ÁGU-BÓṬ, "steamer" (? "cargo-boat," onomatopoetic).—B., *Ed.*

† The word VUREŃ, which also is found in Sentences III. 1 : 12, 15, and 18, after the Dative, is not clear to me. [Possibly connected with the Siṇhalese expletive *viru*.—B., *Ed.*]

Finally, it seems as if the same case were used to express the *agent*, in the construction of *Passive Sentences.*

To this category belong the Sentences AHARAMENNA' MAGU NU-BELÉNÉ VARAKA', "the road by us is not (to be) seen" (III. 2 : 21) = S. *apa-ṭa maga no-peṇena tarama-ṭa ;* ÉNÁYA' . . . NU-IVÉTE, "by her . . . is not heard" (III. 2 : 18) ; TIMANNAYA' DARI NU-LIBÉNÉ, "by me the child is not taken" (III. 3 : B 5).

4.—Ablative.

GAHUŃ, "(falls) from the tree" (III. 1 : 28) ; RAṚUŃ, "(came) from the town" (III. 1 : 22) ; MAGE BARUŃ, "(a part) of my load" (III. 3 : A 3) ; VILÁTUN, "from Europe" (Málim's Letter) ; MAHÁ-RADUN, "from the great King" (Sultán's Missive).

A suffix to indicate the Ablative is KUREŃ : *e.g.*, AŃHENUŃ KUREŃ EKAKU, "one of the women" (III. 3 : B 4) = S. *é strín-gen ekiyak ;* MAGE RAHUMAITTERÍN KUREŃ EKAKU, "one of my friends" (III. 2 : 16) = S. *magé mitrayek.*

Of course, KUREŃ corresponds to the S. *keren.* With regard to this, compare my *Etymologie des Singhalesischen*, No. 381.*

As an Ablative form, I mention VIYÁFÁRIVERIYAKU FURUŃ, "(sent) by a merchant" (III. 1 : 22).

In Siṇhalese, *pera* means "in front of" (see Clough). Whether *peren* is used in the Ablative sense of "from," exactly corresponding to the Máldivian FURUŃ, I do not know.†

5.—Locative.

The Locative Case is expressed by the suffix -GAI, -GA'. Whether it is connected with the S. *gává*, "near," as Gunasékara, in a private communication to me, suggests, I do not know. In the Dative form the suffix is -GÁTA' ; which does not seem to confirm that connection.

---

* The Ablative with KUREŃ is used, as in Siṇhalese, with the Verb AHAŃ, "to ask" : *e.g.*, HIYAL-KUREŃ EHI, "he asked the jackal" = S. *hivalá-gen ęsuva* (III. 3 : C 7).

† The Siṇhalese form *peren*, "before" (from Eḷu *pere*), does not appear ever to have the force of S. *lavá* = Máldivian FURUN, "by," or "from."—B., *Ed.*

Examples of the Locative are MI GAHU-GA', "to this tree" (III. 1: 5); BADGÉ-GAI, "in the kitchen" (III. 2: 2); AHARAMEŃ-GE RAṚU-GAI, "in our country" (III. 2: 4): ETA-GAI,* "there" (III. 2: 10; probably E-TAG-GAI = E-TAN-GAI, *cf.* S. *e-tana*); VALU-GAI, "in the jungle" (III. 2: 24); DIVẸHI-RÁJJÉ-GAI, "on the Máldives" (III. 2: 3); HITU-GAI, "in mind," "in spirit" (III. 2: 23).

A Locative is also dependent on the Verb TAḶAN, "to strike" (BALU-GA', "the dog"), and on DÁE-GANNAŃ, "to bite" (III. 1: 26).

The Plural form E RATTAKU-GAI, "on those Islands" (III. 2: 7), which has risen from RAṚ-TAKU, is worthy of note.

The expression KOŃ RAṚEŃ-HÉ, "in what town?" is not very clear (III. 2: 29).

6.—Emphatic Case.

The Máldivian Language also has an Emphatic Case, which ends in -í. Thus: MI GAHÍ, "this tree"; as well as MI GAS (III. 1: 13 and 14); MI HARUFAYÍ, "this snake" (III. 1: 9).

I also consider MIÍ, in the sentence MIÍ KALÉ-GE NIYÁKAŃ VÍYÁ, "if this is Your (Honour's) decision" (III. 3: B 5), as such an Emphatic Case.

7.—Prepositional Connections.

In conclusion, some relationships with Prepositions may be quoted.

Among these, of course, may be noticed: BURIKAṚI MACCA, "on the back" (III. 3: A 2); BIM MACCE, "(he fell) to the ground" (III. 3: A 5); AHU MACCA, "on the horse" (III. 3: A 6); MÍSMÍHUŃ MACCA, "(be merciful) to people" (III. 3: A 7); EMME KUJJAYAṬ-ṬAKÁI, "on account of a child" (III. 3: B 1); KUḌA IRU-KOLU FAHUŃ, "a short time afterwards" (III. 3: A 5) = S. *madu vélávaka-ṭa pasu.*

The Preposition MACCA is doubtless connected with S. *matu, matté, mattehi,* "above," "on." *Cf. Etymologie des Singhalesischen,* No. 1,043.

---

* *Cf.* ETÁ-GAI (III. 2: 30).

II.—ADJECTIVES.

1.—*Attributive.*

The Attributive Adjective is found: *e.g.*, in VARA' BOḌU GAHE, "a very large tree" (III. 1 : 13); FEHI FAI, "green leaves" (III. 1: 29); ÉNÁ-GE HAGU AŃHEŃ-DARI, "her youngest daughter" (III. 2 : 16); KUḌA ETIKOLEI, "a small part" (III. 3 : C 6); AU BOḌÁ-SÁHIBEN (*i.e.*, -BE'), "a new Governor" (Málim's Letter).

2.—*Predicative.*

The Predicative Adjective occurs: *e.g.*, in MI MÉVA RAHA FONYÉ, "the taste of this fruit is sweet" (III. 1 : 11); MI HEDUŃ HUDU, "this dress is white"; MI VELI RÍNDU, "this sand is yellow"; LÉ RAI, "blood is red"; UḌU NULE, "the sky is blue" (III. 1 : 30).

3.—*Comparative.*

Examples of the Comparative of Adjectives are quoted under I. (b).

Our word "very" corresponds to the Máldivian VARA' (also written VARAŃ). Thus, *e.g.*, VARA' BALI VEJJEVÉ, "he became very tired" (III. 3: A 2); NÁṚI VARAŃ HARÉ, "the coconut shell is very hard" (III. 1 : 16).

III.—NUMERALS.

1.—Cardinal Numbers.

The Máldivian Cardinal Numbers are mentioned by Ranasiṇha in *Journal, R.A.S., Ceylon Branch,* 1882, VII., No. 25, p. 241.

On pages 253 and 254 (*idem*) Bell deals with *The Máldive Numerals,* giving the Numbers from "1" to "100," according to both *Duodecimal* and *Decimal Systems.*

From Ibráhim Dídí's information, I, too, made a complete list, and repeat them here, with connected remarks :—

1 = EKE' ; S. *ek.*	6 = HAYE' ; S. *ha.*
2 = DE' ; S. *dek.*	7 = HATE' ; S. *hat.*
3 = TINE' ; S. *tun.*	8 = AṚE ; S. *aṭa.*
4 = HATARE' ; S. *hatara.*	9 = NUVAYE' ; S. *nava.*
5 = FAHE' ; S. *pas.*	10 = DIHAYE' ; S. *daha.*

The forms probably correspond to the Substantive forms in *-ak* in Siṇhalese, like *dekak, tunak ; e.g., pol-geḍi pahak,* "five coconut trees" (see *Litteratur und Sprache der Singhalesen,* pp. 65–66). The original forms are therefore EKEK, DEK, TINEK.*

It is striking that Pyrard (as printed) gives HEC, DEC, but TINET, ATARET (also, further, ATEC) clearly. In Pyrard's time the final consonants were faintly sounded. †

11 = EGÁRA .. .. P. *ekárasa,* but S. *ekoḷos.*
12 = BÁRA, or DOḶOS .. P. *bárasa,* S. *doḷos.*

---

* The Copenhagen Manuscript (see *Sitzungsber. der K. Bayer,* Akademie d. W., 1900, p. 649), in fact, has HATAREK, FAHEK, &c.

† Gray's salutary warning (*Journal, R.A.S.,* 1879, X., p. 185) is not heeded by Geiger : "I must remind those who peruse it (Pyrard's Vocabulary) that Pyrard was a Frenchman. The Máldive words must, therefore, be pronounced *as if they were French,* in order to sound as Pyrard intended them to."—B., *Ed.*

13 = TÉRA .. .. P. *térasa*, S. *teḷes.*
14 = SAUDA .. .. P. *catuddasa*, but S. *tudus.*
15 = FANARA .. .. P. *pañcadasa*, but S. *pahaḷos.*
16 = SÓḶA .. .. P. *soḷasa*, S. *soḷos.*
17 = SATÁRA .. .. P. *sattarasa*, but S. *sataḷos.*
18 = AṚÁRA .. .. P. *aṭṭhárasa*, but S. *aṭaḷos.*
19 = ONAVIHI .. .. P. (*ek*)*únavísaṇ*, S. (*ek*)*unvisi.*
20 = VIHI .. .. P. *vísaṇ*, S. *visi.*

The Numerals are of interest from the fact that some of them are more closely related to the Páli than the corresponding forms in Siṇhalese.

Instead of SAUDA * (which is historically correct), I heard the expression SÁDA.

The form for "19" is worthy of note. It shows that in the Prákṛit foundation of Siṇhalese and Máldivian a form must have existed which corresponded to the Sanskṛit *úna-viṇsati* (with omission of the *eka*).

The tens beyond 20 are :—

30 = TIRÍṢ .. .. *cf.* P. *tiṇsaṇ*, S. *tis.*
40 = SÁLÍS .. .. S. *sális*, but P. *cattáḷísaṇ.*
50 = FANSÁS .. .. *cf.* P. *paññásaṇ*, S *panas.* †
60 = FASDOḶOS (5 × 12).. *cf.* below.
70 = HAIDIHA (7 × 10) ‡.. Bell has HATTIRI.
80 = AṬIHA (? ADDIHA) (8 × 10) ‡ .. Bell has ÁHI.
90 = NUVADIHA (9 × 10) ‡ Bell has NAVAI.
100 = SATÉKA .. .. Bell has; but L.V., HIYA.
1000 = HÁHE' .. .. HÁS in L.V.

* SAUDA is given by Bell. The form also appears in the Málim's Letter published by Christopher (see *supra*, page 49), and likewise in the "London Vocabulary." *Cf.* on this subject *Sitzungsber. der K. Bayer*, Akademie d. W., 1900, p. 649 *seq.*

† *Cf.* my *Litteratur und Sprache der Singhalesen*, p. 93. In Bell (*The Máldive Islands*, p. 121) I find also FANAS and FANSAS.

‡ Clearly new formations, which are just being introduced.

I also give the Numbers between 20 and 30 ; as well as between 30 and 40, 40 and 50 ; and the hundreds, as I recorded them :—

21 = EKÁVÍS.
22 = BÁVÍS.
23 = TÉVÍS.
24 = SAUVÍS.
25 = FANSAVÍS.
26 = SABBÍS.
27 = HATÁVÍS.
28 = AṚÁVÍS.
29 = ONATIRÍS.
31 = ETTIRÍS.
32 = BATTIRÍS.
33 = TETTIRÍS.
34 = SAURATIRÍS.
35 = FANSATIRÍS.
36 = SATIRÍS.
37 = SATUTIRÍS.
38 = AṚUTIRÍS.
39 = ONASÁḶÍS.

41 = EKÁḶÍS.
42 = BAYAḶÍS.
43 = TEYAḶÍS.
44 = SAURAYAḶÍS.
45 = FANSAYAḶÍS.
46 = SAYAḶÍS.
47 = SATÁḶÍS.
48 = AṚÁḶÍS.
49 = ONAFANSÁS.
200 = DUISATTA.
300 = TIŃSATÉKA.
400 = HATARUSATÉKA.
500 = FASSATÉKA.
600 = HASATÉKA.
700 = HAISATÉKA.
800 = ASSATÉKA.
900 = NUVASATÉKA.

Of these Numbers, FASDOḶOS, "60," is of importance, because it confirms the existence of a *Duodecimal System.*

As I observed before, Bell (*Journal, R.A.S., Ceylon Branch*, No. 25, pp. 253–254) has quoted two complete Series of Numbers (up to "100"), a *Duodecimal* and a *Decimal :* the latter, on the whole, agrees with the one quoted by me.

Single derivations are to be seen in both the forms under consideration.

In the former, "20," for instance, is DOḶOS-AṚE (= 12 + 8) ; "24," FASSEHI (?) ;* "30," FASSEHI-HAYE' (= 2 × 12 + 6) ;

* Geiger queries FASSEHI doubtfully for "24" ; but it is, or was, thus used in the *Duodecimal System* of the Máldivians. Thus, Pyrard has PASSEE as equivalent to "*vingtquatre.*" It may also have been = S. *pas-visi*, "25" ; and possibly partook, then, of like confusion in accounting, as nowadays between the "Indian four anna piece" (= 24 pice) and the "Ceylon twenty-five cent piece."—B., *Ed.*

"36," TIN-DOḶOS (= 3 × 12); "40," TIN-DOḶOS-HATARE' (= 3 × 12 + 4), &c. It is concluded with HIYA (= 100), which comes close to 96 (= 8 × 12).

The "London Vocabulary," with some errors, has the same Numerals. For example, "20" is given as DOḶOS-AṚE', "21" as DOḶOS-NUVAYE.

So, too, in the case of the "Copenhagen Vocabulary," which contains only twenty-one Numerals.

Ibráhim Dídí's communications confirm Bell's statement (*The Máldive Islands*, p. 121) that the *Duodecimal System* has begun to die out; but they also show that for the number "60," where *Decimal* and *Duodecimal* notation are both found, the form 5 × 12 has become generally naturalized.*

For the combination of Numerals and Substantives, my Texts offer sufficient examples.

The Numeral stands in its original form, and precedes the Substantive.

Thus, HA BAKARI, "six sheep" (unedited Text); FANSÁS HATARU RUK-É, "fifty-four coconut palms" (III. 1 : 6); TÍM-MÍHU', "three men" (III. 1 : 7); FAS KUDIŃ, "five children" (III. 1 : 8); FANSÁS KÁṚI, "fifty coconuts" (III. 2 : 5); HATARU DARI, "four children" (III. 2 : 16); DE AŃHENUŃ, "two women" (III. 3 : B 1); TIM-BAYA' BAHÁŃ, "divide in three parts" (III. 3 : C 2); SAUDA DUVAHU, "fourteen days" (Málim's Letter); TIN DUVAS, "three days" (*Journal, R.A.S., Ceylon Branch*, No. 24, p. 122).

2.—*Ordinals.*

The Ordinals are derived by means of the suffix -VANA. In Siṃhalese of the present day the corresponding ending is *veni*; in Eḷu it is *vana*, or *vanna*.

---

* Ibráhim Dídí told me that DOḶOS, "12," belongs to the "common language," but BÁRA to the "better language."

"First" is FURATAMA, L.V. = Sans. *prathama*.

We have :—

1st = FURUTAMA.	10th = DIHAVANA.
2nd = DÉVANA.	11th = EGÁRAVANA.
3rd = TINVANA.	12th = BÁRAVANA.
4th = HATARAVANA.	20th = VIHIVANA.
5th = FASVANA.	30th = TIRÍSVANA.
6th = HAVANA.	40th = SÁḶÍSVANA.
7th = HAIVANA.	50th = FANSÁSVANA.
8th = AVVANA.	60th = FAS-DOḶOS-VANA.
9th = NUVAVANA.	&c.

IV.—PRONOUNS.

1.—*Personal Pronouns.*

Ibráhim Dídí gave me the following forms :—

MA, "I"; KALÉ, "thou"; ÉNÁ, "he," "she"; AHAREMEŃ, "we"; KALÉMEŃ, "you"; EBÁE-MÍHUŃ, "they."

From the Text we get the following forms :—

(*a*) *Pronoun of the First Person.*—MA, "I" (MI in Málim's Letter); Genitive, MA-GE, "from me," "mine"; Dative, MAṚA, "to me"; AHAREŃ (III. 2 : 24), or AHARAMEŃ (III. 2 : 6), "we"; Genitive, AHAREŃ-GE (III. 2 : 2), or AHARAMEŃ-GE (III. 2 : 4), "of us," "our"; Dative, AHAREMENNA', "to us" (III. 2 : 22).

(*b*) *Pronoun of the Second Person.*—We have forms of two kinds : TIYA,* "thou" (III. 1 : 24), and the more respectful KALÉ, "thou" (III. 1 : 23 ; III. 3 : A 3) ; Genitive, KALÉ-GE, "of thee," "thine"; Dative, KALÉYA', "to thee" (III. 2 : 26); Plural, KALÉMEŃ, "you."

In more polite speech one can unite KALÉ-TIYA.*

IMBA (*sic*) corresponds to the Siṇhalese *um̃ba* in IMBA AMÁ, "thy mother" = S. *umbé ammá* (III. 2 : 1). Here, KALÁ-GE AMÁ would be more polite, and KALÉGEFÁNU-GE AMÁ most polite of all.

(*c*) *Pronoun of the Third Person.*—ÉNÁ, "he," "she" (III. 2 : 15); Genitive, ÉNÁ-GE, "of him," "of her," "his," "her" (III. 2 : 16) = S. *ẹ-ge* ; Dative, ÉNÁYA', "to him," "to her."

Of animals, one uses ETI (III. 1 : 26); and the same of things (III. 1 : 3). *Cf.* also EYITI, referring to KUJJÁ, "child" (III. 3 : B 3).

---

* I do not know how TIYAHEŃ (III. 3 : C 7) is to be explained.

[Abdul Hamid Dídí Effendi writes :—"TIYAHEN means 'like that.' TIYA, 'that,' is quite distinct from TIYÁ, 'you' (last syllable long). Further, KALÉ, 'you,' cannot be combined with TIYA." See *supra*, page 34, note 24.—B., *Ed.*]

For the Plural, the above-mentioned EBÁE-MÍHUŃ, and for the Feminine EAŃ HEŃ, appear to be used, according to Ibráhim Dídí.

2.—Reflective Pronouns.

The Reflective Pronoun, also, is employed, clearly in more modest modes of expression, in place of the First Person: TIMAŃ, "I" (III. 1 : 3); TIMAŃMEŃ, "we" (III. 2 : 11), where it alternates[1] in the same sentence with AHARAMEŃ; Genitive, TIMAŃMEŃ-GE, "of us," "our" (III. 2: 11). In Sentence III. 3 : C 6, TIMANNAYA', shows that TIMAŃ (= S. *tamá*) is also used in Máldivian as a Reflective.

The use of the Reflective for the First Person is also found in Siṇhalese; for *apí*, "we," corresponds to the Prákṛit *appá*. See *Etymologie des Singhalesischen*, No. 44.

3.—Demonstrative Pronouns.

In numerous places in our Text MI (= S. *me*) corresponds to our "this."

In contrast, as the more distant Demonstrative, is E = S. *e* (III. 1 : 14). This E is employed just like an Article (III. 1 : 21).

A more respectful mode of expression, in reference to a woman, is E-KABULÉGE (Dative E-KABULÉGEYA') = S. *ẹ-ṭa* (III. 3 : B 6). For males, KALÉGE * is the corresponding honorific; at least, one says FIRI-KALÉGE, in contrast to ABI-KABULÉGE—perhaps equivalent to "gentleman" and "lady."

4.—Other Pronouns.

The Reflective Pronoun TIMAŃ was mentioned above.

"The other" is ANE' : *e.g.*, ANE' (written ANEN) AMBI, "the other woman" (III. 3 : B 5); EKAKU-ANEKAKU, "the one," "the other" (employed both for Masculine and Feminine), are used in contrast to one another.

---

* A still higher rank is KALÉGEFÁNU: *e.g.*, in MÁLIMÍ-KALÉGEFÁNU, "Captain" (Málim's Letter). For formation, *cf.* MANIKUFÁNU, "nobleman," "distinguished man"; Plural, MANUKU FANUME'; Dative, MANUKA FANUMENNAI (Sultán's Missive). For more about honorifics, see Bell, *The Máldive Islands*, p. 63.

"All" is EMME (Málim's Letter), or EMMEŃ (III. 1 : 25); *cf.* ITURU HURIHÁ,* "all the rest" (III. 3 : C 6). In EMME, doubtless, the numeral E' (EK) is contained; to ITURU the S. *itiri* is comparable. See *Etymologie des Singhalesischen*, No. 170.

The Interrogative Pronoun is KOŃ, "which?"

For instance, KOŃ-ECCE, "what?" literally, "what thing?" (III. 2 : 12); KOŃ-KAHALA, "what kind of?" (III. 2 : 3); KOŃTAKUŃHÉ, "where?" (III. 1 : 24); KOŃ-IRU, "when?" (III. 2 : 27); KOBÁHÉ, "where?" (III. 2 : 1).

The -HÉ at the end of several of these words is the Interrogative Particle.

In conclusion, I mention the following :—

KÍŃ-HÉ, "what?" (III. 2 : 10); KÍ-VEGEŃ, "why?" "what for?" (III. 1 : 27); and KITA (or KIHÁ), "how many?" in KITA KUDIŃ, "how many children?" (III. 1 : 8); and KIHÁ DUVAHUŃ, "in how many days?" (III. 2 : 28); *cf.* KIHÁVARU (III. 2 : 30).

---

* HURI, or HUṚI (both are well attested) signify chiefly "is," "exists" (III. 2 : 4 and 7; Málim's Letter).

V.—VERBS.

In Máldivian, as in Sinhalese, the Verb offers the greatest difficulty.

The materials accessible to me allow of no systematic representation of verbal inflexions. Much—indeed the greater part—still remains obscure, and to try to explain too much would be rash, and scarcely profitable to the subject itself.

1.—Close and unmistakable agreements of the Maldivian with the Sinhalese.

In Máldivian, as in Sinhalese, the Transitive and Intransitive (Passive) Verb-roots are different.

1.—Passive.

In HADAŃ, "to make," the Passive form is HEDEŃ, "to be made," "produced," "cultivated"; FAFFALÓ-TA' HEDENI, "fruits are cultivated" (III. 2: 3, with Note). In L.V. (p. 70) I find GOVÁŃ HEDENÍ, "seed is cultivated," as a paraphrase of "field," "cultivated land."

In Sinhalese *hadanu* and *hẹdenu* correspond. The latter signifies, like the Máldivian HEDEŃ, "to grow" (of plants).

Another interesting word is VEṬṬEŃ, "to fall" (L.V., p. 83): E MÉVA VETENI (l.: -ṬṬ-) GAHUŃ, "the fruit falls from the tree,"* S. *vẹṭenu*.

Passive, also, is FEŃ BEDENI, "it freezes" (L.V., p. 10), literally, "the water is bound," S. *bẹṇdenu*. For meaning, *cf.* np. BASTA YAX.

BELAŃ, "to be seen," "to be visible," is the Passive of BALAŃ, "to see" (III. 2: 21). With JEHEŃ, in MÓSAMU-VÁI JEHUNI, "the monsoon has burst" (III. 2: 27), *cf.* JAHAŃ, "to strike"; KEḌEŃ, "to be wounded" (L.V., p. 24), with

---

* Ibráhim Dídí gave me VETENI for "fell" and VETUNI for "falls"; but I believe that the reverse is correct.

KAḌAŃ, "to strike," "to hew down" (*ibid.*, p. 104): *cf.* further, TEMEŃ, "to be moist" (L.V., p. 139) = S. *temunu*; TIBEŃ, "to be," "to live" = S. *tibenu*.

2.—Infinitive.

In Máldivian, as the examples given above show, the Infinitive ends in -AŃ (perhaps written -EŃ), more frequently -ÁŃ, -ÉŃ. These forms doubtless correspond to the S. *-anu*, *-enu*, and, like them, go back to the verbal forms in *-ana* of Páli. See Geiger, *Litteratur und Sprache der Singhalesen*, p. 75.

Short end vowels, which are still preserved in the Siṃhalese (S. *kapanu* is derived from P. *kappanaṃ*), appear, according to the law of sound, to fall off in Máldivian.

Examples of the use of the Infinitive in our Texts are KURÁŃ (III. 3: C 1) = S. *karaṇṭa*, "in order to make"; as well as BAHÁŃ (III. 3: C 2, C 5) = S. *bedaṇṭa*, "to divide," dependent on AMRU-KOFFIYAVÉ, and BUNEPPÉ, "he commanded," "told."

In AHAREŃ MARUVÁŃ VÁNÉ (III. 2: 24) = S. *apa nasiṇṭa óṇẹya*, "we must die," VÁNÉ appears to me to have a close correspondence, etymologically, with the S. *óṇẹ*; but I have found no satisfactory derivation of the word.*

3.—Gerunds.

The formation of the Gerunds also agrees in Máldivian and Siṃhalese.

To this I add that the use of Compound Verbs (in the sense of page 67 of my *Litteratur und Sprache der Singhalesen*), in which the preceding Verb appears in the Gerund form, is extremely frequent in Máldivian.

---

* The Professor could have found it in Malayáḷam *ẹṇḍum* (*ẹṇam*; *ẹṇe*) of the Indian West Coast, corrupted from Tamiḷ *vẹṇḍum*.

The Máldivians have absorbed very many foreign phrases, owing to their intercourse with India, &c. Hence such hybrids, *inter alia*, as GORUNU DOREVE (Sultán's Missive, *supra*, page 54) = GOVERNOR-TURAI (English + Tamiḷ), and GÉGE SÁMÁN, "house-goods," "furniture" (Siṃhalese + Tamiḷ).—B., *Ed.*

Four types noticed.—(*a*) The Gerund NÁHÁ, "without hearing" (III. 3: A 4) = S. *kan-no-dí*, corresponds to the first type of Sinhalese Gerunds *kapá*.

So, in the front rank of Compound Verbs, KAKKÁ-FÍM, "we cooked" (III. 2: 11). *Cf.* KAKKANI, "she cooks" (III. 2: 2); GOVÁ-GEŃ, "having called" (III. 3: B 3); FALÁ-GEŃ, "having divided," "having cut up" (III. 3 : B 3).

In NIDAI FÍME, "I have slept" (III. 2: 19), and VIHAI FÍMEVÉ, "I have borne" (III. 3 : B 2), AI shows the length of the vowels: *cf.* VIKKAI-GEŃ, "having sold" (Málim's Letter); FAṚÁI-GEŃ, "beginning" (III. 3 : B 5) = S. *paṭangeṇa*.

(*b*) The second type of Gerund (= S. *beṇda, baṇdinu*, "to bind") I think I find in BEHI-GEŃ, "wrecked" (Sultán's Missive) = S. *bahinu;* and in DENI-GEŃ, "having recognized" (III. 3 : B 6) = S. *dẹna, dannu* (from *daninu*).

If my idea is correct, the Máldivian form would be of interest. It still possesses the sound of I, which on account of the vowel modification is considered as originally present in Sinhalese forms like *bẹṇda* (Geiger, *loc. cit.*, p. 74).

(*c*) The third type (= S. *idimí, idemenu*, "to swell") occurs in EHI, "having heard" (III. 3: B 4) = S. *asá;* which, as a collateral form by the side of NÁHÁ (see above), is certainly remarkable, and presupposes a Verb EHEŃ by the side of AHAŃ.

For Compounds, I mention VEṬṬIGEŃ, "falling" (III. 3: A 5); OSSI-DÁNÉ, "will set" (III. 1: 20): *cf.* OSSEŃ; also TIRIVI-DÁNÉ, "will set" (III. 2: 20): *cf.* TIRIVÁŃ (S. *venu*), "to become low," "to sink," "descend."

(*d*) We also find the "Irregular" Gerunds of the Sinhalese again in Máldivian. Thus, KO', "having made" = S. *koṭa* (III. 3 : C 2) : *cf.* EKKO', "having gathered" (III. 3 : C 3), and in Compound Words EKKOFFÁ (EK-KO'-FÁ) (III. 3 : C 2), both = S. *ekkoṭa*.

The Máldivian Adverb KO', as in GINA-KO', "frequent very," is formed like the Sinhalese *koṭa*.

Also GOS (= S. *gos*), "having gone" (III. 2 : 13; Sultán's Missive), occurs, and is found in Compounds like OḌI-GOS-LEFÍ (III. 2: 28), "having gone (in a ship)," and GEṆ-GOS-FÍM, "we brought" (III. 2 : 11) = S. *geṇávemuva*.

4.—Compound Verbs.

As regards Compound Verbs, these appear especially frequent as Auxiliary, *i.e.*, in the concluding part of a Compound Verb which seems to correspond to the S. *piyanu*.

Thus, to the forms quoted above, like KAKKÁ-FÍM, "we cooked," &c., I add RÓ-KOF-FÍM, "we kindled fire" (III. 2: 11) : also the Gerund forms DÍ-FAYA',* "having given" (III. 3: B 6) = S. *dí;* NAGÁ-FAYE', "having taken" (III. 3 : C 6) = S. *arageṇa*.

Another Auxiliary Verb is DÁŃ, "to go" (= S. *yanu*), in OSSI-DÁNÉ, "(the sun) set," ARÁ-DÁNÉ, "(the sun) rose"; in the Present, too, OSSI-JJÉ, "sets" (III. 1: 19 and 20), where JJ must have originated from DY.

Also LAŃ (= S. *lanu*), "to put," "place," "lay," is used : *e.g.*, MARÁ-LEYIPPÉ,† "he killed" (III. 3: C 4). As the Siṃhalese *lanu* gives an occasionally Causative meaning to the Verb with which it is connected, so the Máldivian LAŃ, in VEṬṬÁILAŃ, "to fell," does to VEṬṬEŃ, "to fall."

In conclusion, I should like to note that, like the Siṃhalese *geṇa*, in Máldivian the Gerund GEŃ very frequently is seen at the end of a Compound Word, without perceptibly modifying its meaning.

I mention DENI-GEŃ, "having recognized" (III. 3 : B 6); FAṚÁI-GEŃ, "having begun" (III. 3: B 5); FALÁ-GEŃ, "having divided" (III. 3: B 3); GOVÁ-GEŃ, "having called" (III. 3: B 3); VIKKAI-GEŃ, "having sold" (Málim's Letter); VEṬṬIGEŃ, "fallen down" (III. 3: A 5); BEHI-GE'-GOS, "wrecked" (Sultán's Missive).

---

* *Cf.* -FÁ, in EK-KOF-FÁ (III. 3 : C 2).

† LEYIPPÉ = LAIPPÉ; *cf.* FORUVAIPPÉ, LÁIPPEVÉ, VIHAYEPPEVÉ (III. 1 : 17; III. 3 : A 6; III. 2 : 16).

2.—Tenses and Moods.

I restrict myself here to quoting the forms as they occur in the Text, and as I have noted them down, with occasional explanatory remarks.

(a) *Forms with a Present Significance.*

Singular, First Person.—I distinguish three types in my collection; which, however, it is clear are very closely connected.

(i.) With the ending -NA, I noted MA VASGANNA, "I kiss," "smell." Forms of this kind must lie at the foundation of the present Siṃhalese *karana-vá*, *ganna-vá* (colloquial language), if my attempt to explain it (*Litteratur und Sprache der Singhalesen*, p. 81) is correct.

(ii.) The forms in the ending -NI appear to be more frequent.

Thus, MA DANI, "I go"; MA AHANI, "I ask"; MA HUNNANI, "I live"; MA HADANI, "I make"; MA RONI, "I weep"; MA HENI, "I laugh"; MA VEṬṬUNI (*sic;* but *cf.* Note, *supra*), "I fall"; MA DINI, "I give"; also from the Text (III. 2: 23), MA GANNANI, "I take" (? perhaps a new formation).

(iii.) Contracted forms appear with simply a nasal at the end: MA BÓŃ, "I drink"; MA NÁHAŃ, "I do not hear."

Singular, Second Person.—The form agrees with the second form of the First Person: KALÉ HUNNANI, "thou livest"; TIYA KURANI, "thou doest"; as also in the Text (III. 1: 24), TIYA ANNANI, "thou comest."

From DÁŃ, "to go," there is derived, according to my Notes, the Second Person Singular DÉ; and from RÓŃ, "to weep," RONÍTA; whilst for all other Persons and Numbers the one form RONI is used.

An Interrogative form, which appears to belong here, is KALÉ DANNUMHÉ, "do you know?" "do you understand?" (III. 2: 26).

Singular, Third Person.—Here, too, we find the forms in -NI most frequently used.

Thus, (IRU) ARANI, "the (sun) rises" (III. 1 : 19); (KOKKÁ) KAKKANI, "(the sister) cooks" (III. 2 : 2); ULANI, "(she) is" III. 2 : 15) = S. *siṭí ;* (MÉVA) VEṬṬUNI, "(the fruit) falls" (III. 1 : 28), but perhaps it should be changed into VEṬṬEN (see *supra*, page 78, footnote *).

Also ÉNÁ DIYA, "he goes" : with which I connect (IRU) OSSI-JJÉ, "(the sun) sets," JJ from DY, as in Siṇhalese (Geiger, *loc. cit.*, Section 13, 2 *b*), the final É being added, as is frequently the case, to mark the end of the sentence.

Plural, First Person.—From my Collections : AHARAMEŃ KANI, "we eat" ; AHARAMEŃ RONI, "we weep" ; AHARAMEŃ DANI, "we go" ; AHARAMEŃ IṚINNAŃ, "we sit."

Also a form in the Text (III. 2 : 6) which is difficult to bring into connection with the foregoing, AHARAMEŃ AḶAMEVÉ = S. *api sádamuva*, "we build."

Plural, Second Person.—I noted KALÉMEŃ RONI, "you weep" ; KALÉMEŃ IṚINNAN, "you sit" ; KALÉMEŃ DÉ, "you go."

Plural, Third Person.—From the Texts, HUNNANI (*sic*), "they are," "they live" (III. 2 : 24) ; HEDENI, "they are made," "they grow" (III. 2 : 3).

I myself noted RONI, "they weep" ; IṚANNAŃ, "they sit" ; DIYA (or DIYEYI), "they go." Also TIBI, "they are" ; TIBÚHÉ (Interrogative), "do they belong ?"

Present Tense.

We can, therefore, next give with certainty a paradigm of the Present Tense of HADAŃ, "to make," in which the form HADANI is the same for all Persons of both Numbers.

There is in this, again, a close connection between the Máldivian and popular Siṇhalese, in which the one form *karanavá* is also used similarly for all Persons (Present).

Further, I can put together, from Ibráhim Dídí's statements, the Present Tense of the Verb DÁŃ, "to go," which apparently is irregular :—

Singular.	*Plural.*
(1) MA DANI.	(1) AHARAMEŃ DANI.
(2) KALÉ DÉ.	(2) KALÉMEŃ DÉ.
(3) ENA DIYA.	(3) EBÁE MIHUŃ DIYA (DIYEYI).

(*b*) *Forms with a Future Significance.*

Singular, First Person.—TIMANNÁ FONUVÁNAME, "I will send" (III. 2 : 26) = S. *evannemi* ; VÁNEME, "I shall be" (III. 3 : A 3) = S. *siṭinnemi* ; FURÁNEMEVE (or FURÁNEMEVÉ), "I shall depart" (Málim's Letter). With the adjoined -É concluding the sentence, I also noted MA BAI KÁNVÁNÉ, "I shall eat rice" ; AHAREŃ HIFÁŃVÁNEYÉ, "I shall catch," which, however, has almost the meaning "I must catch."

Singular, Second Person.—Ibráhim Dídí gives HIFÁNÚVÉ, "thou wilt catch" ; KALÉ BAI KÁŃVÁNÉ, "thou wilt eat rice." The first may, indeed, be the specific Future form.

A periphrastic construction, apparently, is seen in KALÉ HADÁŃ ULANI, "thou wilt make" (III. 2 : 12, Note).

Singular, Third Person.—There are many good examples of this in the Text: (IRU) ARÁNÉ, "(the sun) will rise" (III. 1 : 19) ; ETI DÁE-GEŃ-FÁNÉ, "he (dog) will bite" (III. 1 : 26) ; (IRU) TIRI-VI-DÁNÉ, "(the sun) will set" (III. 2 : 20) ; (ADIRI) BOḌU-VI-DÁNÉ, "(the darkness) will be great" (III. 2 : 21). Also, in my Notes, ÉNÁ BAI KÁNÉ, "he will eat rice" ; and with the É at the end of the sentence, HIFÁNEYÉ, "he will catch."

Of Intransitive Verbs we have (IRU) OSSÉNÉ, "(the sun) will set" (III. 1 : 20) ; NU-LIBÉNÉ, "(the child) will not (by me) be taken" (III. 3 : B 5) ; also (MAGU) NU-BELÉNÉ, "(the road) will not be seen" (III. 2 : 21).

Plural, First Person.—The ending seems to be -NÚ or -NUŃ. With this AHARAMEŃ BAI KÁNUŃ, "we will eat rice," in my Collection agrees; also HIFÁNÚVÉ, "we will catch," with the -É marking the end of the sentence.

The form in the Text, AHARAMEŃ ARÁNUME, "we will embark" (III. 2: 13), contains the Emphatic Particle -ME, which is common in Máldivian.

Plural, Second Person.—The two forms in my Collection, KALÉMEŃ BAI KÁNÉ, "you will eat rice," and KALÉMEŃ HIFANÚVÉ, "you will catch," do not seem to agree.

In the Text there is found a periphrastic form, KALÉMEŃ HADÁŃ ULUVANI, "you will do" (III. 2: 12) = S. *uṁba karanné.*

Plural, Third Person.—I have only written down the one form EBÁE MÍHUŃ VAI KÁNÉ, "they will eat rice."

Future Tense.

The construction of the paradigm of the Future is not free from doubt. I give it with all reserve:—

Singular.	*Plural.*
(1) MA HADÁNAME.*	(1) API HADÁNÚ.
(2) (KALE HADÁNÚ.)	(2) (KALÉMEŃ HADÁNU.)
(3) ÉNÁ HADÁNÉ.	(3) EBÁE MÍHUŃ HADÁNÉ.

(*c*) *Forms with a Preterite Significance.*

Singular, First Person.—The forms MA EHÍ, "I asked" (III. 1: 1), and MA HEDÍ, "I made," show us that in the Transitive Conjugation the structure was just the same as in Siṇhalese. The Preterite goes back to the old Past Participle of the type *patita* (Geiger, *loc. cit.*, Section 55, 2 *a*).

The Máldivian also shows the vowel assimilation in the root syllable (EHÍ, as opposed to the present AHANI; HEDÍ,

---

* -ME is perhaps an Emphatic Particle again.

as opposed to the present HADANI), brought about by the I of the following syllable, just as the S. *ẹhuvá* and *hẹduvá :* it is, however, somewhat more ancient, inasmuch as it has still kept the I, whilst in Siṇhalese it has been turned into *u*.

The Intransitive Conjugation shows just the same type as the S. *idime-, idimunu-*. To this form belongs MA DENI,* "I gave" (III. 1 : 4)—which, according to Ibráhim Dídí's assertion, may be also MA DINI—colloquial for MA DÍNÍM, which occurs in III. 1 : 3. Probably MI LIYUNI (Málim's Letter), MA LIYUNÍ-ME, "I wrote" (III. 1 : 23), are formed in the same way, as Intransitive.

Of forms which deviate from the regular type, I have noticed MA GATÍ, "I bought" (like the S. *gattá*, from *gannu*) *;* also with the ending -IŃ instead of -I (as in Future Plural (1), -UŃ occurs with -Ú) : MA DUṚIŃ, "I saw" (S. *duṭuvá*)*;* MA BÚIŃ, "I drank"; MA RÚIŃ, "I wept." Irregular, also, is MA DIYÁ-ME, "I went"; VEJJÉ-ME, "I became," in MA TEDUVEJJÍ-ME, "I rose" (III. 2 : 19).

Finally, Compound forms frequently appear in the Preterite, in which the Auxiliary Verb corresponding to the Siṇhalese *piyanu* is employed : MA AHÁ-FIŃ, "I heard"; MA HÍ-FIŃ, "I laughed"; MA VIKKÁ FIŃ, "I sold." In the Texts, too, MA-NIDAI-FÍ-ME, "I slept" (III. 2 : 19); TIMANNÁ VIHAI-FI-MEVÉ, "I have borne (that child)" (III. 3 : B 2).

Singular, Second Person.—The form is difficult to establish. According to KALÉ OḌI-GOS-LEFÍ, "thou hast sailed" (III. 2 : 28), it would agree with the First and Third Persons Singular. But the following forms were given to me : KALÉ BÚIMU, "thou drankest"; KALÉ KÉMU, "thou atest"; KALÉ RUIMU, "thou hast wept"; KALÉ DIYÁMU, "thou wentest"; KALÉ GATÍTA, "thou boughtest."

---

* The root DÁ (*cf.* Geiger, *loc. cit.*, Section 53, 3) is only included in the Intransitive Conjugation for external reasons.

Singular, Third Person.—The forms like BUNI, "he said" (III. 3 : B 3 and B 5) ; EHI, "he asked" (III. 3 : C 7) ; INÍ, "(she) has married" (III. 2 : 16), are clear.

Of the Intransitive forms, we have MÉVA VEṬṬENU (or VEṬṬUNI, *cf. supra,* Note), "(the fruit) fell" (III. 1 : 28) ; JEHUNI, "(the monsoon) burst" (III. 2 : 27).

Also Irregular : ÁI, "(he) came" (III. 1 : 22) = S. *ává ;* and GENÁI, "(he) brought" (III. 1 : 21) = S. *geṇává.*

But a new type in -PPÉ also appears, which can scarcely be explained at first sight : BUNEPPÉ, "he spoke" (III. 3 : C 3, C 5, C 6) ; FORUVAIPPÉ, "covered" (III. 1 : 17) ; MARÁ-LEYIPPÉ,* "he killed" (III. 3 : C 4).

Enlarged forms in -PPEVÉ are clearly related to these, as in the Future, those in First Person Singular in -AŃAMEVÉ, and Third Person Singular in -AŃEYÉ, are related to those in -AŃAME, perhaps -ÁNÉ. Such enlarged forms are AHEPPEVÉ, "he asked" (III. 3 : A 3) ; LÁIPPEVÉ, "he laid" (III. 3 : A 6) ; VIHAYEPPEVÉ, "(children she) has borne" (III. 2 : 16).

In the same way forms of the first type are enlarged : FONUVÁ-FIYEVÉ, "he sent" (III. 3 : B 6) ; AMRU KOF-FIYAVÉ, "he commanded" (III. 3: C 2); as well as VEJJEVÉ, "was," "he became" (III. 2 : 14 ; III. 3 : A 2). *Cf.* MARU-VEJJEVÉ, "he died" (III. 3 : A 5 ; Málim's Letter) ; also the forms HINGI-EVÉ, "he went" (III. 3 : A 4), and ATU-EVÉ, "he has come" (Málim's Letter), are to be taken into consideration.

Periphrastic is NUBUNE HURI, "(she) did not speak" (III. 3 : B 4). Doubtful forms, resembling the Future rather than the Preterite, are (IRU) ARÁ-DÁNÉ ; also OSSI-DÁNÉ, "(the sun) has risen," also "is set" (III. 1 : 19, 20).

---

* From the Compound Verb MARÁ-LAŃ, in which LAŃ has a Causative significance.

Plural, First Person.—The form appears to end in -M, -MU, -MUŃ. In the Texts AHARAMEŃ EKU-KOFFÍM, "we gathered"; AHARAMEŃ-GENGOSFÍM, "we brought"; AHARAMEŃ RÓ KOFFÍM, "we kindled"; AHARAMEŃ KAKKÁFÍM, "we cooked" (all in III. 2 : 11).

I have recorded AHARAMEŃ BÚIMUŃ, "we drank"; AHARAMEŃ RÚIMUN, "we wept"; AHARAMEŃ HINGÍMUN, "we went."

Plural, Second Person.—A single form, KALÉMEŃ KOḶEFÍM (perhaps = KÓ'-LEFÍM), "you did" (III. 2 : 10).

Plural, Third Person.—The simple form BUNI, "they said," is attested (III. 3 : B 2). Also we have, quite analogous to the corresponding forms of the Third Person Singular, HINGI-EVÉ, "they went" (III. 3 : A 1), and ATU-VEJJEVÉ, "they came," or "had come" (III. 3 : B 1). *Cf.* further, VEDÉ, "they went" (III. 3 : C 1), which probably is connected with the S. *vidinu.*

All the forms told me have the final -TA added to them. I should like to write this -TA', and simply look upon it as the Plural Particle spoken of above, were it not also occasionally found in my Notes in the Singular. Such forms are EBÁE MÍHUŃ BÚITA, "they drank"; EBÁE MÍHUŃ RÍUTA, "they wept"; EBÁE MÍHUŃ DIYATA, "they went"; IYYEGÁ EBÁE MÍHUŃ KÉTA BAI, "they ate rice yesterday."

Past Tense.

The paradigm of the Preterite of HADAŃ, "to make," if we wish to put it in tabular form, would perhaps be formed in the following way :—

Singular.

(1) MA HEDÍ, or MA HADÁFIŃ.
(2) KALÉ HEDÍ (or ? KALE HEDÍMU).
(3) ÉNÁ HEDÍ (or ÉNÁ HADAIPPÉ, or ÉNÁ-HADEPPÉ).

Plural.

(1) AHARAMEŃ HEDÍM (-UŃ), or AHARAMEŃ HADÁFÍM.
(2) (? KALÉMEŃ HADÁFÍM.)
(3) EBÁE MÍHUŃ HEDÍ.

Of DÁŃ, "to go," the following conjugation of the Preterite was given to me :—

Singular.	*Plural.*
(1) MA DIYÁIŃ.	(1) AHARAMEŃ HINGÍMUŃ.
(2) KALÉ DIYÁMU.	(2) KALÉMEŃ DIYÁMUTA.
(3) ÉNÁ DIYA.	(3) EBÁE MÍHUŃ DIYATA.

(*d*) *Imperative Forms.*

There are clearly two forms, (i.), (ii.), to be distinguished: a simple one, which, as in Sinhalese (Geiger, *loc. cit.*, Section 62, 1 *a*), represents merely the root of the Verb; and a longer one, to which the syllable HAṚE is added, which I cannot further explain.

(i.) DÍ, "give" (III. 1 : 2); NIDÍ, "sleep" (III. 1 : 27); HADA, "make" (III. 2 : 21) = S. *karapan.*

In NUGANÉ (III. 2: 25) and HURÉ (HUṚE) (III. 3: A 7) the -É may be explained by the position at the end of the sentence; or is it a plural?

(ii.) NAGAHAṚE, "take up," "lift" (III. 3: A 3); NU-TALAHAṚE, "do not strike" (III. 1 : 26); NU-MARAṚE, "do not kill" (III. 3: B 5); DEHEṚE, "give" (III. 3: B 3); and finally, in my Notes, DAHAṚE, "go."

(*e*) *Conditional Forms.*

A Conditional unmistakably occurs in (HARUFÁ) DÁ-GATIYÁ, "in case (a snake) bites (us)" (III. 2 : 24); (MIÍ KALÉGE NIYÁKAŃ) VÍYÁ, "if (this) is (your judgment)" (III. 3: B 5). Here also belongs MÁT-KALÁGE RUSSE-VÍYAI, "if God wills it" (Málim's Letter); to which the S. *russanu*, "to have pleasure in," "to like," is comparable.

The foregoing Notes on Máldivian Grammar give us, of course, only a general and incomplete picture of the Structure of the Language. They are a first attempt, and should be judged as such.

He who knows the many purely external difficulties and obstacles with which one meets in the East in researches which lie at the foundation of work such as mine; he who has experienced how the best intentions and the most enthusiastic zeal are constantly checked and crippled by a thousand petty trifles, will judge the deficiencies of my work kindly.

Knowledge must be indulgent. It may be an easy thing to point out and criticise this or that defect; but of greater worth than criticism is energetic co-operation.

SECTION III.*

I.—MALDIVIAN VERBAL INFLEXIONS.

Through my Colombo friend, A. Mendis Gunasékara, Mudaliyár, I have received a list of paradigms of Máldivian Verbs from my helper, Sheik Ali.

I publish it, in the corresponding form, all the more gladly because the inflexions of Máldivian Verbs are extremely remarkable; and because my own compendia (Z.D.M.G., L.V., Section 383 *seq.*) are in many respects completed and improved by the new material.

At the same time, I avail myself of the opportunity of correcting my former statements about the personality of Sheik Ali. He is not a Bengáli, but is descended from an Arab family which emigrated from Cairo to India. Also, he does not follow any mercantile pursuit in the Máldives, but filled the important position of Supreme Muhammadan Judge there, and was a Member of the Cabinet for ten years.†

This correction is really of importance, inasmuch as Sheik Ali, from his position of KÁZÍ, of course, had opportunities of getting into far more intimate relationship with the Máldivian people than would have been possible to a trader. His notes, being those of a man of rank and education, carry authority.

---

* See *Sitzungsber. der K. Bayer*, Akademie d. W., 1900, p. 641 *seq.*; Z.D.M.G., L.V., p. 371 *seq.* *Máldivische Studien*, III., Von Wilhelm Geiger (Vorgelegt in der Philos.-Philol. Classe am 3. Mai, 1902).

† Sheik Ali ibn (son of) Sheik Abdul Kádir, died at Colombo in January, 1907. He was FAḌIYÁRU, or Chief Judge, of the Máldive Islands, when living on the Group.—B., *Ed.*

Selected Verbs.

The Verbs selected, as examples, in the Present, Preterite, Future, and Imperative Tenses, are:—

(*a*) HADAN, "to make."
(*b*) KÁN, "to eat."
(*c*) BALAN, "to see."
(*d*) ANNAN, "to come."
(*e*) DÁN, "to go."
(*f*) IṚÍNNAN, "to sit." *

1.—Present.

In order to avoid misunderstanding, if possible, I have, as a rule, inserted "now," "at present," Máldivian MIHIDU (MI = S. Pronoun *me* + HIDU, or HINDU, "time"; really = S. *saṇda*). *Cf.* E-HIDU, "then" = S. *e-saṇda.*

(*a*) HADAN, "to make," "prepare" = S. *hadanu* :—

Singular.

(1) TIMAN .. .. .. MIHIDU HADANÍ.
(2) IBA .. .. .. MIHIDU HADANÍ.
(3) ÉNÁ (*Masculine*) .. .. MIHIDU HADANÍ.
(3) E-KABULÉGE (*Feminine*).. MIHIDU HADANÍ.

Plural.

(1) TIMANMEN .. .. .. MIHIDU HADAMÉ.
(2) KALÉMEN .. .. .. MIHIDU HADAMU.
(3) E-MÍHUN .. .. .. MIHIDU HADANÉ.

(*b*) KÁN, "to eat" = S. *kanu* :—

Singular.

(1) TIMAN .. .. .. M. KANÍ.
(2) IBA .. .. .. M. KANÍ.
(3) ÉNÁ .. .. .. M. KANÉ.

---

* The following forms in ordinary colloquial use were recorded at Málé by Mr. Bell in 1879 :—

Present : HADANÍ, KANÍ, ANÁNÉ, DANI, IṚINÁNÉ. Preterite : HADIYA, KÁFI, AYI, DIYA, IṚI(N)DIYA. Imperative : HADAHAṚÉ, KAHAṚÉ, ÁDÉ, ANAHAṚÉ, ANNÁṚÉ, BAHI(G), DAHAṚÉ, IṚINNAWAHAṚÉ. Past Participle : HADÁFÁ, KÁGIN, KÁFÁ, AISGIN, AISVÁ, GOSGIN, GOSVÁ, IṚI(N)DAWÁFÁ. —B., *Ed.*

Plural.

(1) TIMANMEN .. .. .. M. KAMU.
(2) IBUREMEN .. .. .. M. KAMU.
(3) E-MÍHUN .. .. .. M. KANÉ.

(c) BALAN, "to see" = S. *balanu* :—

Singular.

(1) TIMAN .. .. .. M. BALAMÉ.
(2) IBA .. .. .. M. BALANÍ.
(3) ÉNÁ .. .. .. M. BALANÍ.

Plural.

(1) TIMANMEN .. .. .. M. BALAMÉ.
(2) IBUREMEN .. .. .. M. BALAMU.
(3) E-MÍS-TA' .. .. .. M. BALANÉ.

(d) ANNAN, "to come" = S. *enu* :—

Singular.

(1) TIMAN .. .. .. M. ANNANÍ.
(2) IBA .. .. .. M. ANNANÍ.
(3) ÉNÁ .. .. .. M. ANNANÍ.

Plural.

(1) TIMANMEN .. .. .. M. ANNAMUVÉ.
(2) KALÉMEN .. .. .. M. ANNAMU.
(3) E-MÍS-TA' .. .. .. M. AUDÉ.

(e) DÁN, "to go" = S. *yanu* :—

Singular.

(1) TIMAN .. .. .. M. DANÍ.
(2) IBA .. .. .. M. DANÍ.
(3) ÉNÁ .. .. .. M. DÉ.

Plural.

(1) TIMANMEN .. .. .. M. DAMÉ.
(2) IBAREMEN .. .. .. M. DAMUVÉ.
(3) E-MÍHUN .. .. .. M. DEYÉ.

(*f*) IṚÍNNAN, "to sit" = S. *hiṭinu*. The L.V. writes IRÍNAN; my helper, IRINNÁN :—

Singular.

(1) TIMAN	.. .. ..	M. IRÍNNANÍ.*
(2) IBA	.. .. ..	M. IRÍNNANÍ.
(3) ÉNÁ	.. .. ..	M. IRÍNNANÍ.

Plural.

(1) TIMANMEN	.. .. ..	M. IRÍNNAMU.
(2) IBUREMEN	.. .. ..	M. IRÍNNAMU.
(3) E-MÍHUN	.. .. ..	M. IRÍDEYÉ.

2.—Preterite. †

(*a*) *Singular.*

(1) TIMAN	.. .. ..	IYYE HADAIFÍN.
(2) IBA	.. .. ..	IYYE HADAIFÍMU.
(3) ÉNÁ	.. .. ..	IYYE HADAIFI.

Plural.

(1) TIMANMEN	.. .. ..	IYYE HADAIFÍMU.
(2) IBUREMEN ‡	.. ..	IYYE HADAIFÍMU.
(3) E-MÍHUN	.. .. ..	IYYE HADAIFÚ.

(*b*)

Singular.	*Plural.*
(1) T. I. KEÍ.	(1) T. I. KAIFIMÚ.
(2) I. I. KEÍ. §	(2) I. I. KAIFÍMU.
(3) É. I. KEÍ.	(3) É-M. I. KAIFÚ.

---

* Written IRÍ'NANÍ.

† The verbs HADAN, KÁN, BALAN, ANNAN, DÁN, and IRINNAN, with the addition of IYYE, "yesterday."

‡ IBUREMEN (or IBAREMEN) is, according to choice, interchangeable with KALÉMEN, just as, in the Third Person, E-MÍS-TA' alternates with E-MÍHUN.

§ Sheik Ali here writes KEKEÍ; probably from oversight.

(c) *Singular.*

(1) T. I. BELÍMU.
(2) I. I. BALAIFÍMU, or DEKEFÍMU.
(3) É. I. BALAIFI, or DEKEFI.

Plural.

(1) T. I. BALAIFÍMU, or DEKEFÍMU.
(2) I. I. BALAIFÍMU, or DEKEFÍMU.
(3) É-M. I. BALAIFÚ, or DEKEFÚ.

(d)

Singular.	*Plural.*
(1) T. I. AIN.	(1) T. I. AIMU.
(2) I. I. AIMU.	(2) I. I. AIMU.
(3) É. I. AI.	(3) É-M. I. AÚ.

(e)

Singular.	*Plural.*
(1) T. I. DIYAIN.	(1) T. I. DIYAÍMU.
(2) I. I. DIYAIMU.	(2) I. I. DIYAIMU.
(3) É. I. DIYA.	(3) É-M. I. DIYAÚ.

(f)

Singular.	*Plural.*
(1) T. I. INÍN.	(1) T. I. INÍMU.
(2) I. I. INÍ.	(2) I. I. INÍMU.
(3) É. I. INÍ.	(3) É-M. I. INÚ.

3.—Future.*

(a) *Singular.*

(1) TIMAN MÁDAN HADÁFÁNAN.
(2) IBA MÁDAN HADÁNÍ.
(3) ÉNÁ MÁDAN HADÁFÁNE.

Plural.

(1) TIMANMEN MÁDAN HADÁFÁNAMU.
(2) IBUREMEN MÁDAN HADÁFÁNAMU.
(3) E-MÍHUN MÁDAN HADÁFÁNE.

---

* The same verbs in connection with MÁDAN, "to-morrow."

(*b*)

Singular.	Plural.
(1) T. M. KÁNÍ.	(1) T. M. KÁNÚ.
(2) I. M. KÁNÍ.	(2) I. M. KÁNÚ.
(3) É. M. KÁNÍ.	(3) É-M. M. KÁNE.

(*c*) *Singular.*

(1) T. M. BALÁNAN, or DEKÉNAN.
(2) I. M. BALÁNE, or DEKENE.
(3) É. M. BALANE, or É. M. DEKÉNE.

Plural.

(1) T. M. BALÁNAMU, or DEKÉNAMU.
(2) I. M. BALÁNAMU, or DEKÉNAMU.
(3) É-M. M. BALÁNE, or DEKÉNE.

(*d*)

Singular.	Plural.
(1) T. M. ANNÁNAN.	(1) T. M. ANNÁNÚ.
(2) I. M. ANNÁNÍ.	(2) I. M. ANNÁNAMU.
(3) É. M. ANNÁNE.	(3) É-M. M. ANNÁNE.

(*e*)

Singular.	Plural.
(1) T. M. DÁNAN.	(1) T. M. DÁNÚ.
(2) I. M. DÁNÍ.	(2) I. M. DÁNAMU.
(3) É. M. DÁNÉ.	(3) É-M. M. DÁNÉ.

(*f*)

Singular.	Plural.
(1) T. M. IRÍNNÁNAN.	(1) T. M. IRÍNNÁNAMU.
(2) I. M. IRÍNNÁNÍ.	(2) I. M. IRÍNNÁNAMU.
(3) É. M. IRÍNNÁNÉ.	(3) É-M. M. IRÍNNÁNÉ.

4.—Imperative.

(*a*)

Singular.	Plural.
HADÁ, "make."	HADDAVÁ, "make."

(*b*)

Singular.	Plural.
KAI, "eat."	KÉN BALLAVÁ, "eat."

	Singular.	Plural.
(c)	BALÁH, "see."	BALLAVÁ, "see."
(d)	ANNÁṚÉ, "come."	ANNÁṚÉ, "come."
(e)	DÉ, "go."	DÉ, "go."
(f)	IRÍDÉ, "sit."	IRÍNNAVÁ, "sit."

5.—Compound Verb Paradigm.

I add here the paradigm of the Compound Verb VAṬṬAILÁN, "to cause to fall," "to fell," "to drop":—

Present.

Singular.	Plural.
(1) T. VAṬṬAILANÍ.	(1) T. VAṬṬAILAMU.
(2) I. VAṬṬAILANÍ.	(2) I. VAṬṬAILAMU.
(3) É. VAṬṬAILANÍ.	(3) É-M. VAṬṬAILAI.

Preterite.

Singular.	Plural.
(1) T. VAṬṬAILÍ.	(1) T. VAṬṬAILÍMU.
(2) I. VAṬṬAILÍ.	(2) I. VAṬṬAILÍMU.
(3) É. VAṬṬAILÍ.	(3) É-M. VAṬṬAILÚ.

Future.

Singular.	Plural.
(1) T. VAṬṬAILÁNÍ.	(1) T. VAṬṬAILÁNÚ.
(2) I. VAṬṬAILÁNÍ.	(2) I. VAṬṬAILÁNÚ.
(3) É. VAṬṬAILÁNÍ.	(3) É-M. VAṬṬAILÁNE.

Imperative.

Singular.	Plural.
(2) VAṬṬAILÁH.	(2) VAṬṬAILAVVÁH.

6.—Single Verbal Forms and Short Sentences.

(*a*) He dies : ÉNÁ MARUVANÍ.
She died : E-KABULÉGE MARUVÍ.
He will die to-morrow : ÉNÁ MÁDAN MARUVÁNÍ.

(*b*) He is eating rice now : ÉNÁ MIHÁRU BAT KANÍ.
He ate rice yesterday : ÉNÁ IYYE BAT KAIFI.
He will eat rice to-morrow : ÉNÁ MÁDAN BAT KAIFÁNE.

(*c*) All men must die : EMMEHÁ MÍS-TAKUN MARUVÁN VÁNÍ.

(*d*) Thou drinkest water now : KALÉ MIHIDU FEN BONÍ.
Thou drankest water yesterday: IBA IYYE FEN BOIFÍMU.
Thou wilt drink water to-morrow: IBA MÁDAN FEN BOIFÁNE.
Drink water (*Singular*) : IBA FEN BÓI.
Drink water (*Plural*) : KALÉMEN FEN BAFFAVÁ.

(*e*) We need rice to-day: TIMANMENNAṚ * MI-ADU BAT BÉNUN VEJJE.

(*f*) Put (*Plural*) the load down on the ground : BIN-MATTAṚ * BURABOḌI VAṬṬAILAVVÁH.
Put (*Singular*) the dish on the table : MÉZU-MATTAṚ * BÓ-TAṚI VAṬṬAILÁH.

---

* Pronounced TIMANMENNA'. *Cf.* Z.D.M.G., L.V., p. 375; as well as below, in "Study of Sounds."

II.—MALDIVIAN LINGUISTIC SOUNDS.

[*Preliminary Remarks.*—By Christopher, I refer to Christopher's *Vocabulary of the Maldivian Language, Journal, R.A.S.*, 1841, VI., Section 42; by Pyrard, I refer to Pyrard's list of words, elaborated by Gray, *Journal, R.A.S.*, 1878, new series, X., p. 173 *seq.*; by L.V., to the *Vocabulary, Persian and Hindústání*, of the India Office Library, with a manuscript Máldivian translation; by K.V., to the Vocabulary in the Copenhagen Library. *Cf. Sitzungsber. der K. Bayer*, Akademie der Wiss., Cl. I., 1900, p. 647 *seq.* By Geiger, I refer to my own collections; by E.S., to my *Etymologie des Singhalesischen*, Abhdl. der K. Bayer, Akademie der Wiss., Cl. I., Bd. XI., Part 2, p. 177 *seq.*]

My account of the Máldivian Study of Sounds rests, I believe, on about four hundred and thirty authenticated comparisons. A glance at the list at once shows the close connection between Máldivian and Siṃhalese.

Máldivian Grammar offers difficulties of many kinds.

We shall be obliged to admit in it the influence of the language of the original non-Áryan inhabitants of the Islands, or of intercourse with foreign nations.

But for a linguistic classification of a Language, the *Study of Sounds* is decisive.

Máldivian Word Forms.

Máldivian words now show in their form all the influences which were fixing the character of Siṃhalese down to the Tenth Century after Christ.*

(i.) Máldivian has lost all the original double consonants, all long vowels, and all aspirates. Double consonants and long vowels, as in Siṃhalese, are new secondary formations.

* Geiger, *Litteratur und Sprache der Singhalesen, Ind. Grdr.*, I., 10, p. 40.

(ii.) The loss of the nasal before consonants takes place in Máldivian as in Siṇhalese; and the process, regarded from the point of view of dialect, has progressed further.

(iii.) The same is the case with the change of the sibilant S into H, and the loss of the latter.

(iv.) Mutes occurring between vowels had totally disappeared at the time when Máldivian branched off from its parent language.

(v.) Palatals had also gone through their characteristic transformation (C to S, H and J to D).

(vi.) Finally, the effects of vowel-assimilation and change are just as recognizable as in Siṇhalese.

In one word, *Máldivian must have separated from Siṇhalese at a time when the latter had already, in respect of Sound, assumed the form which it has at present.* And this, as I think I have proved, was about the year 900 A.D.

Siṇhalese Word Forms.

The secondary support of a nasal by the addition of the mute of corresponding sound doubtless belongs to the most recent specimens of the Siṇhalese language.

I am thinking of word-forms like *paṇḍuru*, "present" (E.S., No. 765) = P. *paṇṇákára; bam̆bara*, "wasp" (E.S., No. 964) = P. *bhamara.**

Professor Ed. Müller justly lays stress on the fact that such forms first occur in the Mihintále Inscription † (No. 121); which belongs to the end of the Tenth Century. ‡

But this Sound change also belongs to the period before Máldivian branched off.

This, at least as regards the changing of the *m* into *m̆b*, is proved by the Máldivian word KABURU, "smith" (Christopher; L.V., 83) = S. *kam̆buru*, P. *kammára;* TABURU, "lotus flower"

* Geiger, *Litteratur und Sprache der Singhalesen*, p. 48, Section 25, 5.

† *Wiener Zeitschr. f. d. Kunde des Morgenlandes*, XVI., Section 79.

‡ Geiger, *loc. cit.*, p. 20.

(L.V., 68) = S. *tam̃buru*, P. *támarasa;* also by the Máldivian MABUṞU, "bee" (Christopher), which—with a more recent difference of sound—resembles the S. *bam̃buru*, P. *bhamara.* In all these cases the Máldivian (*cf. infra* about this) has subsequently discarded the nasal altogether.

Lastly, there is another, certainly relatively recent, phenomenon in the Siṃhalese language, of which it may be inferred that it preceded the branching off of Máldivian.

This is the occasional replacing of *p* by *m̃b*.* We see this in Máldivian KUBU, "mast" (Christopher; L.V., 86), which, again, with the loss of the nasal, corresponds to the S. *kum̃ba*, P. *kúpa*.

Máldivian Words from Prákṛit, &c., Originals.

But it is not entirely surprising that, in spite of its later separation from Siṃhalese, Máldivian possesses words which originate from the Prákṛit foundation of Siṃhalese, but are wanting in Siṃhalese itself. Also, in single words, it shows phonetic derivations from the mother language, which would lead one to decide on a different fundamental form than the one assumed for Siṃhalese.

For example, Máldivian has retained the word FUHEN, "to ask" (L.V., 189), which corresponds to the Prákṛit *pucchati*. In Siṃhalese there is only the word *ahanu*, likewise known to Máldivian.

Máldivian BIS, "egg" (Christopher; L.V., 45), corresponds to the Sanskṛit-Prákṛit *bíja*, according to special Laws of Sound which I shall have to discuss later; but in Siṃhalese the word is not present. Two other words, also, have no equivalent in Siṃhalese: HEKI, "witness" (Christopher; L.V., 105), and HUVAI, "oath" (L.V., 106; Christopher, HUVÁE) = P. *sakkhi*, Sans. *sákshin*, and P. *sapatha*, Sans. *ṣapatha*.

For such phenomena there are different possibilities of explanation.

* Geiger, *loc. cit.*, p. 44, Section 20, 2 *b*.

Even if words we meet with are not present in Sinhalese Literature, and are also unknown in the language of the common people at the present day, the possibility of their being used in former times is not excluded. They may have been replaced by synonyms.

For example, in older Sinhalese it is probable that a word *puhanu*, "to ask," may have existed originally, side by side with *ahanu*, but has fallen into disuse.

In other cases, under the influence of Literature and the Grammar of the learned, the borrowed word has got the upper hand of the true Sinhalese word.

For instance, *bíjaya*, "egg"; *ṣákshí*, "witness"; *sapatha*, "oath," are now used.

But it is also conceivable that the foundation of Máldivian is a Sinhalese dialect which does not find its expression in the literary speech and in the social language of the present day, but differs from the source of these, at least in small details.

Máldivian and Sinhalese Word Forms.

We are also led towards this view from the circumstance that the phonetic form of single Máldivian words points to a different source from the form of the corresponding Sinhalese words.

Thus, for example, Máldivian FIRI, "male" (*e.g.*, FIRI-KANBALI, "bull," L.V., 37); FIRI-KALÉGE, "husband" (L.V., 13), are doubtless more ancient and closer to the P. *purisa* than the S. *pirimi*, with its enigmatical *-mi*.* Pyrard has the earlier form PIRIS.

Likewise HÁS, "thousand," is the direct and regular development from the P. *sahassa;* while the S. *dahas*, from its sound, clearly is related to the Numeral *daha*, "ten."

The two words TABU, "post," "pillar," and TIKI, "something," "a little," are also interesting. With their dental T they agree with the P. *thamba* and *thoka;* but differ from the S. *ṭẽmba* and *ṭika*.

---

* May it not possibly be a contraction from *pirimi(nis)*, "male (human being)" = Máldivian FIRI-MIHUN ?—B., *Ed.*

In old Siṇhalese there must have been equivalent forms, dental and cerebral: the former is continued in Máldivian; the latter in Siṇhalese words of the present day.

Máldivian US, "sugar-cane," compared with S. *uk*, points to an earlier double form. The first corresponds to the P. *ucchu;* the latter, on the contrary, to *ukkhu.* As is well known, the Sanskrit *ksh* has, in Prákṛit, in some cases turned into *cch,* in others to *kkh,* without its being possible to make a sharp separation between the two.

On the other hand, the S. *sohon, són, hón,* "grave" (E.S., No. 1,659), agrees with the P. *susána;* whilst the Máldivian MAHÁNU * presupposes an equivalent form, which occurs in the P. *masáṇa.*

In many cases in which Máldivian shows older forms, this is explained by the fact that in Siṇhalese the more recent form of the word was developed in the period after the separation of Máldivian.

As a rule, the words which in their enunciation show an earlier vowel than the Siṇhalese equivalent, can be accounted for in this way. But, of course, the supposition is not excluded that, in one case or the other, it may be due to radical differences in dialect.

The first idea would only be confirmed beyond doubt, if in a single case in old Siṇhalese—perhaps from earlier inscriptions—a form of word can be referred to which differs from the present form, and agrees with the Máldivian word. But, hitherto, I have not discovered such a case.

Vowel Sounds.

Words where the Máldivian shows a more primitive vowel sound than the Siṇhalese are, for example :—

KURA-FAT, "razor" (L.V., 85) = P. *khura,* but S. *ḳara.*

HUS, "empty" = P. *cuccha,* but S. *his.*

LONU, "salt" = P. *loṇu,* but S. *luṇu.*

FURI, "full" = P. *púrita,* but S. *piri.*

---

* The Á is striking.

MUṚI, " hammer " (Geiger) = P. *muṭṭhi*, but S. *miṭi*.

MINAN, " to measure " = P. *mináti*, but S. *mananu*.

DIRI, " cummin " = Sans. *jíra*, but S. *duru*.

TIN, " three " = P. *tiṇṇ-aṇ*, but S. *tun*.

To this, also, may be added ABURAN, " to turn," " to wind," with the U vowel, contrasted with the S. *aṁbaraṇu*, if the verb goes back to the Sanskrit root *bhur*.

In HILA, "stone," contrasted with the S. *hel*, we might consider that in Prákṛit the equivalent forms *sela* and *silá* are already present.

Noteworthy, also, are some cases in which the Siṇhalese shows a change of sound, which is not caused by the following *i*-sound; whilst, on the contrary, the change of sound is wanting in Máldivian :—

TABU, " pillar " = P. *thambha*, S. *ṭęmba*.

HAU, " cock " (HA'Ú) = P. *capala*, S. *sęvul*.

DAU, " net " = P. *jála*, S. *dęl*.

On the other hand, in Máldivian is found DEKUNU, " on the right," "southern " = P. *dakkhiṇa ;* whilst S. *dakuṇu* does not show the expected change of sound. In NAU, " ship," but S. *nęv*, it may again be a case of accepting double forms, NÁVÁ and NÁVI.

In such isolated cases, in which Máldivian, in contrast to Siṇhalese, gives one an impression of greater age, the general character of the former is, of course, not in question.

Máldivian is a relatively recent dialectic derivation of Siṇhalese: it shares with Siṇhalese all the characteristic linguistic phenomena.

Double Consonants.

Double consonants are wanting, or have only arisen as secondary formations.

Thus, VANNAN, " to enter," " go in," has arisen, after loss of the vowels through assimilation, from VADNAN, and corresponds to the S. *vadinu* (E.S., No. 1,281) = P. *vajati :* also VIKKAN, " to sell," from VIKNAN = S. *vikuṇanu* = P. *vikkiṇáti ;* DAKKAN, " to show," from DAKVAN = S. *dakvanu*.

We have instances of a simple loss of vowels in Máldivian, as in Siṃhalese.

Examples: DANNAN, "to know" = S. *dannu*, from *daninu*; GANNAN, "to buy" = S. *gannu*, from *ganimu*; KONNAN, "to dig" = S. *kaninu*.

But in these three cases, as well as in VANNAN, it seems to be a case of a double Infinitive suffix in Máldivian.

It is difficult to explain ANNAN, "to come," in reference to S. *enu*; and HUNNAN, "to sit," "stay," "remain" = S. *iṃdinu, hiṃdinu*.

Also in KEKKULA, "strong," "hard" (Geiger)—if I have written the word correctly, and it ought not, perhaps, to be written KEKULA*—as well as in KESSAN, "to cough" (Christopher; L.V., 29), the double consonant is striking; but in no case is it ancient.

It is self-evident that double consonants may appear at the point of junction of compound words, through assimilation.

Examples: VAKKAN, "theft," from VAG, "thief" = S. *vag* ("tiger") + KAN, "work," "deed" = S. *kam*; EBBAḌU, "uterine brother," from EK + BAḌU, "womb"; EDDAḶU, "ivory," from ET, "elephant" + DAḶU, "tooth," &c.

Long Vowels.

Also, though long vowels are wanting in Máldivian, they have arisen secondarily by contraction.

Máldivian continues the process, which is to be observed in Siṃhalese, in that, more frequently than in Siṃhalese, an H between vowels is thrown out, and the hiatus removed by contraction.

The sounding of the H in Máldivian, as is shown by other evidence, has become thinner and slighter than in Siṃhalese.

Examples of such lengthenings, due to contraction, are :—

BÉS, "medicine" = S. *behet*, P. *bhesajja*.

BÉRU, "out of doors" = S. *bẹhẹra*, P. *báhiraṃ*.

---

* Abdul Hamid Dídí states :—"The correct spelling is KEKKULA; but the word means 'patient,' not 'hard,' 'strong.'"—B., *Ed.*

BÍRU, "deaf" = S. *bihiri*, P. *badhira*.
FÍRU, "file" = S. *pihiri*.
MÍRU, "pleasant" = S. *mihiri*,* P. *madhura*.
FÁRU, "wound" = S. *pahara*, P. *pahára*.
VÁRÉ, "rain" = S. *vaharé*.
NÁRU, "nerve," "mind" = S. *nahara*, P. *nahára*.
DÚLA, "carpet" = S. *duhul*,† P. *dukúla*.

Contraction also occurs in FÍLA, "board" = S. *paliha:* it must have arisen from a fundamental form, FILIHA, FIHILA.

It is always worthy of note that where the Sinhalese shows a double form, the Máldivian appears only to know the further developed contracted form.

Thus, the Máldivian agrees with the Sinhalese in MÓ, "pestle" = S. *mól*, also *mohol;* BÁ, "arm" = S. *bá*, P. *báhu;* FÁ, "foot" (Christopher) = S. *pá, pada;* FILÁ, "green stuff," "herb," = S. *palá*, P. *palása;* HÁS, "thousand" = S. *dás*, also *dahas*, P. *sahassa;* MÚDU, "ocean" = S. *múdu*, also *muhudu*, P. *samudda;* LÉ, "blood" = S. *lé*, P. *lohita;* ÚRU, "pig" = S. *úru*, P. *súkara*, &c. Also may be mentioned here, NÉ, "nose" = S. *nẹ;* and RÉ, "night" = S. *rẹ*. (*Cf.* E.S., Nos. 757 and 1,225.)

A double form in Máldivian is KÍS and KIYAS, "saw" = S. *kiyat*. ‡

Some long sounds, indeed, remain unexplained. §

Thus, for example, MAHÁNU, "grave" (Christopher) = Prákṛit *masáṇa* (already quoted above); BÁRA, "12" = S. *bara;* TÉRA, "13" = S. *teḷes;* BÁṚI, "night," "shade" = S. *baḷu;* DÓNI, "boat" = P. *dóṇí*.

---

* In S. also *miyuru* (E.S., No. 1,091, 2).

† In S. also *diyul* (E.S., No. 597).

‡ VÁT (L.V., 20), VAI (Christopher), "left arm," is difficult. I believe that it is contracted from VA', "left" = S. *vam*, P. *váma* (*cf.* NA', L.V., 26, "name"), and AT, AI = S. *at*, P. *hattha*.

§ Those long in utterance, arising from the dropping of a final consonant, will be spoken of further below.

The relationship of MÍHU, "human being," "man," to S. *minis* is obscure.

Finally, in monosyllabic words, the vowel appears to be occasionally lengthened.

Examples: BON or BÓN, "to drink"; LAN or LÁN, "to set," "place"; DAN or DÁN, "to go"; O' or Ó', "kernel," "grain."

Nasal.

As regards the dropping of the nasal before a mute, this, again, has gone further in Máldivian than in Siṇhalese. The nasal in Máldivian is frequently quite dropped, where it is still retained in Siṇhalese.

Nevertheless, dialectical variations seem to occur. In my Notes, chiefly, are forms with the nasal, as I heard them from the mouth of my helper, Ibráhim Dídí; whilst in the printed and manuscript Vocabularies forms (of the same words) occur without the nasal.

I have noted BANGU-RÁ, "wine," "arrack" (Sans. *bhaṅga + rasa* *): Christopher; L.V., 55, on the contrary, has BAGU-RÁ. Also I have BANḌU, "body" (= S. *baṇḍa*, P. *bhaṇḍa*); ENDU, "bed" (= S. *ęṇda*); ANDIRI, "dark" (= S. *aṇduru*, P. *andhakára*); INGILI, "finger" (S. *ęṇgili*, P. *aṅguli*); DANḌI, "staff" (S. *daṇḍu*, P. *daṇḍa*); UNGULU, "cinnabar," "vermillion" (S. *iṇgul*, P. *hiṅguli*); TAMBU, "post," "pillar" (S. *ṭęm̃ba*, P. *thambha*): whilst, on the other hand, are to be set BAḌU, EDU, ADIRI, IGILI, DAḌI, UGULI, TABU, given by Christopher; L.V.; K.V.

Other words in which the nasal has fallen out are: ABI, "woman" (Christopher; but Pyrard has AMBY) = S. *am̃bu*; AGURU, "charcoal" (Christopher; L.V., 9) = S. *aṇguru*, P. *aṅgára*; KIBU, "crocodile" (L.V., 45) = S. *kim̃bul*, P. *kumbhíla*; KOTABIRI, "coriander" (L.V., 37) = S. *kotam̃buru*; KUKUN, "saffron" (L.V., 69) = P. *kuṅkuma*;

* In spite of Ed. Müller's objection (*W.Z.K.M.*, XVI., 78), I hold to the derivation of S. *rá* from P. *rasa*. An argument for it is the equivalent Siṇhalese form *raha*. Besides, for Máldivian the form RAS in Pyrard is direct testimony.

VEDUN, "present" (Christopher) = S. *vendum*, "reverence," "adoration."

For further comparison are noticeable: Máldivian TABURU, "lotus flower" (L.V., 68) = S. *tam̆buru;* MABURU, "bee" (Christopher) = S. *bam̆buru;* KABURU, "smith" = S. *kam̆buru;* as well as KUBU, "mast" = S. *kum̆ba* (*cf.* above, pages 100, 101).

Palatals.

The original palatals C (CH) and J throughout show in Máldivian the same changes as in Siṇhalese, *i.e.*, through S, which later becomes H, and occasionally D.*

I notice that, as regards the change of S into H, the Máldivian continues a process in language which had already begun before its separation from Siṇhalese.

In Siṇhalese, double forms frequently occur, in which, as I have mentioned, the forms with *h* must, as a rule, be regarded as the more recent.†

(i.) In Máldivian, forms with S have become extremely rare. Almost everywhere H appears; as much in the place of an original sibilant as of an originally silent palatal—the H being then, in many cases, completely dropped. Only where the S stands at the end, is it, as in Siṇhalese, always retained.

For the change of the silent palatals into H (from S), a few examples may suffice:—

Initial.—HAN, "skin," "hide" = S. *ham, sam,* P. *camma;* HA(N)DU, "moon" = S. *haṇda, saṇda,* P. *canda;* HAT, "screen," "shelter" = S. *hat, sat,* P. *chatta.*

Medial.—FAHUN, "later" = S. *pasu,* P. *pacchá;* MEHI, "flies" = S. *mẹsi,* P. *macchiá;* UHULAN, "to lift up" = S. *usulanu,* P. *uccáleti;* KAHABU, "turtle" = S. *kẹsubu,* P. *kacchapa.*

---

* Geiger, *loc. cit.*, p. 46, Section 23. The Máldivian palatal C is as little connected as the Siṇhalese with the original palatal: like the latter, it has rather arisen from TI. We see this from MACA', MACCA', "on," and MATÍ (S. *matu*), "above": Geiger, *loc. cit.*, p. 38, Section 13, 2.

† Geiger, *loc. cit.*, p. 45, Section 21.

Final.—The s remains: as GAS, "tree," but GAHU-FAT, "tree leaf"; AS, "horse," but AHU-KOTAṚI, "mane"; FAS, "five," but FAHÉI (Geiger), PAHET (Pyrard); US, "sugar-cane" = P. *ucchu*; US, "high" = S. *us*, P. *ucca*.

The H arising from an original sibilant obeys just the same laws.

We have HAKURU, "sugar" = S. *hakuru*, *sakuru*, P. *sakkhará*; HAT, "seven" = S. *hat*, *sat*, P. *satta*, &c. Medial FAHAN, "to sew" = S. *pahanu*, P. *pása*, Sans. *páṣa* and *páṣayati*, "binds"; DIHA, "ten" = S. *daha*, P. *dasa*, &c.

The initial H is quite dropped in UI, "thread" = S. *hú*; as is the medial H, with contraction following, in BÉS, "medicine" = S. *behet*, P. *bhesajja*.

An initial H arising from an original palatal is dropped in IṚÍNNAN, "to sit"—a word in many respects obscure, but which must be connected with S. *hiṭinu*, P. *ciṭṭhati*.

That the H of very different origin, within the word, between vowels, readily disappears, we may see by a comparison with pages 105, 106. I mention here FAUḶU, "clear," "public" = S. *pahaḷa* and *páḷa*, P. *pákaṭa*, where the H fills the gap.

(ii.) As an example of the rarer change of C into D, we have Máldivian EDURU, "teacher" = S. *ẹduru*, P. *ácariya*.

(iii.) Cases of D from J are frequent.

Initial.—DAU, "net" = S. *dẹl*, P. *jála*; DIRI, "cummin" = S. *duru*, P. *jíra*; DÚ, "tongue" = S. *div*, P. *jivhá*.

Medial.—MEDU, "middle" = S. *mẹda*, P. *majjha*; A(N)DUN, "collyrium" = S. *aṇdun*, P. *añjana*; ADU, "to-day" = S. *ada*, P. *ajja*.

(iv.) In two cases H has arisen from J, instead of from D, between vowels: Máldivian RIHE, "pain" = S. *rudá* (*ridenu*), P. *rujá*; and RIHI, "silver" = S. *ridi*, P. *rajata*.

Mute.

For the dropping of the simple mute between vowels, which was completed in pre-Máldivian times, we scarcely need special examples.

Stop-gaps.

To fill a gap, as in Sinhalese, Y, V, and H are employed. That H has then regularly disappeared and a contraction taken place, we have already seen.

(i.) Examples of Y (thus employed) occur in RIYAN, "cubit" = S. *riyan*, P. *ratana ;* and in MIYARU, "dog-fish shark" = P. *makara*, where the Sinhalese, so far as I know, only uses the borrowed word.

(ii.) As contrasted, we have V.

Thus: AVI, "sunshine" (Geiger; L.V., 2; K.V.) = S. *avu*, P. *átapa ;* and HUVAI, "oath" (L.V., 106) = P. *sapatha.* We may also mention here FAURU (= FAVURU), "wall" = S. *pavuru*, P. *pákára ;* as well as HAU (pronounced HA'U, or, more correctly, HA'Ú), "cock" = S. *sẹvul*, P. *capala.*

(iii.) In some words the Máldivian has inserted Y to prevent hiatus, where the Sinhalese has *v*.

Examples: HIYAḶU, "jackal," *cf.* S. *hival* = P. *sigála ;* HIYANI, "shadow" (L.V., 26), *cf.* S. *hevan*, *sevan* = P. *chadana ;* RIYAU, "sail," *cf.* S. *ruval.*

An I precedes the Y, because between the letter preventing hiatus and its preceding vowel there is an unmistakable connection.

In conclusion, it may be noticed that Máldivian, like Sinhalese, is determined in its pronunciation not merely by (*a*) the shortening of originally long sounds—of which we have already spoken—but by (*b*) the influence of accent, and by the two laws of (*c*) vowel assimilation and (*d*) change of sound.

Accent.

We observe the influence of Accent, as in Sinhalese,* in the frequent qualitative alteration of the vowel of the second syllable.

In this way the U in AKURU, "alphabet" = S. *akuru ;* DEKUNU, "on the right" = S. *dakuṇu ;* MAḌULU, "district"

---

* Geiger, *loc. cit.*, p. 31, Section 6.

= S. *maḍulu*, &c., from P. *akkhara, dakkhiṇa, maṇḍala ;* also I in RAKIS(-BOḌU), "bat" = S. *rakas, rakis ; cf.* P. *rakkhasa.*

Occasional derivations of Máldivian from Sinhalese will be spoken of below.

Vowel Assimilation.

Also as regards vowel assimilation,* it may suffice to refer to I(N)GILI, "finger" = S. *ęṅgili*, P. *aṅguli ;* BÍRU, "deaf," through BIHURU = S. *bihiri*, P. *badhira ;* LUI (*i.e.*, LÚ, "as it is said") through LUHU = S. *luhu*, P. *lahu ;* TUNI, "thin" = S. *tunu*, P. *tanu.*

Sound Change.

For change of the sound of A, corresponding to the characteristic ę of the Siṇhalese, we have E, with clear utterance, in Máldivian.

Change of sound also takes place in the formation of the Intransitive (Passive), as in Siṇhalese.

Thus: BALAN, "to see"; BELEN, "to be seen," "appear"; KAḌAN, "to cut down"; KEḌEN, "to be cut down" (like S. *kaḍanu, kęḍenu*).

Examples of single words, in which both languages agree, are particularly numerous :—

DEN, "afterwards," "thereupon" = S. *dęn*, P. *dáni.*
ET, "elephant" = S. *ęt*, P. *hatthi.*
FEN, "water" = S. *pęn*, P. *páníya.*
MEHI, "flies" = S. *męsi*, P. *macchiá.*
RES, "multitude" = S. *ręs*, P. *rási.*
VELI, "sand" = S. *vęli*, P. *váluká.*
VEU, "pond" = S. *vęv*, P. *vápi.*

Above, on page 104, DEKUNU, "on the right," "southern," has been referred to, where—as contrasted with S. *dakuṇu*—the change of sound through the I is founded on the P. *dakkhiṇa.*

In the same way there are words like HAU, "cock" (= S. *sęvul*), and TABU, "pillar" (= S. *tęm̃ba*), in which an ę

---

* Geiger, *loc. cit.*, p. 34, Section 9.

in Sinhalese corresponds to A in Máldivian; but where the Sinhalese ẹ cannot be explained by the influence of an *i*.

In a few cases the Máldivian has I corresponding to the Sinhalese ẹ.

Thus: I(N)GILI, "finger," S. *ẹngili;* and BIRU, "impossible," which I compare with S. *bẹ́ri.*

On the other hand, Máldivian E corresponds to Sinhalese *i* in FELI, "cotton material" = S. *pili*, P. *paṭi.*

Finally, like E answering to the Sinhalese ẹ, É is found corresponding with *ẹ́:* NÉ(-FAT), "nose" = S. *nẹ́;* and RÉ, "night" = S. *rẹ́.*

Thus, it is clear, Máldivian shares all the essential peculiarities of Sinhalese in respect of Sound.

Other Comparisons.

In details, too, the direct dependence of Máldivian on Sinhalese is seen.

In KIBÚ, "crocodile," as compared with P. *kumbhíla*, there is the same arrangement of the vowels as in S. *kim̆bul.* We have the same change of consonants in MÚDU, "ocean" (from MUHUDU), compared with P. *samudda;* and in BILAT, "betel," compared with P. *tambúla;* S. *muhudu* and *bulat.*

The Roḍiyá dialect here has preserved *tabala.*

But the Máldivian shows, besides, certain vocal peculiarities, which must have arisen after the separation from Sinhalese, and determine its dialectal peculiarities.

Vowel Alterations.

The vowels have undergone qualitative alteration of many kinds, through the effect of Sound-environment.

(i.) Thus, the vowel U frequently appears in the neighbourhood of labials: *cf.* BUNAN, "to speak," with S. *baṇinu*, P. *bhaṇati;* BUḶAU, "cat," with S. *baḷal*, P. *biḷála;* BURA, "difficult," with S. *bara*, P. *bhára;* BUMA, "eyebrows," S. *bẹma*, P. *bhamu;* FUNÁ, "comb," with S. *paná;* also, perhaps,

FUṚU, "side," with S. *piṭa*, P. *piṭṭha*.* We might, perhaps, admit the existence of a fundamental form in U as well as one in I, such as we really have in the P. *puṭṭha* and *piṭṭha*.

(ii.) Also, after G and K, the vowel U has developed in many cases.

Thus, in GUNAN, "to reckon," S. *gaṇinu*, P. *gaṇeti ;* GURAI, "parrot," S. *girá ;* KURAN, "to make," S. *karaṇu*, P. *karoti ;* KUḶI, "play," S. *keḷi ;* KUḶU, "saliva," S. *kela ;* KUREN, suffix, "herefrom," S. *keren ;* KEKURI, "cucumber," S. *kẹkiri*, P. *kakkári*.†

(iii.) The vowel O is found in KONNAN, "to dig," "cultivate," S. *kaninu*, P. *khanati ;* and in KOḶU, "end," S. *keḷa*, but P. *koṭi*, the O of which, according to the laws of change of sound, ought really to become E.

(iv.) On the other hand, in many cases a dental causes the appearance of the vowel I.

Thus, DIDA, "flag," S. *dada*, P. *dhaja ;* DIHA, "ten," S. *daha*, P. *dasa ;* TILA, "surface," S. and P. *tala ;* TIMÁ, "self," S. *tamá ;* A(N)DIRI, "dark," "blind," S. *aṇduru*, P. *andhakára*. ‡

(v.) The development of the vowel O from *a*(*ẹ*) in front of Ṛ (= S. *ṭ*) is worthy of note. It occurs in MUGOṚI, "ichneumon," S. *mugaṭi*.

We have the same before the final T, which then, according to the Laws of Sound, must become mute.

Thus, in O' (Christopher, OG ; L.V., 78, ON), "kernel (of fruit)" = S. *eṭa*, P. *aṭṭhi ;* and in VO' (Christopher, VOG ; L.V., 60, VON), "lamp" = S. *vẹṭa*.

---

* O after F occurs in FONI, "sweet," S. *pẹni*. On the other hand, *cf.* FI'Á, "herbs," "green stuff," S. *palá*, P. *palása*.

† On the other hand, KILAU, "soil," "dirt," S. *kalal*.

‡ More isolated cases are HONU, "lizard," S. *húnu ;* HONU, "lightning," S. *hena ;* HUKURU, "Venus (planet)," S. *Sikurá*(*dá*), "Friday," &c. In DUAS (= DUWAS), "day," the U is caused by V, as in NUVA, "nine," S. *davas*, *nava*. The preference for U in the second syllable, as has been observed in Siṇhalese, explains MIRUS, "pepper," S. *miris ;* FORUVAN, "to cover," S. *poravanu*. For NU, "blue," see *infra*.

In MADOṚI, "a (particular) weight," I originally occurs; S. *madaṭa*, P. *mañjiṭṭhá*: in this, the *a* of the Siṇhalese has arisen secondarily, *i.e.*, after the Máldivian separated off.

(vi.) If Máldivian o' is found in place of I, we have a derivation for o', "wax" (Christopher, *oa*; L.V., 47, UN): it corresponds exactly to the S. *iṭi* (E.S., No. 124).

Root Vowel Changes.

In connection with vowel change, I must mention a remarkable difference between Máldivian and Siṇhalese in regard to the vowel of the Root of the Noun.*

I should state, first of all, that in the scarcity of Máldivian texts it cannot always be established, with certainty, in which form, whether of the Root or of the Nominative, helpers have communicated the Máldivian words.

Further, I desire to record that, in my *Etymology of the Siṇhalese*, I was not sufficiently consistent; for in the *Supplement to Clough's Vocabulary* I put down sometimes the Root and sometimes the Nominative of the Substantive. In my later works, *i.e.*, in *Litteratur und Sprache der Singhalesen*, I have avoided this inaccuracy.

With regard to Máldivian, I should like to draw attention to the fact that there is still danger for us at the present time of falling into the same mistake, less through our own fault than through the existing state of our knowledge. Of course, our acquaintance with Siṇhalese always gives us some guidance.

We make, then, the remarkable observation, that in very numerous cases the end of the Root is different in Máldivian and Siṇhalese, and that—

(1) Where Siṇhalese has *u*, Máldivian has I.
(2) Where Siṇhalese has *i*, Máldivian has U.
(3) Where Siṇhalese has *a*, Máldivian has U.†

---

* As regards the formation of the Root of the Noun in Siṇhalese, *cf.* Geiger, *loc. cit.*, p. 52, Section 30 *seq.*

† In all these cases we are dealing with a Root vowel, which has arisen from an originally reduced (undetermined) vowel.

(1) Thus, we find in Máldivian the roots: AḶI, "ashes"; AVI, "sunshine"; BÁṚI, "night-shade"; BOLI, "mussel"; DARI, "child"; FANI, "worm"; DUNI, "bow"; HUNI, "chalk," "mortar"; KAṚI, "bone"; KOṚI, "cage"; KUNI, "dirt"; MAḌI, "smooth rock"; MUDI, "ring"; TARI, "star"; TAṚI, "cup," "dish"; ALI, "bright"; A(N)DIRI, "dark"; BARI, "heavy"; HIKI, "dry"; KUDI, "small"; where the Siṃhalese has *aḷu, avu, baṭu, boḷu, daru, paṇu, dunu, huṇu, kaṭu, koṭu, kunu, maḍu, mudu, taru, taṭu, aḷu, aṃduru, baru, hiku, kudu.*

(2) Directly opposite to these are KIRU, "milk"; BIRU, "impossible"; BÍRU, "deaf"; as against the Siṃhalese *kiri, bęri, bihiri.*

(3) Finally, occur EDU, "bed"; FUṚU, "side"; HA(N)DU, "moon"; HANU, "grinding stone"; KO(N)ḌU, "shoulder"; KUḶU, "saliva"; LADU, "shame"; MADU, "boundary"; MAḌU, "dirt"; MAGU, "way"; NÁRU, "sinew," "nerve"; TABU, "pillar"; TUḌU, "point," "top"; VAḶU, "hole"; MADU, "slow"; MEDU, "middle"; but in Siṃhalese *ęṃda, piṭa, haṃda, haṇa, koṃḍa, keḷa, lada, mada, maḍa, maga, nahara, tęm̃ba, tuḍa, vaḷa, mada, męda.*

Among these differences in vowel formation between Siṃhalese and Máldivian there may, of course, be many cases where, with the former, it is a case of a secondary change of form, while the Máldivian represents the direct continuation of the old form.

We scarcely need lay stress on the fact that, in many cases, of course, the Root Vowel in Máldivian and Siṃhalese agree.

Consonant Changes.

More far reaching in their influence are certain specific Máldivian Laws of Sound governing the consonants.

In some few words N has come in, in place of the Siṃhalese *l.* One finds interchange of the two sounds in Siṃhalese and in Páli.*

---

* Geiger, *loc. cit.*, p. 48, Section 25, 3.

In Máldivian KAKUNI, "crab" = S. *kakuḷu*, P. *kakkaṭaka;* MAKUṆI, "spider," S. *makuṇu* and *makul* = P. *makkaṭa:* also VIDANI, "lightning" = S. *viduli;* whilst Siṇhalese *vidu* corresponds to the Máldivian VIDU.

General laws are :—

(1) Change of Siṇhalese *p* into Máldivian F.

(2) Change of Siṇhalese *ṭ* into Máldivian Ṛ, a sound peculiar to Máldivian, difficult to describe.

(1) For the gradual appearance of the change of *p* into F we have interesting chronological support.

Pyrard, who spent from 1602 to 1607 on the Máldives, always, in fact, writes P for F. The change of sound is of quite recent date.

Examples (of the change from *p* into F) have already been given. I add :—

Initial.—FAS, "dust" = S. *pas*, P. *paṇsu.*
FENI, "vision" = S. *peṇenu*, P. *paññayati.*
FIYA, "foot" = S. *piya*, P. *pada.*
FÍ-VÁN, "to become rotten," "to stink" = Sans. *púta, púyati.*
FOT, "book" = S. *pot*, P. *potthaka.*
FURÓ, "axe" = S. *porova, poró* (E.S., No. 922).
FUTU, "son" = S. *put, pit*, P. *putta.*

Medial.—KAFA, "cotton" = S. *kapu*, P. *kappása.*
HAFAN, "to chew" = S. *hapanu.*
UFULYAN, "to lift up" = S. *upulvanu.*
UFURAN, "to pluck out" = S. *upuraṇu*, P. *uppáṭeti.*
BAFA, "father" (Geiger) = S. *bapa.*

(2) Examples of the change of *ṭ* into Ṛ—Christopher writes RH—are the following :—

AṚA, "eight" = S. *aṭá*, P. *aṭṭha.*
AṚI, "under," "underneath" = S. *yaṭi*, P. *heṭṭhá.*
FAṚAN, "to begin" = S. *paṭan.*
FUṚU, "side" = S. *piṭa*, P. *piṭṭha.*
KAṚI, "sting," "prick" = S. *kaṭu*, P. *kaṇṭaka.*

KOṚAN, "to cut down" = S. *koḷanu*, P. *koṭṭeti*.
KOṚI, "cage" = S. *koṭu*, P. *koṭṭha*.
MADOṚI, "a weight" = S. *madaṭa*, P. *mañjiṭṭhá*.
MUGOṚI, "ichneumon" = S. *mugaṭi*.
NAṚAN, "to dance" = S. *naṭanu*, P. *naṭṭa*.
MUṚI, "hammer" = S. *miṭi*, P. *muṭṭhi*.
VAṚAN, "to turn," "to twist" = S. *veṭi*.

In a few cases my authorities varied between Ṛ and R.

For example, I heard IṚINNA, "to sit"; on which account I considered the word as related to S. *hiṭinu*: Sheik Ali writes the word IRÍNNÁN: in L.V., 183, we have IRÍNA.*

I have noted FAṚUI, "silk," which I conceive to be a compound of FAṚA = S. *paṭa*, and UI, "thread": the L.V., 49, also writes it thus: but Christopher has FARUI.†

The regular replacing of the Sinhalese *ṭ* by the Máldivian Ṛ is very striking, both in the verb VEṬṬAN, "to fall"; L.V., 183, VEṬṬEN, Transitive VEṬṬÁILÁN, "to fell," which appears to be comparable to the Sinhalese *veṭenu* (E.S., 1,404); as well as in ÍṬU, "tile" = Sans. *ishṭaká*, P. *iṭṭhaká*.

In conclusion, I have to make some special remarks about the treatment of Initial and Final Letters.

Initial Letters.

In initials the media and tenuis are interchanged.

(i.) Máldivian GIGUNI, "bell," and GUDU, "hump-backed," "crooked," may be compared with Sinhalese *kikiṇi* and *kudu*. In Christopher we find TOṚI, "bowl," "shell (of egg)"—for which I do not know any etymology to propose; in L.V., 64, there is DOṚI.

(ii.) In AṚI, "below," compared with Sinhalese *yaṭi*, we have, perhaps, the falling off of an initial Y: possibly the word

* The Málé written standard requires Ṛ for IṚINNAN, or IṚÍNNAN: thus, IṚÍNNA(Å) ANNÁṚE (or A(Å)NÁṚÉ), "Come and sit down."—B., *Ed.*

† The proper spelling of FAṚUI is (as noted by Geiger) with Ṛ, not R: FAṚUI FÉRÁN, "silk cloth."—B., *Ed.*

goes back to an original form with H which corresponds to the Páli *heṭṭhá*.

(iii.) More remarkable is it that in several words there is a change of an initial Y into D.

Such words are DAGAḌU, "iron" = S. *yakaḍa ;* DAN, "watch," as a division of time = Sans. *yáma ;* DAN, DÁN, "to go" = S. *yanu*, P. *yáti ;* DATURU, "journey" = S. *yaturu*, Sans. *yátrá*.

(iv.) In addition, I mention, too, JAHAN, "to strike," which seems to correspond to Siṃhalese *gahanu, gasanu ;* and where, perhaps—I give the comparison as an isolated one, with all reserve—turning of the initial into a palatal has taken place.

Final Letters.

For the ending of words, the most characteristic feature of all lies in the consonants T, K, Ṛ, and L becoming mute.

(i.) As regards T, it has, as a rule, become I, but the words are still (in historic writing) written with a T in the L.V.; as well as in the few (published) texts written in the Máldivian Alphabet; and also by Pyrard.

Thus, the *written* forms are AT, "hand"; BAT, "rice"; DAT, "tooth"; FAT, "leaf"; RAT, "red"; but they are *pronounced* AI, BAI, DAI, FAI, RAI; and so they stand in all my recent Notes from verbal communications.

For GAI, "body" (Christopher); GOI, "manner," "account" (Geiger); MEU, "pearl," we must accept the writing GAT, GOT, MUT = S. *gat, got, mutu*.

On the other hand, HAT, "sunshine" (L.V., 111) = S. *hat*, P. *chatta*, has the pronunciation HAÍ.

Where such a T is removed to become medial it is, of course, retained in the pronunciation; as, for example, RATU-LÓ, "red metal," "copper."

(ii.) The I which occurs at the end of words like GUI, "cottage"; HUVAI, "oath"; VAI, "wind" = P. *gútha, sapatha, váta*, is to be regarded quite differently. In these instances —since it is a case of the simple *t* (*th*) of Páli, not of a double consonant—the consonant must have been dropped in pre-Máldivian times. In fact, we have in Siṇhalese, too, *gú*, "cottage," and *vá*, "wind."

The I in Máldivian is scarcely more than a sign of the lengthening of the final vowel.

A whole scries of such spellings may be recorded.

Thus: BAI, "share" = S. *bá*, P. *bhága*; FAI, "leg" (L.V., 20; Christopher, FÁ) = S. *pá*, P. *páda*; KURUBAI, "young coconut" (L.V., 66) = S. *kurum̆bá*; LEI, "blood" = S. *lé*, P. *lohita*; REI, "night" (L.V., 9; Geiger and Christopher, RÉ) = S. *rẹ́*, from *ráti*; OI, "stream" = S. *ó*, P. *sota*; UI, "thread" = S. *hú*; LUI, for LŬ, "light," "easy" = S. *luhu*, P. *lahu*.

(iii.) After E in ET, "elephant," the T has not become I, but closing of the top of the throat has come in. We shall see that the same is the case with the other consonants becoming mute.

The word ET must be written E' if we wish to record the present pronunciation. Christopher has E*G*, and by his italic capital *G* he only wishes to indicate the closing of the top of the throat. Strange to say, Pyrard writes this sound as EL—and he gives it also in other words where there was certainly not an L originally present at any time—instead of the closing of the top of the throat of modern pronunciation.*

(iv.) Incidentally, I mention here a change of T into S, which, indeed, is only apparent.

Examples: BÉS, "medicine" = S. *behet*, P. *bhesajja*; KIYAS, KÍS, "saw" = S. *kiyat*.

I know no etymology for the latter word; but in the case of BÉS we have to deal with a D appearing at the end of a word, and originating from J; which probably would be used quite differently from the T of the words compared with it above.

---

* Quite possibly Pyrard may have written T, which his early Seventeenth Century publishers misprinted L. Christopher, in his manuscript, *writes* G without modification, having made it clear that G final was = the AVIENI sign with *sukun* (Å), and should not be *pronounced*. It was Dr. Wilson who changed G to italic *G* in *printing* Christopher's Vocabulary in *Journal, R.A.S.*, 1841, VI.—B., *Ed.*

The likeness to BÉS at once gives us the etymology of the word BIS, "egg," which belongs to the Sanskṛit *bíja*.

K and Ṛ also become mute, and doubtless closing of the top of the throat comes in. Historic writing has here been only sporadically preserved.* We may, indeed, conclude from this that the disappearance of final K and Ṛ is older than that of T.

(v.) Examples for the disappearance of K are RU', "tree" (Pyrard, ROUL) = S. *ruk*, P. *rukkha;* FUVA', "areca-nut" (Christopher, FUVAG) = S. *puvak*.

Here belong the numerous cases where there is a Substantive with a so-called Indefinite Article dependent on it, which corresponds to the Numeral EKA. In Siṇhalese it is pronounced *-ak*, *-ek*, in Máldivian -A', E'; *e.g.*, MÍHE, "a man"; MALE', "a flower"; GAHE', "a tree." †

Instead of FUVA', quoted above, the L.V., 68, gives FUVAN. The nasal sound appears here in place of the closing of the top of the throat; and I notice that the nasal is always pronounced (in this word): the exact transcription of the pronunciation would thus be FUVAŃ.

Such nasal pronunciation is not unfrequently found in Máldivian at the end of a word. Thus, for example, FAHUN, "later," "afterwards," corresponds to the S. *pasu*.

(vi.) At the end of the Root of a Noun M becomes N.

Examples: BIN, "earth"; DAN (DAM in Pyrard), "night watch"; DUN, "smoke"; FÁLAN, "bridge"; HAN, "skin," "hide"; VEDUN, "present," &c. = S. *bim*, —, *dum*, *pálam*. *ham*, *vęṇdum*, &c.

(vii.) But a nasal change, alternative to the closing of the top of the throat, under conditions which previously have not been fixed, appears specially often.

In the Sentences III. 2 : 7 (Section I., p. 36) the two Plural forms MÍDA-TAN and MÍDA-TA', "the rats"—spelt according

---

* See *supra*, page 98, in the examples, Sentences (*e*) and (*f*).

† But, if no longer at the end, *e.g.*, HIYALAK-Á VAGALAK-Á, "a jackal and a lion," with vowel A; also FUÑÑAKA' (Dative), "on a heap"; DÓNIYAKA', "to a boat."

to the pronunciation—stand side by side, and in general the Plural suffix is pronounced, sometimes -TA', sometimes -TAN.

Similarly, there is variation in the suffix which means "towards," in the case of the expression GÁTA' (Section I., p. 43: III. 3: A 3) and GÁTAN (*loc. cit.*, p. 36: III. 2: 8). Instead of MI-TAN, "to," MI-TA' is spoken and written thus (*loc. cit.*, p. 54).

Side by side with MÍHUN, "people," we find MÍHU'; and -E' by the side of -EN, as, for example, SÁHIBEN (*loc. cit.*, p. 50).

We may, indeed, say that for pronunciation, closing of the top of the throat and the nasal are interchangeable (in practice). The exact circumstances under which one or the other is found will only be understood when more extensive and exactly noted texts are at our disposal.

(viii.) Closing of the top of the throat, or, in its place, the nasal sound, appears instead of the Ṛ.

In this way the Máldivian Dative in -AN or -A is explained; which, as I have stated (Section II., p. 66), corresponds with the Sinhalese Dative in *-ṭa*. Thus, Máldivian GAHA' = S. *gahaṭa*, "to the tree"; VALA', "to the forest" = S. *valaṭa*.

Just so we have closing of the top of the throat instead of Ṛ (= Sinhalese *ṭ*) in KO' of the verb KURAN, "to make" = S. *koṭa*.

Roots of Nouns in Ṛ are RA',* "land" = S. *raṭa*; O', "kernel," "seed" = S. *eṭa*; O', "camel" = S. *oṭu*; perhaps also O', "wax" (which I mentioned above) = S. *iṭi*. In Christopher we find, again, the spelling RAG, ÓG, OG: in L.V., with the nasal, RAN, RON, RUN, but certainly RA': in Pyrard, RAL, OL.

(ix.) Finally, (as regards) the behaviour of the sound L in Máldivian.

After A it becomes U, and has also experienced a change, which is perhaps analogous to that of T.

---

* Within the word, retaining the Ṛ: *e.g.*, RAṚUN, "from the land"; RAṚU-GAI, "in the land."

Accordingly, we have BUḶAU, "cat" = S. *baḷal;* DAU, "fisherman's net" = S. *dẹl;* FUḶAU, "broad," "wide" = S. *palal;* GAU, "stone" = S. *gal;* KILAU, "dirt," "clay" = S. *kalal;* MAU, "flower" = S. *mal;* RIYAU, "sail" = S. *ruval*; VAU, "forest" = S. *val.** Also TEU, "oil" = S. *tel.*

If U or O precedes the original L, only a lengthening of the final vowel takes place.

Thus, MÚ, "root" = S. *mul;* KAKÚ, "knee" = S. *kakul;* KIBÚ, "crocodile" = S. *kim̆bul;* Ú, "fork" = S. *ul;* BÓ, "skull" = S. *boḷu;* BÓ, "thick," "coarse" = S. *bol;* MÓ, "pestle," "pounder" = S. *mohol, mól.*

The correct spelling, also, should be NAGÚ, "tail," from NAGUL = S. *nagul;* and HAÚ, "cock," from HAᵛUL = S. *sẹvul.*

In the solitary case known to me in which an I precedes L, the latter is turned into U. Thus, we have NÚ, "blue" = S. *nil.*

* Here, again, within the word L is retained; *e.g.*, MALE', "a flower"; VALU-VAGU, "tiger."

APPENDICES.

A.—PIONEERS IN MALDIVIAN LINGUISTIC RESEARCH.

B.—THE LEYDEN VOCABULARY.

C.—THE OLD AND MODERN MALDIVIAN ALPHABETS.

D.—MALDIVIAN LETTERS.

By H. C. P. Bell, C.C.S. (*Retired*).

APPENDIX A.

PIONEERS IN MALDIVIAN LINGUISTIC RESEARCH.

Professor Wilhelm Geiger's acquaintance with the efforts of preliminary explorers—more or less serious—in the field of Máldivian Linguistics is, not unnaturally, incomplete, and, to some extent, quite excusable.

But his references to Pyrard, to Christopher, and to Gray —all three well known to him, and the chief sources of our information prior to the learned Professor's own masterly "Studies"—are surprisingly inadequate, in view of their exceptional respective merits.

It may be well, therefore, to put on record at least a brief synoptical "Bibliography" of contributions to our present knowledge of the Máldivian Language, in justice to the "spade work" done by earlier workers, however humble.

The notices of these "pioneers" and their labours, given below, are curtailed as far as desirable ; it being left to those who wish for supplementary information to follow up the references to the original authorities.

1.—Ibn Batuta.

The famous Moroccan, Abú Abdulláh Muhammad, usually styled Ibn Batúta, "the Traveller, *par excellence*, of the Arab nation," was at the Máldives for eighteen months, in A.D. 1313–1314.*

In his Narrative are found some forty (40) Máldivian, or semi-Máldivian, words, somewhat disguised under Arabian garb.

The most notable is the early mention of two words in particular, now classed as modern "Anglo-Indian terms":—†

(i.) COMBILI-MAS: "Máldive fish," or "the dried *bonito*, which has for ages been a staple of the Máldive Islands"

---

* Gray, *Ibn Batúta in the Máldives and Ceylon :* translated from the French of MM. Defrémery and Sanguinetti. (*Journal, C.A.S.*, 1882, Extra Number, VII.)

† See Yule and Burnell, *Hobson-Jobson*, 1886.

(Máldivian, KALUBILI-MAS ; Pyrard, COBOLLY, or COMBOLLY, MASSE ; Ibn Batúta, KOULB-AL-MAS).

(ii.) GUNDARA : Term applied to the Trading Boat of the Islanders, from which is acquired their present-day Siṇhalese appellation, *Gundarakárayó* (Ibn Batúta, CUNDURAH).

2.—Francois Pyrard.

François Pyrard, a native of Laval, in Bas-Maine, France, sailing for the East in 1601, as "one of a company of French adventurers," was wrecked on the Máldives, July 2, 1602.

"The crew were taken captive : a few escaped ; some were executed ; many died from sickness." Pyrard himself spent five years (A.D. 1602–1607) in captivity on the Group, before being released by an expedition of "the King of Bengal," which attacked Málé, and slew the Sultán.

"By conducting himself discreetly Pyrard won, as did Robert Knox some sixty to seventy years later in Ceylon, the favour of his guardians, and finally of the King."

The unique opportunity thus afforded enabled him to acquire a sound knowledge of—or, as he puts it, "a sufficiently large and exact acquaintance with"—the Máldivian Language, during his enforced sojourn at the Islands.

The result took shape, a few years after Pyrard had at length safely returned to France in 1611, in the publication of the Vocabulary, entitled *Un Petit Dictionaire de la Langue des Maldives ;* which was printed at the end of the Third Edition of his *Voyage* (2 vols., 8vo., 1619).*

This very valuable Vocabulary of the early Seventeenth Century consists of nearly three hundred (300) Máldivian words : to these should be added at least half as many again, found scattered up and down Pyrard's book ; making a sum total of well-nigh five hundred (500) words and phrases.

Pyrard prefaced his Vocabulary by this short Introduction :—

> I have remarked in many places in my book on the diversity of languages which are current throughout the East Indies. . . . As for the Máldives, they have a language apart, which is spoken only in these Islands ; and the best is spoken in the Northern Islands, more immediately under the King. For, towards the South they speak barbarously, being further from the coast and from traffic with other nations.
>
> Besides the vulgar tongue, there is also the Arabic, for the affairs of religion and the sciences, as Latin is with us ; and is only spoken and understood by the priests and the learned.

---

* Hakluyt Society's Edition of the *Voyage of François Pyrard.* See footnote * on page 7, *supra.*

I could have made a complete dictionary of the vulgar tongue, as my long residence had given me a sufficiently large and exact acquaintance with it; but, not to weary my readers, I will content myself with giving some of the principal and more necessary words, which will satisfy even the most curious.*

Pyrard's thoughtful consideration for his "readers" has, unfortunately, deprived modern students interested in Eastern languages of a wealth of Máldivian phraseology, which would have been of much philological value at the present day.

Elsewhere Pyrard wrote :—

There are two languages in use.

The first is that peculiar to the Máldives, which is a very full one. In the five years and more which I spent there I had mastered it as though it were my mother-tongue, and was quite familiar with it.

The second is the Arabic, which is much cultivated, and is learnt by them as Latin is with us. It is also used in their daily prayers.

Besides these, there are other languages, such as those of Cambaye, Guzerati, of Malalaca, and the Portuguese, which some learn for the sake of trade, and by reason of the communication they have with those peoples. In the Atoll of *Souadou* (Suvádiva), and towards the South, they speak a language hard to understand, rough and barbarous; but still it is the common (Máldive) language.*

3.—The Leyden Vocabulary.

The book containing this Vocabulary belonged to the *Bibiliotheca Leydeniana*, or Library of that distinguished scholar, Dr. John Leyden, who studied most branches of Southern Indian, and kindred, archæology.†

From its having subsequently found its way into the India Office Library, London, it is styled by Professor Geiger "The London Vocabulary."

---

* Gray, *The Máldive Islands:* with a Vocabulary taken from François Pyrard de Laval, 1602–1607. (*Journal, R.A.S.*, 1878, new series, X., pp. 181–182.)

† A. C. Burnell (*South Indian Palæography*, 1878, p. 49) quotes his epitaph at Batavia.

It runs: "Sacred to the memory of John Casper Leyden, M.D., who was born at Teviotdale, in Scotland, and who died in the prime of life at Molenvliet, near Batavia, on the 29th August, 1811, two days after the fall of Cornelis.

"The poetical talents and superior literary attainments of Dr. Leyden rendered him an ornament of the age in which he lived. His ardent spirit and insatiable thirst after knowledge were perhaps unequalled: and the friends of Science must ever deplore his untimely fate. His principles as a man were pure and spotless; and as a friend he was firm and sincere. Few have passed through this life with fewer vices, or with a greater prospect of happiness in the next."

The full title of the book (which Geiger does not give) is :—

"*A Vocabulary, Persian and Hindoostanee* [to which '*and Máldivian*' was added in manuscript, to cover the Máldivian words and phrases subsequently inserted by hand]. Calcutta. Printed by Thomas Hubbard, Hindoostanee Press. MDCCCVIII." *

The period when the Máldivian words, &c., were interpolated cannot have been later than the opening years of last century.

As will be seen, Professor Geiger, throughout his "Studies," sets particularly great store by this "London Vocabulary"—a confidence which has to be discounted, *quâ* the correctness of the Máldivian words and phrases *as true equivalents for their Hindústání and Persian counterparts* given in the book, by the *contra* opinion of I. Ahmad Dídí Effendi, a Máldivian nobleman of exceptional intelligence and reliability, son of A. Ibráhim Dídí Effendi, Prime Minister at Málé, Dorhiméná-kilagefánu.*

4.—The Copenhagen Vocabulary.

Nothing very definite, or of value, is known regarding it.

From Professor Geiger we learn (*supra*, page 11) the bald fact that "a short manuscript *Vocabulary of the Máldivian Language* is found in the Library of Copenhagen"; with the personal note that he had, "by the kind mediation of Professor Fausböll, received the manuscript," and copied "its contents."

He adds that "the Máldivian Writing employed in this Vocabulary has a quite unique style."

In regard to the extent, and probable date, of the Vocabulary, the Professor affords no information. Here and there he utilizes it in his "Studies."

The inclusion in the Manuscript of a Missive of Sultán Muhammad Muin-ud-din (A.D. 1799–1833) may perhaps throw its date back to the first quarter of the Nineteenth Century.

5.—James Prinsep.

To a *Note on the Nautical Instruments of the Arabs*,† the world-renowned Oriental scholar, James Prinsep, added a short *Note on the Máldive Alphabet*, accompanied by a lithographed Plate (XLIX.), in which the regular eighteen consonants (some with vowel signs added) are given, and about a dozen words.

---

* For further particulars, see Appendix B.

† *Journal, A.S. Bengal*, 1836, V., pp. 784–794.

Of nine letters, or half the Alphabet, Prinsep noted that—

They are, in fact, the nine Arabic numerals, with a dash above them to distinguish them from the ciphers . . . .

The system of vowel marks is partly an imitation of the Arabic and partly of the Indian method; the long vowels being denoted by doubling the diacritical stroke: the nasal N is marked like the Sanskṛit *anuswara*, but the letter N is also inserted.

Prinsep closes with an ingenuous admission :—

I pretend to no more knowledge of the Alphabet, or Language, than is comprehended in the Plate itself.

This doubtless accounts for his *reversing the writing* in the Plate, and his startling assertion in regard to the GABUḶI TÁNA, or Modern Máldivian Script, that "the order of writing is from *left to right*, contrary to the Arabic mode"—the truth being just the other way.

6.—Willmott Christopher.

In 1834,* during a Marine Survey of the Máldives by the British Government, Lieutenants W. Christopher and I. A. Young, of the Indian Navy, were able to spend two or three months on Málé Island.

In that short period, and despite attacks of "Máldive fever," which shortened their stay, these two observant Naval Officers drew up a valuable *Memoir* on the Islands.†

In addition, Christopher compiled a very full *Vocabulary of the Máldivian Language*, running to close on eleven hundred (1,100) words.

This Vocabulary, together with a Máldive Letter in the original (reproduced *supra*, pp. 49–51), with transcript and translation, was placed in the hands of Dr. J. Wilson, in 1838, and appeared a year or two later in the *Journal, R.A.S.*, 1841, VI., pp. 42–76.‡

Further, Christopher had supplied Dr. Wilson with—

Two facsimiles of writing in the Ancient Characters, or EVÉLA AKURU, not re-written, as they probably are more faithful in the present form.

---

* There is some confusion as to the year—whether 1834 or 1835. The *Memoir* (page 55) says the two Lieutenants landed on Málé on June 4, 1834: a footnote adds that Young had to leave on August 17, owing to continuous fever; and that, "after struggling against the fever for some time," Christopher himself was forced to quit "on the 9th September, 1835."

† See footnote * on page 8, *supra*.

‡ *Journal, R.A.S.*, 1841, VI., pp. 42–76.

I also send a specimen of the sculpture of the former mode of carving the Arabic on stone. Whether this may enable a person to trace the time of the first visit of the Muhammadans to the Islands, I am not aware. The stone bears date 994 of the Hegiri.

Perhaps the Muezzin Tower (drawing) and Inscription may be interesting. The Inscription was written round the Tower, so that from my ignorance of Arabic I probably have not begun at the real commencement of it.*

None of these, except the Máldive Málim's Letter, saw the light; they are probably no longer in existence.

Christopher's continuous Naval duties, culminating in a noble death, before the walls of Multán, in 1848,† were probably responsible for the non-fulfilment of that expressed intention, which would have further added to the scholarly debt he has laid all students of the Máldivian Language under, and, in some degree, doubtless have anticipated Professor Geiger's "Studies" by half a century:—

I propose hereafter to arrange, in a tabular form, the Substantives, Adjectives, &c., and hope to give a general Introduction to the Grammar, as time permits; so that if any person should visit those Islands from a philanthropic, or any other, motive, he may have a help towards the acquisition of the Language.*

Christopher's remarks on the transliteration, &c., of the Máldivian Language were summarized by Dr. Wilson; and that summary has been partially reproduced by Gray.‡

---

* Christopher's Manuscript Vocabulary (now in the Ceylon A.S. Library, Colombo).

† In the terrible night attack of the 9th September, 1848, Christopher received his death-wound.

"Captain Christopher," wrote Sir H. Edwardes (*A Year on the Punjaub Frontier*), "had, from his first arrival with the steamers at Mooltan, shown the usual willingness of his profession to co-operate with his brother officers on shore.

"On the night in question he had once already conducted some reinforcements to Colonel Pattoun's assistance; but the fighting at the outposts still raged with unabated fury. Another reinforcement came up, but had no guide. 'Will no one show us the way?' asked the officer of the party, looking round on the tired occupants of the trenches. 'I will,' replied Christopher, and putting himself at their head, steered them with the steadiness of a pilot through ditches and gardens, under a roaring fire of musketry. A ball hit him in the ankle, and shattered the joint to pieces.

"A few weeks later (9th October, 1848) he was borne by the grateful British officers to a rude grave, beside a well, near the village of Sooraj Khoond, and I myself read the service over him.

"A better or braver man fell not beneath the walls of Mooltan."

‡ See footnotes ‡ and § on page 9, *supra*.

But to do Christopher full justice, his *ipsissima verba** should be quoted *in extenso* :—

MALDIVE ALPHABET.†

The native name is AKURU FILI. The consonants are as under, in the order the natives uniformly write them :—

	Name.	*Value.*	
1.	HAVIENI ..	H.	The ordinary aspirate.
2.	RHAVIENI ..	RH.	This cannot be represented by a single letter. It, with the sign °, doubles the next consonant, and has no sound when itself a final. Its former sound was *shri.*
3.	NAVIENI ..	N.	This letter, with the sign ° over it, has the sound of *n* in "man," and of the nasal *ng* in "hang."
4.	RAVIENI ..	R.	The usual sound in "roar."
5.	BAVIENI ..	B.	As in "bab." All the vowels derive from this, when coming before it, the sound of *m*, excepting *o.*
6.	ḶAVIENI ..	Ḷ.	Reverting the tongue on the palate.
7.	KAVIENI ..	K.	As in "kid."
8.	AVIENI ..	—	This letter takes the sound of the vowel affixed ; but with the sign ° over it, *g.*
9.	WAVIENI ..	W.	Or v.
10.	MAVIENI ..	M.	As the common one in "moon."
11.	FAVIENI ..	F.	As in "fife," interchanged at times with the aspirate *h.*
12.	DAVIENI ..	D.	The dental *d*, as in "dew."
13.	TAVIENI ..	T.	The dental *t.* The *sukung* (°) gives this letter the short sound of *i.*
14.	LÁMU ..	L.	This letter is, in some connections, pronounced with the sound of *lya,* but generally this peculiarity is unobservable.
15.	GAVIENI ..	G.	The common sound ; always hard.
16.	ṆAVIENI ..	Ṇ.	As LÁMU (L) above, this letter sometimes has the sound of *nya.*
17.	SAVIENI ..	S.	Common, with the *sukung* (°) as *ss* final in "lass" ; never as *s* in "has."
18.	ḌAVIENI ..	Ḍ.	With the tongue reverted on the palate. This letter constantly gives a nasal sound to the vowel preceding it.

* See footnote * on page 130, *supra.*

† As the GABUḶI TÁNA and DIVES AKURU characters appear in the Plates, they are not reproduced here.—B., *Ed.*

In addition to the former, some few letters have been adopted from other Alphabets. (They are) classed as follows :—

Persian.	*Arabic.*
CH. As in "church."	Z. As in "zone." Y. As in "year."
P. As in "prop."	J. As in "joy." GH. A guttural *g*.
Ṭ. Reverting the tongue on the palate.	(TH, DH.) A sound between the dentals *t* and *d*.

Some of the above are not in ordinary use, while others are continually occurring.

The vowel-marks are as follows, and require particular attention, as they usually govern the pronunciation of the words. They are called FILI by the natives :—

ABA FILI .. A (ʹ) .. This sound is more like *u* in "mud," the short *u*. It never can be sounded like *a* in "mad," "bad," or in "can," "man": it is placed over the consonant.

ÁBÁ FILI .. Á (ʺ) .. As in "father": placed over the letter.

EBE FILI .. E (ʻ) .. Exactly the English short *e* in "men," or French *e*: placed over the letter.

ÉBÉ FILI .. É (“) .. The *ai* in "main," "pain": placed over the letter.

IBI FILI .. I (,) .. The short *i* of "pin": placed under the letter.

ÍBÍ FILI .. Í (,,) .. The long sound in "seen," "me": placed under the letter.

OBO FILI .. O (ʺʻ) .. The *o* in "dote." It is never sounded as in "dot," "lot": placed over the letter.

ÓBÓ FILI .. Ó (ʻʻ,) .. The long sound of *o*: placed over the letter.

UBU FILI .. U (ʼ) .. As *oo* in "food"; this never has the sound of *u* in "mud," "cud": placed over the letter.

ÚBÚ FILI .. Ú (”) .. The same sound prolonged: placed over the letter.

A consonant following the double (long) vowels, when final, is scarcely heard, merely adding its softening influence to the terminating vowel. There are only six consonants which can terminate a syllable or word; and they do so only when the *sukung* (°) is placed over them. None but these six are used with the above sign °.

They sound as under: AVIENI, as *g* in "bag"; N, as *n* or *ng* in "man," "fang"; Ṇ, the same as the last; RH repeats, or doubles, the consonant succeeding it, giving the emphasis to the syllable it terminates; unless the last letter of the word, when it has no sound, and seems totally unnecessary, except for the division it causes between words, and (because) the natives cannot understand writing without its due insertion; S, as before mentioned, sounds as our *ss* in "pass," "grass," &c.; T only remains: it is sounded like a very short *i* with the *sukung* above: the word (GENAT, pronounced) GENAI offers an easy illustration.

I was a long time searching out and comparing words to discover some uniform plan for the sound of the letters used with the *sukung* (°) over them; and at last was determined by the words in most common use, all concurring in one method of spelling, such (words) as FUWAG, "betel nut"; RAG, "island"; HANG, "skin."

Christopher's Vocabulary stands to-day as the fullest and most reliable of all *published* up to date.

Professor Geiger has been so unduly obsessed, in these "Studies," with the peculiar merits he claims to have discovered in the "London Vocabulary" that Christopher's — possibly less pretentious, but at least as deserving—work has suffered in comparison, and failed to receive at the Professor's hands that high commendation it so justly demanded.

7.—Simon Casie Chitty.

In the *Ceylon Government Gazette* of December 11, 1830, above the signature "Indiophilus," appeared the following remarks.

They introduced a list of thirty-five (35) Máldivian words, side by side with their Siṇhalese and English equivalents:—

It is commonly supposed that the Islands called Máldives, or *Malayadwípas*, lying South-west of Cape Comorin, were peopled by a colony of Siṇhalese from Ceylon, probably at a very early period, anterior to their embracing the Muhammadan religion. The chief circumstance that seems to support this supposition is the striking affinity between the DÍVÍ language spoken by the natives of those Islands and the Siṇhalese; although the former had received an accession of words from the Arabs and Bengalese, with whom they have great commercial intercourse.

In November last a Máldivian boat arrived at Calpentyn; and having been given to understand that the *Nakuda* spoke Hindoostanee with tolerable proficiency, I sent for him, and, through the medium of an interpreter, succeeded in collecting a number of DÍVÍ words, which I here exhibit, with their corresponding ones from the Siṇhalese.

The writer of the above was presumably Simon Casie Chitty, Mudaliyár, the author of that useful work (now out of print) *The Ceylon Gazetteer*, 1834.

For in *The Ceylon Magazine*, 1840–1841 (p. 10), there was published a very similar list of forty-two (42) comparative words (Máldivian, Siṇhalese, and English) contributed to that Periodical by the Mudaliyár.

8.—James de Alwis.

Among the papers left unpublished by the late Honourable Mr. James de Alwis (the editor of the erudite Siṃhalese-English version of the *Sidat Saṇgaráwa*, as well as of other valuable works) was discovered a short *Note on the Máldivian and Siṃhalese Languages*, accompanying a list of two hundred and fifty (250) parallel words in English and Máldivian—taken from Christopher's Vocabulary — with the Siṃhalese equivalents of some 140.

This Note must have been written shortly before 1866, in which year Mr. de Alwis brought out his English translation of the *Attanagaḷu-vaṇsa.*

The Note was obviously left unfinished. It breaks off at the commencement of a sentence.

Note.

During one of my trips to Galle, I was peculiarly struck, on hearing some Máldivian people speak, by the similarity which numerous words in their tongue presented to the vernacular Siṃhalese. Curiosity thence led me to an investigation as to the relation which the former bore to the latter; and the following is the result, which I have great pleasure in communicating to this Society.

The Rev. Dr. Stevenson, of Bombay, in an *Essay on the Language of the Aboriginal Hindús,* considers the Siṃhalese, "as well as the language of the Máldivo Islands," a branch of the *Dekkan,* or Southern Family, of languages.

I have already devoted a portion of the Introduction to my forthcoming publication, entitled the *Attanagaḷu-vaṇsa,* to prove the error of the *Siṃhalese* being placed in the Southern class, there being unequivocal testimony to show its relation to the *Páli,* or the Northern class of languages; and as regards the *Máldivian,* all the testimony which may be deduced from the development of that tongue goes to establish the fact of its being a dead (?) derivative of the Siṃhalese.

The following Comparative Table * of Máldivian and Siṃhalese vocabularies establishes this fact beyond all manner of doubt.

It is compiled from the materials furnished by the *Vocabulary of the Máldivian Language* in the Royal Asiatic Society's *Journal,* 1841, Vol. VI., pp. 46–72; and it proves most important facts :—

1. That nearly the whole of the Máldivian Language is derived from the Siṃhalese.

The Vocabulary from whence the above list was framed is extensive; and it is probable that I have overlooked many words

---

* Not reproduced. Mr. de Alwis was, therefore, in a humble way, the pioneer in the field of comparison, more fully worked by Gray and Geiger later.

which had a Sinhalese origin, but which now bear meanings different from those which they originally bore.

2. That Máldivian was formed some time after Sinhalese commenced to draw from Sanskrit; which was about the Twelfth Century A.D. See my *Sidat Sangaráwa*, pp. clxiv, clxv.

(i.) Sinhalese *u* is changed into Máldivian I: *e.g.*, "lime" (S. *hunu*; M. HUNI), "all" (S. *mulu*; M. MULI), "dirt" (S. *kunu*; M. KUNI).

(ii.) Sinhalese *p* is changed into Máldivian F: *e.g.*, "axe" (S. *poro*; M. FURÓ), "book" (S. *pot*; M. FO(T)).

(iii.) Sinhalese *i* is changed into Máldivian U: *e.g.*, "bare" (S. *hus*; M. HIS), "blue" (S. *nil*; M. NÚ).

(iv.) Sinhalese *l* is changed into Máldivian N: *e.g.*, "crab" (S. *kakulu*; M. KAKUNI).

(v.) Sinhalese *j* is changed into Máldivian S: *e.g.*, "egg" (S. *biju*; M. BIS).

3. That this language is mixed with Tamil: *e.g.*, "ladder" (T. *éṇi*; M. ÉNI).

4. That the . . . .

9.—Louis de Zoysa.

The heirs of Louis de Zoysa similarly found, amid the manuscript Notes of the deceased Mahá Mudaliyár, a *Vocabulary of Máldivian Words and Sentences* — 700 odd in all — transcribed in Sinhalese writing, with meanings, entered opposite each, also in Sinhalese.*

This rough and undigested Vocabulary was evidently intended to be divided under separate Headings (of which a dozen are given); but other words and phrases, supplementing those entered in their respective divisions, appear in the list, quite haphazard.

The Vocabulary (which remained unrevised, and has never been published) naturally suffered in its orthography from the words being not recorded in the Máldive characters, but merely taken down according to sound.

It would, however, be not without some value to any one who, wishing to acquire a knowledge of ordinary Máldivian, is content to study it through the medium of every-day Sinhalese.

---

* His heirs kindly placed the collection of words, &c., at the writer's disposal; and a copy was made.

Mr. Albert Gray wrote (*loc. cit.*, p. 176) in 1878 :—

"No attempt can yet be made to discuss the question of Máldive Grammar; though, if my information is correct, Louis de Zoysa, Mudaliyár, is collecting materials for the purpose."

In reply to an enquiry by Mr. Bell, in 1881, the Mahá Mudaliyár replied, May 1, 1881 :—

"I have no notes on Máldivian Grammar. I had a collection of Máldivian words and a few phrases, but unfortunately I have mislaid them." These came to light after his death.—B., *Ed.*

10.—Albert Gray.

In 1878 Mr. Albert Gray, late of the Ceylon Civil Service, published in the *Journal, R.A.S.*, new series, X., pp. 173–209, an Article entitled : *The Máldive Islands : with a Vocabulary taken from François Pyrard de Laval.*

The *raison d'être* for his Paper is given at the outset by Mr. Gray :—

It was Dr. Goldschmidt's task to investigate the history of the Siṇhalese Language back to its Indian sources, to define as accurately as might be the influences of Sanskṛit and Páli, and to note its correspondence and kinship with the other descendants of those ancient tongues ; and, finally, to mark its history through the period when it was known as Eḷu down to the Siṇhalese of to-day.

A study of Siṇhalese and of the Siṇhalese Inscriptions was, of course, the first and principal stage. But the work would not have been complete without an examination of the dialect of the Máldive Islands, where, as has long been known, a race of Siṇhalese origin resides, and a language of Siṇhalese descent is spoken.

It was duriṇg Dr. Goldschmidt's first year in Ceylon, while I was in almost daily intercourse with him, that a visit to the Máldives was suggested, which was fated never to be performed.

On my return to England, in 1876, it struck me that the Vocabulary which I now offer might be of some use to Dr. Goldschmidt, before he could visit the Islands himself, and it was chiefly with this view that I compiled it.

I presume that some advance in the knowledge of the Máldive Language may be made by re-publishing the interesting Vocabulary of Pyrard.

The only other Vocabulary with which I am acquainted is that given by Lieutenant Christopher, R.N., in the *Journal, R.A.S.*, VI., o.s., p. 42. Mr. Christopher was engaged under the Indian Government in the Survey of the Atolls, and during his residence there he seems to have obtained a considerable acquaintance with the language.

As it will be of great importance to scholars to compare the language of the beginning of the Seventeenth Century with that of the Nineteenth, I have placed, side by side with Pyrard's, the words given (whenever given) by Christopher to express the same idea.

I have not thought it necessary to copy the whole of Christopher's Vocabulary, for two reasons : (*a*) the *Journal, R.A.S.*, is accessible to all scholars ; (*b*) the language as given by him is that of to-day, and any one who visits the Atolls will find living dictionaries of more than the thousand words or so given by Christopher.*

---

* See footnote * on page 135, *supra.*

Before proceeding to give Pyrard's Vocabulary, Gray adds these useful hints :—

I must remind those who peruse it—

(i.) That Pyrard was a Frenchman: the Máldive words must, therefore, be pronounced as if they were *French*, in order to sound as Pyrard intended them to sound.

(ii.) That in *old French* printing *v* is used only as an initial: elsewhere in a word *u* is invariably used.

I am enabled to give, on the Plate opposite this page,* lists of the Sinhalese and Máldivian letters in parallel columns, from which the resemblance between the Old Máldivian and Old Sinhalese will be apparent. The last nine of the Old Letters have been abandoned in favour of the first nine Arabic Numerals. Formerly the Máldivian Language was written from left to right, but since the supremacy of Muhammadan literature it has been written from right to left. It will be hard to find another historical instance of so radical a change.

Gray adopts the following convenient division, under two heads :—

I.—Pyrard's Máldive Vocabulary.

II.—Máldive Words and Expressions used in the course of Pyrard's Narrative.

Under II. the words, &c., are further grouped into—

(i.) Atolls.
(ii.) Islands.
(iii.) Names and Titles.
(iv.) Religion.
(v.) Maritime Terms.
(vi.) Judicial Terms.
(vii.) Botanical Terms.
(viii.) Diseases.
(ix.) Social and Miscellaneous.

Gray's Paper—as Geiger curtly admits in his all too brief reference to it—is "the first (published) attempt to discover the connection between the Máldivian and Sinhalese Language"—a "first attempt," in truth, but none the less of real importance as marking a very distinct step forward.

11.—A. Ibrahim Didi Effendi.

Presumably Professor Geiger intended to include, albeit anonymously, that most courteous and obliging of gentlemen, A. Ibráhim Dídí Effendi, Dorhiméná-kilagefánu, the present

* See Plate II.—B., *Ed.*

Prime Minister to His Highness the Sultán of the Máldives, in the obscure footnote of acknowledgment in his "Studies" (see *supra*, page 11).*

The full extent of the Professor's debt to the Prime Minister —whom he had no compunction in "tiring"† by a flood of questions lasting for "three days"—must be left to supposition; though there are manifest indications of its value to be found in an occasional reference to "my helper Ibráhim Dídí," "Ibráhim Dídí," or bare "Dídí," in the "Studies."

Be that and the Professor's conscience as they may, it is both just and pleasing to record the fact that very substantial aid to a study of the Máldivian Language has been otherwise rendered, in his own unobtrusive manner, by the able, but unassuming, Prime Minister to His Highness the Sultán of the Máldives.

There was issued, in 1883, an "*English and Máldive Vocabulary: a Practical Guide for His Highness the Sultán of the Máldives,* Edited by Ebráhim Dorhiméná-kilagefánu. By His Highness' Command."

This book, which is quarto in size, has the English Words and Phrases printed on the outer third of the pages, leaving space on the other two thirds for the Máldivian spelling of the English words with their actual Máldivian equivalents, entered in manuscript opposite, and divided into parallel columns.

The following summary of the contents of a Vocabulary so unique will sufficiently testify to its high aim and value.

On the three preliminary (unnumbered) pages is given the English "Alphabet" in ten varieties of type, capitals and ordinary, with the Máldive pronunciation entered above; the

---

* In this he merely writes in general terms at the commencement: "It is with pleasure that I avail myself of this opportunity of publicly thanking my active helpers"; and then proceeds incontinently to induce undesirable and embarrassing comparison by specifically naming one of the three.

Was it not said forcibly of a well-known "History of Frederick the Great":—

"It would have been a graceful and proper thing to acknowledge the help in a *Preface;* but Neuberg, his generous aider, was too modest to ask for this, and Carlyle too egoistic to think of it."—B., *Ed.*

† See footnote § on page 60, *supra*.

following page (also unnumbered) has "Figures" 1 to 100, and one to a billion, running up in multiples of ten.

Then follows the "Index" of sub-heads.

This may be quoted in full, as well displaying the extent and broadness of this most valuable Vocabulary :—

The whole book consists of 77 pages, with 24 lines to a page, besides the first 7 containing the Alphabet, Figures, and Index. The total number of *words* given amounts to 1,600 and upwards, in addition to 250 *sentences.**

Truly an undertaking of which the esteemed Prime Minister should have every reason to be vastly proud.

---

* A bound copy of this unique Vocabulary, written up in full in the standard dialect of Málé, the Capital of the Máldive Islands, was most generously presented to the writer by the Prime Minister some years ago. It has proved of great assistance in furthering study.

12.—Abraham Mendis Gunasekara.

In addition to very valuable aid—indispensable aid, to a great extent—rendered to Professor Geiger by A. Mendis Gunasékara, Mudaliyár, both as "intermediary" between the German Savant and his other "active helpers," the Máldivian Prime Minister and the late Sheik Ali, the scholarly Mudaliyár proved himself a tower of strength in helping the Professor in his comparative study of the two Languages, by his translation of numerous sentences into Sin̥halese, and by suggesting the Sin̥halese equivalents and derivations of Máldive words.*

The Mudaliyár has recently supplemented his good work, on behalf of Professor Geiger and his "Studies," by publishing, in his very useful little *Sin̥halese-English Dictionary*, 1915, a list of Máldivian-Sin̥halese words, with their English meanings. The list runs to 407 words.

---

* See footnote * on page 11, *supra*.

APPENDIX B.

THE LEYDEN VOCABULARY.

Certain statements made by Professor Geiger (*supra*, pages 12, 13, and 15) in connection with the above book (which he calls the "London Vocabulary," owing to its present location at the India Office Library, London) being misleading, it is desirable to examine them.

This can best be done by the very "searchlight" which, under the Professor's manipulation, unaccountably gives a very blurred vision of the facts, *viz.*, that "bundle of letters," received by him from Mr. C. H. Tawney, Custodian of the India Office Library.

Fortunately, the *original* letters bearing on the question (copies of which the bundle contained) are still available in Ceylon.

They are quoted below; and speak for themselves with exceptional clarity. (Letters I., II., III., IV.)

Taking the learned Professor's assertions *seriatim* :—

A.

Mr. Tawney was so kind as to send the book to me, and with it a bundle of letters; from which it appears that some years ago, according to Mr. Bell's wish, it had been sent to Colombo.*

Mr. Bell expressed no "wish," and made no application to the India Office, at any time, for the loan of the Vocabulary.

It came to him—unfortunately too late to work on himself, as he had left Colombo—*gratuitously*, from the ever-helpful hands of Dr. R. Rost, then in charge of the Indian Office Library; "*at the suggestion*," it would seem, of "Professor E. Kühn, of Munich University" (with whom Mr. Bell was never acquainted), after that Savant had himself had the use of the book.† (See Letter I.)

---

* Mr. Tawney hatte die Güte, mir das Buch zu übersenden und dazu ein Konvolut von Briefen, aus denen hervorgeht, dass es vor etlichen Jahren auf Wunsch Herrn Bell's nach Colombo geschickt wurde. (Geiger, *Máldivische Studien* I., pp. 649, 650.)

† In a Letter, to the writer, of March 19, 1890, the late Mr. D. W. Ferguson quotes Professor Kühn as stating that he had "received the Máldivian Vocabulary from the India Office Library."—B., *Ed.*

B.

He (Mr. Bell) showed it to some native Máldivians, who were to examine the Vocabulary; but they came to the conclusion that it was full of mistakes and errors, and of little or no value.*

When the Vocabulary reached Ceylon, in June, 1890, Mr. Bell, a Member of the Ceylon Civil Service, had been already transferred to Anurádhapura, as Archæological Commissioner, to start operations in the Archæological Survey of Ceylon, of which he finally relinquished charge in 1912.

In the interval of twenty-two years, he had neither the spare time, nor the opportunity, of prosecuting his Máldivian Studies.

All that he could do, he did: he sent the Vocabulary to his generous friend, I. Ahmad Dídí Effendi, elder son of the Máldivian Prime Minister, who had, with much kindness, aided him very greatly, from time to time, in Máldivian matters, when attached to His Majesty's Customs at Colombo and Galle, in the Seventies and Eighties.

It is surely the irony of fate that the German Professor should cast a slur on a worthy son of a worthy father, A. Ibráhim Dídí Effendi, one of the Professor's three "active helpers" when in Ceylon, to whose patience and condescension the latter owed so much in the development of his own "Studies."

"Some native Máldivians"—to whom Mr. Bell is alleged to have shown the Vocabulary—have, in reality, like Falstaff's "rogues in bukram," swollen from a single individual—no ordinary "native" of the Islands, but one of the ablest of Máldivian noblemen.

Letters II., III., IV.—as the Professor must have been aware, from the copies filed in the "bundle of letters" sent to him, though he ignores them—clearly establish the fact that the whole burden of Ahmad Dídí's and his Himití referee's condemnation of "the book" rests on this, *viz.*, the *incorrectness* of the work *as a Comparative Vocabulary of the Hindústání, Persian, and Máldivian Languages.*

Professor Geiger is himself fain to make the confession: the "London Vocabulary is, indeed, not free from errors; and a considerable number of words contained in it can be rejected at once as worthless." †

---

* Bell legte es einigen eingeborenen Máldivianern vor, welche das Vocabular prüfen sollten, aber zu dem Ergebnisse kamen, dass es voll sei von Fehlern und Irrtümern und nahezu keinen Wert besitze. (Geiger, *loc. cit.*, p. 651.)

† Das Londoner Vocabular, mit dem ich mich nun auf grund der eigenen Beobachtungen zu beschäftigen habe, ist freilich nicht frei von Irrtümern, und eine beträchtliche Zahl von Wörtern scheidet für uns als wertlos von vornherein aus. (Geiger, *loc. cit.*, p. 650.)

To the Professor, however, "the mistakes" are not due to "ignorance"—regarding which Ahmad Dídí and his Persian *Paṇḍit* apparently have no shadow of doubt — but to a "praiseworthy, though naturally impracticable endeavour" —and, therefore, unprofitable and foolish—"to give, wherever possible, a translation for every Persian and Hindústání word."

"There are," adds the Professor—a naïve admission—"in this Vocabulary numerous words (technical terms, &c.) for which there neither are, nor can be, found equivalents in Máldivian."

Be it placed, nathless, to his credit, that Hasan-bin-Adam seems honestly, despite his "heavy handicap"—employing for the nonce the expressive metaphor of the Hunting Field—to have made a plucky attempt, "mounted" at times on "Paraphrase," at times on "Transliteration," to "take impossible fences"—at which he, naturally enough, "came a cropper"—thereby showing us (as the Professor considers, with unconscious humour) that he quite "understood his task." *

C.

I regret to be obliged to say that the Máldivians whose aid Mr. Bell sought, clearly did not take much pains in the matter: perhaps they did not possess the necessary knowledge of Persian and Hindústání.†

The unworthy insinuation against "the Máldivians whose aid Mr. Bell sought" (*i.e.*, Ahmad Dídí alone, though the

---

* Aber die Irrtümen erklären sich zum Teil als blosse Schreibfehler und entschuldigen sich damit, dass es eine durchaus feststehende Orthographie im Máldivischen überhaupt nicht gibt, und die Wörter, welche ich als wertlos bezeichne, fallen nicht der Unwissenheit des Uebersetzers zur Last, sondern erklären sich aus dem an sich ja löblichen aber natürlich undurchführbaren Bestreben, wo möglich zu jedem Persischen und Hindustani-Wort eine Uebersetsung beizuschreiben.

Nun finden sich aber in dem Vocabular zahlreiche Wörter, z. B. technische Termini u. s. w., für die es im Máldivischen kein Aequivalent gibt, noch geben kann. Da half sich denn Hassan bin Adam auf doppelte Weise: entweder gab er statt der Uebersetzung eine erklärende Paraphrase oder er setzte das Persische (bezw. Arabische) oder Hindustani-Wort in Máldivische Buchstaben um.

Von den "Paraphrasen," um diesen Ausdruck der Kürze halber zu gebrauchen, sind übrigens viele ganz verständig und beweisen uns zum mindesten, dass der Uebersetzer seine Vorlage verstand. (Geiger, *loc. cit.*, pp. 650, 651.)

† Ich bedauere, sagen zu müssen, dass die Máldivianer, an welche Herr Bell sich gewendet hatte, sich die ihnen gestellte Aufgabe offenbar nicht allzu schwer machten, vielleicht auch nicht die nötigen Kenntnises im Persischen und Hindustani besassen. (Geiger, *loc. cit.*, p. 650.)

latter justifiably invoked the extraneous aid of a *Paṇḍit* at Himití), as the Letters II. to IV. in the bundle must have apprised the Professor, without possibility of misconception, and the veiled sneer, no less at that Máldive nobleman's knowledge of *Hindústání*, than his travelled friend's knowledge of *Persian*, may best be left without comment.

Copies of this Special Number of the Journal of the Ceylon Asiatic Society will, however, be sent to I. Ahmad Dídí Effendi (now an honoured Minister at Málé), and to his father, A. Ibráhim Dídí, Dorhiméná-kilagefánu, the Prime Minister, "equally for the delight and amazement of good men"—as the *Mahávaṇsa* quaintly puts it.

D.

At any rate they ("some native Máldivians") were in error in calling in question Hasan-bin-Adam's knowledge of their mother-tongue.*

This is deliberately setting up the proverbial "man of straw"—with the usual result.

Nowhere, and at no time, have Ahmad Dídí and his Himití authority called in question Hasan-bin-Adam's "knowledge of their *mother-tongue*."

The unjustifiable charge is the more strange, in view of Ahmad Dídí's express and voluntary declaration (see Letter II.), that "the man seems never to have been acquainted with any other language than *Máldivian*," albeit apparently perfunctory in his methods.

E.

It is natural that I (in Germany), so many thousand miles away from the land of origin, was not in a position to verify all the new words of the "London Vocabulary"; and for this reason especially deplore the fact that this could not be done at the time that the "London Vocabulary" was in Bell's hands, and his Máldivian helpers were there.†

---

* Jedenfalls thaten sie Unrecht daran, die Kenntnis der eigenen Muttersprache bei Hassan bin Adam in Zweifel zu ziehen. (Geiger, *loc. cit.*, p. 650.)

† Es ist aber natürlich, dass ich, so viele tausend Meilen vom Ursprungslande entfernt, nicht im stande war, alle neuen Wörter des LV. zu verifizieren, und aus diesen Grunde vor allem beklage ich es, dass dies nicht geschah zu der Zeit, als das LV. in den Händen Bell's und seinar Máldivischen Gewährsmänner sich befand. (Geiger, *loc. cit.*, p. 652.)

During the time the "Leyden Vocabulary" was in Mr. Bell's hands it could not be put to direct use. He was, as stated above, stationed then, under Government orders, at Anurádhapura, in the North-Central Province, an interior district of Ceylon; and fully occupied with Archæological work.

To have sought to muster "*Máldivian* helpers," of all people, to "a pleasant walk, a pleasant talk," amid the distant ruins of that "Buried City"—the ancient Capital of *Laṅká*—would have met with success equaling that of the cynical invitation by a certain Walrus and Carpenter to the luckless "Oysters," when—"answer came there none!" For—

> Green Earth has her sons and her daughters,
> And these have their guerdons; but we
> Are the wind's and the sun's and the water's
> Elect of the Sea.

F.

The book was returned by Ahmad Dídí, from Málé, at the close of 1895.

It was restored by Mr. Bell to the India Office a few months later, with a letter of frank apology—distinctly due for the very great delay which had ensued, and for which full personal responsibility was, of course, accepted unreservedly.

To the apology was added expression of real regret that it had not been found possible to turn the Vocabulary to account, it having been "condemned as incorrect and valueless" in the copies of Ahmad Dídí's Letters (II., III., IV.) annexed to Mr. Bell's Letter.

Some particulars regarding the Vocabulary (not given by Professor Geiger) were jotted down by Mr. Bell in a brief Note, before finally despatching the book to England:—

The Leyden Vocabulary.*

In the Indian Office Library is—

"*A Vocabulary, Persian and Hindoostanee* [to which was subsequently added, in pencil, '*and Máldivian*']. Calcutta. Printed by Thomas Hubbard, Hindoostanee Press. MDCCCVIII."

Size, 8vo., $9\frac{5}{8}$ in. by $6\frac{1}{2}$ in.; binding, brown leather, mottled; cover, plain; back, six urn figurines between seven ornamental bands, all gilt.

This book, now the property of the Indian Office Library, London, belonged to the "*Bibliotheca Leydeniana,*" formed by the learned Dr. John Leyden.

---

* See *supra*, Appendix A, pages 127-128.

It contains 216 pages, of 18 lines (with exceptions) to the page. Each line consists of a *Persian* word ; as well as (to some extent) its *Hindústání* equivalent, opposite, in "Devanágari" character. Beyond this is given the *Máldivian* version, written clearly in the GABUḶI TÁNA, or modern Máldive, characters.

Many *lacunæ* occur in the book.

Inside the cover, at the beginning of the book and on the fly-leaf, is written out, irregularly, the GABUḶI TÁNA syllabary (vowels and consonants), starting thus: MA, MI, MÍ, ME, MO, MA(N), MI(N), ME(N), MO(Ṛ), MÉ(Ṛ), MÓ(Ṛ), and ending with ṬA, ṬI, ṬÍ, ṬE, ṬO, ṬA(N), ṬI(N), ṬE(N), ṬO(Ṛ), ṬÉ(Ṛ), ṬÓ(Ṛ).

The blank page before the Title Page bears some Persian (?) writing, with date A. H. 1223.

On the pages of the fly-leaf at the end of the book there are transcribed, in two separate columns, what look like archaic variants of the GABUḶI TÁNA Alphabet—that on the first page giving the consonants from M to Ñ ; that on the second page the syllables from MA to ṬA, with dots and dashes, headed by the title "The Divas Alphabet." *

Of both these columns of antique writing, a very careful tracing was made by Mr. D. A. L. Perera, Head Draughtsman (now Muhandiram and Native Assistant) of the Archæological Survey. They have been reproduced by photography, and appear on Plate V., 1 and 2.

ANNEXURES.

I.

(*Letter, June 6, 1890, from Dr. R. Rost.*)

India Office, Whitehall, S.W.,
June 6, 1890.

MY DEAR SIR,

Professor E. Kühn, of Munich University, informs me that you are working at Máldive. At his suggestion, I send you a Máldive Vocabulary, which turned up in our Library some time ago.

As you may wish to have the use of it for some time, I enclose the usual voucher, which I would ask you to sign and return.

Ever sincerely yours,
R. ROST.

H. C. P. BELL, Esq.,
Ceylon Civil Service.

---

* See footnote † on page 21, *supra*.

II.

(*Letter, November 13, 1890, from I. Ahmad Dídí.*)

The Vocabulary has been printed in the Hijra 1223 (and the Hijra now is 1308), or eighty-five * years ago.

A man, by name Hasan-bin-Adam, of Himití (Nilandú Atoll), has given the *Máldive equivalents* to the Author, as he thought right; but I am confident that there are not ten correct in every hundred, having some acquaintance with the *Hindústání* language.

I found, to my surprise, that the *Máldive equivalents* were greatly wrong, as the man mentioned above seems never to have been acquainted with any other language than Máldive; and even in the Máldivian sentences some are not completed.

I think it would be useless labour for you to take the trouble to edit this work.

III.

(*Letter, November 26, 1890, from I. Ahmad Dídí.*)

I have now gone through the whole Vocabulary.

Not being fully competent in *Hindústání*, and not knowing *Persian*, I am unable to judge whether *all* the words are correct or not.

I am able to judge of those which I understand, by comparing them with Hindústání, but not with Persian.

I shall write for you the equivalents in *Siṇhalese* of the correct words I am able to make out.

The person who has given the *Máldive equivalents* in the book has done so through *interpretation*, it seems: that is why so many of them are wrong.

IV.

(*Letter, December 7, 1895, from I. Ahmad Dídí.*)

Regarding the Hindústání, Persian, and Máldivian Vocabulary, which you handed me when I was in Ceylon, for translation either into English or into Siṇhalese.

---

* Lunar years. By the Christian Era reckoning, eighty-two years (A.D. 1890-1808).—B., *Ed.*

When I examined the book it was found to be a Persian and Máldivian Vocabulary. Two or three pages only contained the translation in Hindústání; and, therefore, it was not possible for me (being not competent at that time in the Persian language) to go on comparing whether the Máldivian translations were correct or not.

When I came here, I heard about a man in Himití, who had for many years visited India, and had acquired a knowledge of the Persian language. To him, therefore, I forwarded the book for examination.

He wrote to me saying that the *Máldivian translations* are mostly incorrect, and do not agree with their *Persian equivalents*; and that, it seemed to him, the work had been done by a man who did not know the *Persian* language properly; or that he might have translated through the aid of *Hindústání*, even which language he may not have known well.

As the Himití man says that the book is worth nothing, I have to return it without the promised translation.

APPENDIX C.

THE OLD AND MODERN MALDIVIAN ALPHABETS.

In the compass of a limited Appendix, it is not possible to cover all the ground required for a full treatment of the Old and Modern types of the Máldivian Alphabet.

It must, therefore, suffice for the time being to offer an outline sketch, intended to bring out at least the salient features noticeable in the use of each, respectively.

Without question, Professor Geiger's learned "Máldivian Studies" have very materially advanced general knowledge of the Construction and Grammar of the Máldive Language, besides, to some degree, extending our acquaintance with its Vocabulary; and these are chiefly material.

But, as touching the collateral branch, its Epigraphy—both the "DIVES (or DIVEHI) AKURU," or Old, and the "GABUḶI TÁNA," or Modern, forms of Máldive writing — the Professor, from no fault of his own, has been unable to add appreciably to the stock of information — in the case of the Ancient Alphabet confessedly very imperfect—already existing.

So far as concerns the GABUḶI TÁNA Alphabet, as given by Christopher, of eighteen (18) Máldivian letters—or, including the Persi-Arabic modified incorporations, twenty-six (26) in all—with its *Semitic* vowel system of detached accents, &c., nearly all particulars have long been recorded. The influence of the *Arabic Numerals 1 to 9*, or the first section of the Alphabet, on its *written character*, as well as the *right-to-left mode of writing*, are now-a-days well-established facts; rightly attributed to the influence of the Muslim conversion of the Islands, which took place about the middle of the Twelfth Century.

In regard, however, to the DIVES AKURU (literally, "the Island Letters"), the pristine alphabet of "DIVEHI RÁAJE," or "The (Máldive) Island Kingdom" — unless, perchance, one of the older forms of *Bráhma lipi* script should yet be discovered on the Group—the case is very different.

What little is known about the DIVES AKURU is based almost entirely on two authorities.

These are Christopher and Young's communications made to the Geographical and Royal Asiatic Societies, between 1836 and 1841, or more than three-quarters of a century ago; and Gray's Paper, which was penned some five and thirty years later, and printed in the Royal Asiatic Society Journal of 1878.*

Beyond the welcome, and *pro tanto* successful, effort of Gray to show, by Tabulated Comparison (see Plate II.), the more or less close connection between this EVÉLA, or "Ancient," Alphabet and that of Mediæval Siṇhalese lithic inscriptions, nothing has been printed tending to elucidate the real origin of the DIVES AKURU Alphabet.

Writing in 1900–1902, Professor Geiger, despite his very persistent and highly important researches into the Structure of the Máldivian Language (conducted first at Colombo itself, during a three months' sojourn in Ceylon during 1895–1896, and subsequently in Germany), has to content himself, and his readers, with falling back wholly on (*a*) Christopher's partial syllabary of that well-nigh unknown Alphabet, and (*b*) Christopher and Young's joint assertion regarding an alleged special peculiarity, *viz.*, that "the separate letters appear in a different form according to the vowels to which they are joined."

I.—"Dives Akuru" Alphabet.

As stated, all that has been *published* up to date regarding the Old Máldivian script is contained in a short reference, found in the *Memoir* compiled by Naval Lieutenants Young and Christopher (*Transactions, Geographical Society, Bombay*), to "the most ancient character, called by the natives the DEWEHI HAKURA"; and the valuable, but incomplete, delineation (eighteen letters only) of the Alphabet communicated to Dr. Wilson by the latter officer (*Journal, R.A.S.*, 1841, pp. 42–76).

In the above *Memoir* (see *supra*, page 20) it is said that these characters "in all likelihood were used by the first inhabitants"; but "the knowledge of them," not being remembered in the Northern Atolls, was even then (1835 *circa*) "nearly lost," though partially used for "orders" to the Southern Atolls, where "the writing appears to have been retained longest"; that "no old manuscripts with this character (which is *written from the left hand*) are preserved"; and, finally, that "one peculiarity in the Alphabet is that some of the consonants change their form according to the various vowel sounds with which they are united, the construction of the letters being altogether different."

---

* (i.) *Transactions of the Bombay Geographical Society*, 1836–1838 (reprint, 1844); (ii.) *Journal, R.A.S.*, 1841; (iii.) *Id.*, New Series, X., 1878.

This last-mentioned "characteristic phenomenon" of "the Ancient Máldive Alphabet points," according to Professor Geiger (*supra*, p. 25), "towards a writing which is very closely related to the Aṣóka Alphabet."

The above represents, then, virtually the sum total of present-day outside acquaintance with the DIVES AKURU.

It will be shown below, briefly, that this tantalizing dole of information, made eighty years ago, can at this day be considerably augmented.

Even now "old manuscripts" in DIVES AKURU character might very possibly come to light, here and there, in the Southern Atolls, were these more distant groups exploited judiciously by systematic search.

At least it is certain that the Ancient Alphabet continues to be used, on occasions, in those Atolls; and songs, &c., written therein may probably yet be obtainable.*

(i.) *Origin of the "Dives Akuru" Alphabet.*

The obvious affinity of the old writing—not so much with Mediæval Sinhalese as to the Tuḷu of the Malabar Districts of Southern India, which lie opposite the Lakkadive and Máldive Islands; or, doubtless, even more nearly to an older Grantha type of Tuḷu-Malayáḷam, or *Árya Eḷuttu*, to which the DIVEHI AKURU may well have been closely akin — strongly suggests the former existence of a fuller list of characters, including aspirates.†

The DIVES AKURU Alphabet, so far as it is utilized at the present day, has manifestly been made to fall into line with the modern GABUḶI TÁNA Alphabet, both in the current order, as well as the limit, of its characters.

Evidence has not been forthcoming hitherto — if such exists still on the Islands — concerning its *original extent* as compared with Sanskṛit and other Indian alphabets; but it seems most probable that it once possessed, like them, a more complete complement of letters, embracing not only aspirated consonants, but additional sibilants also.

With the acceptance of Muhammadanism, and the adoption of an alphabet based on a compromise with Semitic script and mode of writing, the need for aspirated letters, and the palatal (ṣ) and—except rarely—the cerebral (*sh*) sibilants of Indian systems vanished. The dental surd s with sonant z sufficed usually.

---

* Thirty or forty years ago Mr. Bell procured a few songs, &c., from Máldivian Islanders, both in DIVES AKURU and GABUḶI TÁNA writing.

† Unless the DIVES AKURU followed the limitation of the Eḷu Alphabet, which dispensed with aspirates.

Hence, as will be seen by Plate VI., the DIVES AKURU Alphabet, as now surviving, is confined to the narrowed limits and changed order of the GABUḶI TÁNA.

(ii.) *Syllabary.*

There is evidence on record that Christopher must have been acquainted with all the basal " vowel-consonants " (*i.e.*, those with inherent short A), as well as the vowel system, of the DIVES AKURU Alphabet ; but that, with characteristic modesty, he confined himself in his manuscript (from which Dr. Wilson printed) to giving only the equivalent *aksharas* for the first eighteen (18) letters of the GABUḶI TÁNA Alphabet.*

Inquiries pressed by the writer, when attached to H. M. Customs at Colombo and Galle in the Seventies and Eighties, elicited definite information that DIVES AKURU *characters exist corresponding virtually to the entire* GABUḶI TÁNA *Alphabet*, the only exceptions being (see Plate II.) the two so-called "adopted" or "borrowed" Arabic letters *gh*, and *th* or *dh*, sub-scribed with three dots, given by Christopher and reproduced by Gray.

Of what survives of the original DIVES AKURU Alphabet, a duplicated syllabary of consonants (with short A only; except H, which is shown, *exempli gratiâ*, fully inflected) and vowels is now presented in Plates VI., VII.

The upper letters of each division exhibit the form (probably the purest) obtained from the *Southern Atolls*, the lower that of those from *Málé*, the centre of the Group.†

From these the main characteristics of the Old Alphabet may be fairly grasped.

The basal forms — twenty-six (26) in all, inclusive of the *sukun* as a nasal — will be found illustrated on Plate VI., in

---

* Lieutenant Christopher met the travelled French savant, Monsieur Antoine d'Abbadie, at Tujurrah, in 1841.

" I never *saw* Christopher ; for I was blinded by ophthalmia when he called on me. He promised to send me a copy of the Old Máldive syllabary ; and I thanked his messenger warmly the following day, a few hours before Christopher set sail to receive his death wound on the Indus (1848). When I recovered my eyesight, I saw with regret that he had sent me a list of consonants (34), vocalized only in A, followed by a tantalizing '&c.' I boarded the Indian Navy Warship ; but Christopher was then gone." (Extract from a letter to Mr. Bell, dated February 2, 1887, Basses Pyrenées.)

The letters in Christopher's list, as copied by Monsieur d'Abbadie, show 18 with short A, and 16 with either long Á or short I.

† The letters as written in the Southern Group were given by Ahmad Dídí, of *Fua Mulaku* Island ; the others were kindly supplied by Ibráhim Dídí Effendi, Dorhiménà-kilagefánu (now Prime Minister), from *Málé*.

which (*a*) the letters ("*vowel-consonants*") commencing with H (according to modern usage) and ending with Y, and the *sukun*, are set out; besides (*b*) some variants.*

These are supplemented in Plate VII. by (*c*) the five *initial vowels*, short and long; their (*d*) *medial signs*; together with (*e*) the consonant H (the first of the Alphabet), as modified by all its vowel inflexions; and (*f*) a few compound letters.

Finally, (*g*) specimens of the writing are added.

(iii.) *Consonants.*

The inflected forms of H, as shown in Plate VII., definitely explode the long-standing "myth," *viz.*, that "the separate letters appear in a different form according to the vowel to which they are joined"; except in so far, and only in so far, as the addition of vowel signs necessarily modifies the outlines of the consonants affected, as in Sanskṛit, Siṇhalese, &c.

Ex uno disce omnes. Some consonants may assume a variant shape (see Plate VI.); but, whatever the shape adopted, the addition of *vowels*, or the *sukun*, in no way affects them, beyond the inevitable modification resulting from the attachment of the vowels, &c.

A radical difference between the Old type of character and the New lies in the DIVES AKURU base-consonants being, as stated above, like those of Sanskṛit, Siṇhalese, and other Indian cognate alphabets, actually "*vowel-consonants*" (*i.e.*, each contains the short vowel A); whilst the GABUḶI TÁNA letters are *pure consonantal* signs, quite vowel-less until vivified by the super-script, or sub-script, accents common to Persian, Arabic, &c.

The only indication of aspirates (H excepted) and extra sibilants once forming part of Máldivian script is furnished by the occurrence in both Alphabets of *aksharas* for P and F (the simple breath-sound of the aspirated digraph PH), and the occasional employment of SHA in GABUḶI TÁNA.

---

* No uniformity has ruled so far for the order of the "adopted," or "borrowed," consonants of the Modern Máldive Alphabet as contrasted with the first eighteen letters. These should start with H and end with D correctly; though the latter half (M to D) has been sometimes (as by Gray) transposed with the first half, making the last letter V.

Christopher (reproduced by Gray; see Plate II.) gives (from Persian) C, P, T, (from Arabic) Z, Y, J, GH, TH (or DH); omitting Ñ. Geiger (adopting—for these nine only—the order of the pseudo-GABUḶI TÁNA in the "Leyden Vocabulary") prints (Plate I.) Y, Z, C, J, Ṭ, Ñ, P, *Greek* γ for GH, and T underlined for TH (or DH). In Plate VI. the order of the first seven (as copied from the DIVES AKURU manuscript alphabets obtained by Mr. Bell) runs Ñ, Ṭ, C, Y, Z, J, P; but definite authority is not claimed for this obviously unsystematic jumble.

(iv.) *Vowels and Vowel Signs.*

The Old Máldivian *Vowel-sign* variations (the natural sequences of the markedly divergent forms of the *Initial Vowels*, as written in the *Southern Atolls* and at *Málé*) are well exhibited in Plate VII.

The distinctive shapes of the Southern-type vowels have manifestly given place elsewhere to a vowel system based on the A consonantal sign (the GABUḶI TÁNA A), adapted so as to form the other vowels by the addition of the several inflexions.*

Abnormal, and even contradictory, usages seem prevalent. These vagaries are doubtless due to the want existing of a recognized standard in a very elongated series of Atolls, which stretch for over four hundred miles from North to South.

The Eight Vowels.

Initial and Medial forms are employed for both the short and long Vowels A, Á, I, Í, U, Ú, E, É, O, Ó, in accordance with the Sanskṛit canon; but not for the diphthongs AI, AU, which, seemingly, have to be formed by the respective conjunct vowels.

A, Á.

The short A, as stated, is inherent in the consonant; the sign for long Á is written separately, and, like the Siṃhalese *ẹlapilla*, to right of the letter.

I, Í.

The invariable broad rule followed in *Devanágiri* and similar Indian scripts, of using the *super-script* medial signs for I, Í, meets with unlooked-for exception in the case of the DIVES AKURU Alphabet.

As will be seen (Plate VII.), these signs differ only from that for long Á in that, whilst the latter is detached, I, Í should be *united to* the consonant (in the case of long Í with a slight kink at start), and *carried below it partially, or, in cursive script, fully round, to the left*, after the manner of the Siṃhalese *uttara rakárânṣaya* (peculiar *r* sign) in ශ්‍රී, *ṣrí*, and Old Máldive SRÍ.

A not-improbable explanation of this anomaly may be that the Máldivians adopted Medial signs of the rare ṚI, ṚÍ vowel signs (which are written below the consonant in several old Indian alphabets) in lieu of those for I, Í.†

---

* See the lower line of Vowels on Plate VII.

† See Burnell, *South Indian Palæography*, 1878; Faulmann, *Das Buch der Schrift*, 1880; Holle, *Tabel van Oud-en-Niew Indishe Alphabetten*, 1882.

U, Ú.*

These signs are usually attached to the consonants below in accordance with that form (hook to right) of the *pápilla* used with certain Sinhalese consonants; but the alternative adoption for short U of a superscript form appears to be allowable for several, if not all, letters.

E, É.

The Sinhalese practice rules nearly. The vowel-consonant with short A, following a small circle, serves for short E; and for long É a similar double circle looped: these being the substitutes for the Sinhalese *kombuwa* and its manner of employment.

O, Ó.

Here the usage is apparently irregular. The *kombuwa* symbol is followed by the consonant inflected with either I or U vowel signs;† whereas the Sinhalese and Indian fixed rule is to employ the consonant with short *a* and long *á* respectively.

SUKUN.

The wavy semi-diagonal symbol (possibly an evolution of the two kinds of Sinhalese *al* mark rolled into one) employed for the *sukun* of the DIVES AKURU—as distinct from the small open superscript circle (Sinhalese, *bindu*) in GABUḶI TÁNA—is written not merely above, but to the right of the letter with which it is used.

Undoubtedly the former should be classed with the stroke-like Sanskṛit *viráma* and upright *al* of Sinhalese; whilst the later *bindu*, or dot, is common as well to South Indian Prákṛit manuscripts, and goes as far back as the early *lipi* of India.

For the use and sound-values of the Máldive *sukun*, see *supra*, pp. 27, 28.

(v.) *Writing.*

The DIVES AKURU Character is written in two ways :—

(i.) Ordinary; each *akshara* being formed separately.

(ii.) Cursive; with two *aksharas* united, usually by carrying the Máldive forms of the Sinhalese *ẹlapilla* or *ispilla* signs round the head of its consonant to unite with the next letter.

Samples of (i.), the simpler form of the script, appear in (*a*) a list of *birudas* (eulogistic epithets) of Máldive Sultáns (Plate VIII. 3), and (*b*) the DIVES AKURU transcript of the GABUḶI TÁNA letter on Plate IX.

---

* Note the variant Medial signs for long Ú (Plate VII.).

† In the form employed in the Southern Atolls, a vertical stroke heads the long ó, both Initial and Medial.

*Epithets of Máldive Sultáns.**

1. SUVASTÍ SRÍ-MATTA (? SRÍ-MATA) †
Hail! With beauty endowed,
MAHÁ SRÍ-BARI †
of great fortune the bearer,

2. KUSA FURADÁNA † SRÍ RANNAVALÓKA ‡
in wisdom pre-eminent, glorious war-lord,

3. ABÁRUNA ‡ SIÁKA SÁSTURA
(to the race) the ornament, in arts and sciences
AUDÁNA†
accomplished,

4. KÍRITI KATTIRI BOVANA † MAHÁ RADUN.
renowned, a Kshatriya, of the Universe the Great King.

Stanza.

The following "Stanza" (spelt as written, and quoted from "DIOGE RAIVARU," a favourite Máldivian poem) affords a specimen of both styles: (i.) on Plate VI.; (ii.) on Plate VIII. 4:—

1. TAVAAKÁRI § ERUVI NAO
With sea-coconuts loaded the vessel

2. BÁILATE BÍHETI NAAFU
was taken out, when going aground, into deep water

3. RAṚA DIOGE ADANAAFU.
to sail, O! Dioge, to Aden.

The Máldive Islanders are expert and intrepid mariners, whose picturesque boats (M. OḌI) may be seen in most Indian ports, not infrequently.

At times—"sailing upon different stars (by means of their effective, if primitive, nautical instruments) in lieu of points of the compass"—they make greatly adventurous voyages,

---

* See, too, *supra*, p. 54, and Appendix D.

† See *infra*, Appendix D (Sultán's Missive: A.D. 1795).

‡ Sanskṛit *Raṇávalóka: lit.*, "warfare o'erseer" (*raṇa*, "war," "battle"; *avalóka*, "seeing," "supervising"). A *biruda* of the Rásṭhrakúṭas (Ep. Ind., VI., 189). *Cf. Avalókitéṣwara*, "the lord who looks down (in compassion)." ABÁRUNA (not found in Sultáns' Missives) = perhaps, S. *ábharaṇa*, "ornament."

§ TÁVAAKÁRI, "the hard (shelled) coconut" (*cf.* S. *távara*, "firm"). This, the double-coconut (*Lodoicea Seychellarum*), from its fruits being carried by currents from the Seychelles and cast ashore frequently on the Máldive Islands obtained the names *Coco-de-mer* ("sea coconut") and *Cocos-des-Máldives*.

In former days it was highly valued as an imagined sovereign remedy for all sorts of ailments. See *Hak. Soc. Pyrard*, I., 230.

from the "tempest-haunted" Atolls, in their small, light-built, but most sea-worthy vessels, as far as Aden, Calcutta, Penang, Sumatra, &c., braving the storms and formidable currents which sweep round the Indian Ocean and elsewhere.

Lo! our barque's upon the wave,
Dangers of the deep to brave,
Path 'mid ocean-wilds to pave—
To Aden.

Guiding stars with kindly ray
Will direct us on our way
Through the darkness, day by day—
To Aden.

Seas of strife as wide as deep,
Restless waves that never sleep,
Currents of terrific sweep—
To Aden.

Slender barque of bosom'd sail,
Breasting bold the sternest gale
Till her haven's light she hail—
At Aden.

II.—"Gabuli Tana" Alphabet.

Particulars regarding the GABUḶI TÁNA Alphabet, and its use, were afforded by Christopher (1838): these were partially reprinted by Gray (1878), and have been touched on by Geiger (1900).

Details appear in the "Studies" (*supra*, pp. 20–29), in Appendix A, and in Plates I., II.

Some additional remarks may be offered.

(i.) *Variant uses of "Tána" Scripts.*

Certain variations in the order of TÁNA script are in vogue at the Máldives.

The *Memoir* already quoted says (*supra*, p. 21):—

There are several kinds of TÁNA writing; and we are inclined to think that the one at present used was not so generally adopted until within the last fifty years, as many tombstones are evidently inscribed in a character differing from the GABUḶI TÁNA: the letters, at least, have a different sound, and the signs used for vowels are different.

Nothing seems to be known of tombstone epigraphs other than those in the Old and Modern Máldive character and Arabic. It is possible that Young and Christopher may be referring to the DIVES AKURU as the unknown tongue; or to some chance gravestones of aliens carved in their special script.*

Artificial transpositions of "TÁNA writing," smacking of semi-secret, semi-apparent "codes," employed by social classes or private individuals, are occasionally indulged in to this day — apparently *pour passer le temps*, rather than for any definite object.

Of these are the "HAṚA TÁNA" and "DE-FA(T) TÁNA" systems—*nuances*, pure and simple, of no real importance.†

According to the DE-FA(T) TÁNA mode, the two halves of the GABUḶI TÁNA (I., II.) are exactly interchanged, *i.e.*, H = M, Ṛ = F, and so on; whereas in HAṚA TÁNA the mutation is effected between consecutive letters, *i.e.*, H (HAṚA) = Ṛ (GABUḶI); Ṛ (HAṚA) = H (GABUḶI); N (HAṚA) = R (GABUḶI); R (GABUḶI) = N (HAṚA), &c.

In the following Table, Columns I. and II. give the more usual eighteen (18) letters of the GABUḶI TÁNA Alphabet arranged for DE-FA(T) TÁNA, so that the first nine balance the last nine placed opposite to one another; whilst Columns III. and IV. show the equivalent HAṚA TÁNA letters matching those of GABUḶI TÁNA.

III.		*I.*		*II.*		*IV.*
Ṛ	..	H	..	M	..	V
H	..	Ṛ	..	F	..	D
R	..	N	..	D	..	F
N	..	R	..	T	..	L
Ḷ	..	B	..	L	..	T
B	..	Ḷ	..	G	..	Ṇ
A	..	K	..	Ṇ	..	G
K	..	A	..	S	..	Ḍ
M	..	V	..	Ḍ	..	S

(*a*) GABUḶI TÁNA = Columns I. and II. together.

(*b*) DE-FA(T) TÁNA = Columns I. and II. opposed.

(*c*) HAṚA TÁNA = Columns III. and IV. opposed to Columns I. and II.

---

* When at Málé in 1879, Mr. Bell did not notice any graveyard records inscribed in scripts other than DIVES AKURU, GABUḶI TÁNA, and *Arabic*; but closer search might possibly have revealed such.

† Abdul Hamid Dídí writes :—"The HARA and DE-FA(T) forms of writing and conversation are still in use among the higher classes of Máldivians; sometimes in the presence of ordinary people."

Examples.

(*a*) KULA SUNDURA KAATIRI BOVANA MAHÁ RADUN.
(*b*) ṆUBA UDNUTA ṆASRITI LOḌADA HAMÁ TANUD.
(*c*) UTA ḌURFUNA AKLINI ḶOMARA VAṚÁ NAFUR.

(ii.) *The "Leyden Vocabulary" Alphabets.*

The so-called "archaic variations" (see *supra*, p. 25) of the GABUḶI TÁNA Alphabets attributed to Hasan-bin Adam ("transmogrified" by Professor Geiger in Plate I., both as regards the respective order of their appearance in the "Leyden Vocabulary" and their true delineation; but correctly represented in Plate V.) offer a strange puzzle.

It seems highly improbable, on the one hand, that—

> "Exceeding peace had made Ben Adhem bold,"

and that he, or other unsophisticated Máldivian, would have laid himself out deliberately to invent, from the ordinary GABUḶI TÁNA of his day, spurious alphabets to be foisted on the erudite Dr. John Leyden as the "DIVAS AKURU."

On the other hand, there is the distinct opinion regarding Hasan-bin Adam's linguistic limitations contained in Ahmad Dídí's Letters (see Appendix B, *supra*); coupled with the crushing condemnation, recently put on record by Abdul Hamid Dídí, another son of the Máldivian Prime Minister Ibráhim Dídí, that "the alphabets" are "pure inventions of Hasan-bin Adam," concocted to serve private purposes.*

Be the case—if there be any case—what it may for the genuineness of the two alphabets of the "Leyden Vocabulary" as "archaic variations" of the modern GABUḶI TÁNA, of this, at any rate, there can be no question—they have nothing whatever to do with the Old Character, the true DIVES AKURU.

---

* "The alphabets you have sent me should not be taken seriously as Máldivian letters. They are pure inventions of Hasan-bin Adam, of Himití. He must have composed them in order to prevent others reading his private writings. It is not the first time that I have seen, and known, persons writing or inventing such letters for their own personal use. I enclose herewith a modern specimen of such fancy letters.

"The letters contained in the photographic print (Plate V.) cannot, of course, be called the DIVES AKURU Alphabet: they are, as you say, formed from GABUḶI TÁNA letters." (Extract from a letter to Mr. Bell.)

The "specimen" of TÁNA writing sent — playfully styled INGIRÉSI (English) TÁNA—is formed on the stiffest angular lines, not unlike the form of Column 1 (i.) on Plate V.

(iii.) *Origin of the "Gabuḷi Tána" Alphabet.*

How did the GABUḶI TÁNA Alphabet originate? A simple explanation, *primâ facie* reasonable, is submitted tentatively.

With the gradual influx of Arab trade and the growing influence of settlers on the Islands, which culminated in the Muslim conversion of the Twelfth Century, the continued use of the cumbrous DIVES AKURU script would steadily become more and more intolerable; and must almost inevitably have given way to some *Semitic* mode of presenting the Máldive language in written form easy of expression, besides following the right-to-left practice of Arabia and Persia.

Hence it is but natural that the Old Writing should come to be supplanted, as far as practicable, by a simpler system based on Persi-Arabic lines.

Thus it could easily happen that the devisers of the New GABUḶI, or "Composed," Alphabet, looking for a satisfactory basal substitute for the objectionable indigenous form, found it readily available to a large extent in two sets of *Numerals*.

These were, presumably, (*a*) the *Máldive Numerals for 1 to 9* — some at least variants, without doubt, of the *Siṇhalese Numerals* (Plate V. 3) and *Lit Akuru* (Plate V.* 4),* or other and possibly closer Indian equivalents — which conveniently fell into place as the consonants (ten to eighteen) M, F, D, T, L, G, Ṇ, S, Ḍ; whilst (*b*) the ordinary *Arabic Numerals* of like values were made to serve for the first nine letters H, Ṛ, N, R, B, Ḷ, K, A (or ʌ), V.

For the rest, the Arabic, Persian, and Urdú alphabets would inevitably suggest adaptations for some at least of the remaining consonants needed.†

No alphabetic revolution could be more smoothly effected: happy selection, compromise, and modification would meet all requirements with the least possible inconvenience.

(iv.) *Classified Table of the Máldivian Alphabet.*

The arbitrary arrangement of the GABUḶI TÁNA Alphabet has naturally destroyed that orderly scientific classification (Gutturals, Palatals, &c.) founded upon Pronunciation, and

---

* For the *Siṇhalese Numerals* and *Lit Akuru* (or *Lit Illakkam*), see *C. A. S. Journal*, 1852, Appendix, xlvi., xlvii.

The connection of the *Siṇhalese* 1, 2, 3, and 7 with the *Máldive Numerals* is clear; the others (4, 5, 6, 8, 9) are open to doubt: for them the Máldivians may have preferred some Indian prototypes.

Máldive S may be an adoption from Persi-Arabic.

† Thus: Christopher's Z with one dot above; GH, TH (or DH) with three dots below; P formed by similarly sub-scribing Máldivian F. On the other hand, C, T, Y, J, Ñ appear to be free of Semitic influence.

adopted by Grammarians in dealing with Siṇhalese and other Indian Alphabets, which, there is no reason to doubt, once ruled also with the DIVES AKURU.

Taking the Consonants and Vowels which at the present day constitute the full Máldivian Alphabet—Christopher's GH and TH (or DH) being excluded, but Ñ added—these may be grouped, according to phonetic values, as follows :—*

DIVISIONS.	CONSONANTS.							VOWELS.	
	SURD.		SONANT.					SONANT.	
	Tenues (Hard).	Sibilant.	Mediæ (Soft).	Nasals.	Liquids.	Sibilant.	Aspirate.	Short.	Long.
1. *Gutturals* ..	K	—	G	Λ	—	—	H	A	Á
2. *Palatals* ..	C	—	J	Ñ	Y	—	—	I	Í
3. *Cerebrals* ..	Ṭ	—	Ḍ	Ṇ	Ṛ Ḷ	—	—	—	—
4. *Dentals* ..	T	S	D	N	R L	Z	—	—	—
5. *Labials* ..	P	—	B	M	—	—	—	U	Ú
6. *Gutturo-Palatals*	—	—	—	—	—	—	—	E	É
7. *Gutturo-Labials* .	—	—	—	—	—	—	—	O	Ó
8. *Dento-Labials* ..	F	—	V	—	—	—	—	—	—
9. *Sukun* ..	—	—	—	°	—	—	—	—	—

(v.) *Old "Gabuḷi Tána" Manuscript.*

Various substances have from time to time been utilized in India and the Far East for writing on—prepared cloth, wooden boards, *bhúrja* bark, palm leaves, metal plates.

* The classification by A. Mendis Gunasékara, Mudaliyár, in his *Siṇhaḷese Grammar*, 1891, p. 22, is adopted, being easy of comparison in Ceylon. The *sukun*, in its nasal capacity, like the *bindu* by Gunasékara, is put last, unclassified.

The comparative poverty of their vegetation and products no doubt forced the Máldive Islanders to resort to yet another expedient.

In 1886 the Editor was able, with considerable difficulty, to procure from the Máldives a couple of old manuscripts, which proved to be written on strips, about a foot in length by five inches broad, of the *Pandanus odoratissimus* (Máldivian, MÁ-KAṚIKEYO; Siṃhalese, *veṭakeyiyá*).*

The use of this make-shift material had even then long been superseded by paper on the Group.

The prepared *Pandanus* leaves are formed into continuous booklets, of convenient size, by folding each strip in and out alternately, so as to make the rough inner surface alone available for receiving the writing, which is in some kind of "fast" black ink.

Two leaves, photo-lithographed from the more archaic manuscript,† appear in Plate VIII. Its writing offers striking comparison with that of the modern Commercial Letter of about 1875 (Plate IX.).

The short diagonals and vertical down strokes (specially marked in Ṛ, N, and R), the unusual type of Ḍ, the perpendicular B, with the general rugged boldness of all the characters, carry its age back at least to the first half of the Eighteenth Century, if not earlier.

The writing approaches in style the script of the oldest extant Missives in GABUḶI TÁNA sent by the Máldive Sultáns to the Dutch Governors at Colombo annually: Missives written also to the Commanders at Galle are more recent.‡

A transcript of the Arabic and Máldivian letters on the third leaf (which contains all the first 18 letters of the GABUḶI TÁNA Alphabet) is given below. §

The manuscript is a Máldivian FAḌITA FO(T) (Siṃhalese, *mantra pota*), or "Charm Book" of love spells, into which a fair proportion of Arabic enters.||

---

* There is an interesting reference to the use of *Pandanus* leaves, as a *pis-aller* for writing material, in the *Maháwaṇsa*.

When Ḳing Waṭṭagámiṇi was fleeing from his "Damila" enemies, he hid in the Vessagiri forest, where he was fed by the Ṭhéra Mahá Tissa, of Kuppikala Vihára. "Thereon the king, glad at heart, recording it upon a *kétaka* leaf, allotted lands to his vihára for the use of the brotherhood." (Geiger, *Maháwaṇsa*, XXXIII., 48–50.)

† This little book, as folded, measures 5½ in. by 4½ in., and has 7 pages of 65 lines. The other book is slightly larger.

‡ The oldest GABUḶI TÁNA Missive discovered by Mr. Bell in the Dutch Records Office, Colombo, is dated October 16, 1713.

§ Arabic words are printed in *italic capitals*.

|| For specimens of Máldive TAVÍDU, or "charms," see Bell, *Journal, R.A.S. (Ceylon)*, 1881, VII., No. 24, pp. 119–124.

Professor Geiger devotes a paragraph (*supra*, p. 5) to a quotation from Christopher and Young's *Memoir* regarding "the old animistic worship, the belief in demons and spirits, in exorcism, and in magic," which plays an "important part in the life of the people (Máldivians)," despite the counter injunctions of "Islám, the official religion."

Side by side with Muhammadism there has continued to exist an older creed—not the less real because disowned—in demons and spirits, spells, charms, and the like. Anyone thrown in contact with the ordinary Islanders (particularly those of the Southern Atolls) will find demonolatry and nature worship as rife as of old, if pursued now-a-days less obtrusively.*

Transcript.†

(Top half: right.)

1. *ABGHÁ* VÍ TANA(Ṛ) KIAVAI TIṚ FA
2. HARU AṚHEṚ MÍHÁ MÚNA(Ṛ) FUMELAI
3. AHANI KULAKA(Ṛ) BUṆEI *MUJARRAB*
4. *FASL* VARI TOḶA(Ṛ) KURÁKA(Ṛ) ṆI
5. ADURU FATU TIN FATU *RASÚ*
6. *LULLAHI* GEFÁṆÁI I*YAHÚ*DÍNÁI
7. HAIDURU MASRIṚ*KA MAGHRIBBA*
8. *HAIDU*RU UḌÁI BIMÁI HAI
9. DURU *ALHÁ KUMUTTAKA* SURUHATTÁ

(Bottom half: left.)

10. DURU MIAGE DE VERÍṚ DURU MIHEṚ
11. TIR FATU LIÉNI E(Ṛ) FA(Ṛ) KAṚ
12. ṆÉ DAṚU LANI AṆE(Ṛ) FA(Ṛ) EDU DAṚU
13. VAḶULAṆI AṆE(Ṛ) FA(Ṛ) OḶI DAṚU LA
14. NI VARIVEI *FASL* VARI TOḶU BU
15. NAME AHÁDÉ RUKUṚ Í TIṚ BURI
16. VÍ FANAKU MEDU BURI VARUGAI
17. DE KEṆE(Ṛ) RÚ, KURAHAI DE BO DEKO
18. LA(Ṛ) LAI VÁHAKA VARA OḌUṚ

A translation of the manuscript would be out of place in the present connection.

---

* Bell, *The Máldive Islands*, p. 58.

† Noticeable is the preference given to Ṛ (i.) in lieu of the AVIENI sign Λ, for mute terminations—here printed (Ṛ); (ii.) for the nasal (*e.g.*, TIṚ, AṚHEṚ); and (iii.) for duplicating consonants; also the exceptionally frequent use (as in Sultáns' Missives of early Eighteenth Century) of the cerebral Ṇ.

POSTSCRIPT.

What has been said above, so far as it relates to the GABUḶI TÁNA script, is based mainly on the material put together in 1838 by Lieutenant Willmott Christopher,* of the Indian Navy, and the Plate of the Modern, and a portion of the Old, Máldivian Alphabet which accompanied it, when printed in 1841.

That Plate was reproduced in a Paper, published in 1878, by Mr. (now Sir) Albert Gray, formerly of the Ceylon Civil Service, with a summary, below the Alphabet, of Christopher's remarks regarding the sound-values of the letters. (See Plate II.)

It was only to be expected that, in the fluxion of three-quarters of a century or more, the form of the Máldive written character would undergo gradual evolution. This has been the natural course in the history of all scripts of long-continued life.

A comparison of the forms of the letters in Christopher's Table (Plate II.), and those appearing in the "Máldivian Commercial Letter" of 1875 *circa* (Plate IX.), provides expected testimony to this slow, but no less sure, process of mutation.

Thanks to the courteous aid of Abdul Hamid Dídí Effendí, the Máldivian Government Representative in Ceylon (who has himself carefully penned each character), the Editor is enabled to close this Appendix with a list of the *twenty-four (24) letters which at the present time make up the full* MÁLDIVIAN ALPHABET, and exhibit the GABUḶI TÁNA *as it is written now-a-days*, according to best authority.

That steady evolution has continued even since 1875 is illustrated by the form of the Máldivian characters given in the Table on page 167.

---

* For particulars of the gallant death of this brave Officer at Multán, in 1848, see *supra*, p. 130 †.

One who knew him intimately wrote : "Lieutenant Christopher, of the Indian Navy, was a very old friend of mine—indeed I was his 'best man' at his wedding, at Aden, in, I think, 1844. You may depend on the *accuracy* of whatever *he* put on paper. He was *an earnestly religious man.*" (General H. W. B. Bell, R.E., January 1, 1880.)

The closing words of Christopher's Letter to Dr. Wilson, in forwarding his *Vocabulary of the Máldivian Language* (MS. in C. A. S. Library), pathetically bespeak the "Christian Soldier" fated to give a noble life for his country within a few years : "(May) you continue to prosper under the fostering care of Our Heavenly Father."

In the absence of any standardized fount of cast type, the tendency in manuscript is manifestly towards a "running hand," with its inevitable result—progressive, though unconscious, "slurring" of distinctive forms.

The clear difference between such characters as Ṛ and N, Ṇ and Z, in the GABUḶI TÁNA of the Old *Pandanus* Manuscripts, and the Máldive Sultáns' Missives of the earlier years of the Eighteenth Century—those of the first quarter of the Nineteenth Century—and, finally, the "current script" of the later Nineteenth and present period of the Twentieth Centuries, is strongly marked.

Frankly, it must be admitted that the change, thus almost automatically evolved during a period of two centuries, has not made for greater distinctness or beauty in the writing: instead of amelioration, steady chirographic decline is perceptible. This has been due, without doubt, to *the want of a recognized printed standard;* such, for instance, as has for long ruled—with certain modifications not affecting its general bold attractiveness, *teres atque rotundus*—in the case of Siṇhalese characters of *ola* manuscripts and printed books.

The GABUḶI TÁNA letters which have undergone most change perhaps, during the course of the past two hundred years, are B and J.* These do not seem to be used ordinarily at the present day in their old stilted vertical shape.

The form of cerebral Ṇ given by Christopher, that was holding the field firmly more than a century earlier, appears to have yielded to the nasal more usually transcribed as the presumed palatal Ñ.† It is believed that the older form, as well as the variants of Ṭ and C (see Plate II.), may still be employed at will.

The word KU;HA, among the *birudas* of the Sultáns in their Missives of the Eighteenth Century, was written (when not spelt simply KUSA) alternatively by Máldivian dental S with three dots under, or by the Arabic character for cerebral *sh* super-scribed with triple dots.

The present-day GABUḶI TÁNA Alphabet has been arranged on page 167 in three Columns, *from right to left* according to Máldivian script.

---

* The strange type of Ḍ found in the FAḌITA FO(T) (see Plate VIII.) does not occur in Sultáns' Missives.

† Formerly, at least, association of different classes of nasals was allowable: thus, *e.g.*, HUNṆA (dental and cerebral). Further, the honorific plural suffix in MANIKUFÁNUMENÑA, and the like, appears with its final nasal looped, but bent to left—apparently the form of palatal Ñ (Plate I.) now, and may be of old, utilized also for cerebral Ṇ (see Alphabet, p. 167, and *cf.* DÓÑE, Plate IV., line 10).

Column I. gives the first nine letters of the Alphabet: these are virtually the *Arabic Numerals 1 to 9.*

Column II. shows the next nine, drawn from the *Máldivian Numerals** of like values, several of which find obvious counterparts in Indian, and Ceylon, Numerical symbols.

In Column III., the remaining six letters are set out, presumably in their recognized alphabetic order.

With the list of Máldivian characters, Abdul Hamid Dídí further supplied their Persi-Arabic equivalents *as written by Máldivians,* appending this important Note :—

We do not use Persi-Arabic letters, unless we find it absolutely necessary to give Persi-Arabic pronunciation, when writing an Arabic or Persian word in Máldivian characters. But we could write Máldivian wholly in Arabic letters, with dots here and there to represent Máldivian TÁNA sound.†

This accounts for the absence from the GABUḶI TÁNA alphabet of the comparatively little-used characters transcribed by Christopher (see Plate II.) as GH, TH (or DH).

The following points should be noticed.

The penchant for modifying Arabic forms by *triple dots sub-script* is very marked: see Ṛ, G, Ṇ, Ḍ, C.

The Máldivian sign for P is virtually F, subscribed thrice, or once: from Z the super-script dot (*teste* Christopher, Plate II.) has disappeared.

Ṭ with quadruple dots above is an Urdú form.

The Arabic letter (here subscribed once and utilized as the equivalent of Ḷ) is usually transcribed by *z* with dot or line below.

---

* Sultán Ibráhím Iskandar's Missive of *A.D. 1749* is dated in *Máldivian Numerals* (M Ṇ T Ḍ); as is that of Sultán Ghází Hasan Izz-ud-din's Missive of *A.D. 1765* (M Ṇ G L), in addition to the *Hijra Year 1178* in *Arabic Numerals* (H H K A).

† In proof Abdul Hamid Dídí gave the Máldivian title DOṚIMÉNÁ KILAGEFÁNU written in Persi-Arabic characters.

Maldivian "Gabuli Tana" Alphabet, with English and Persi-Arabic equivalents.

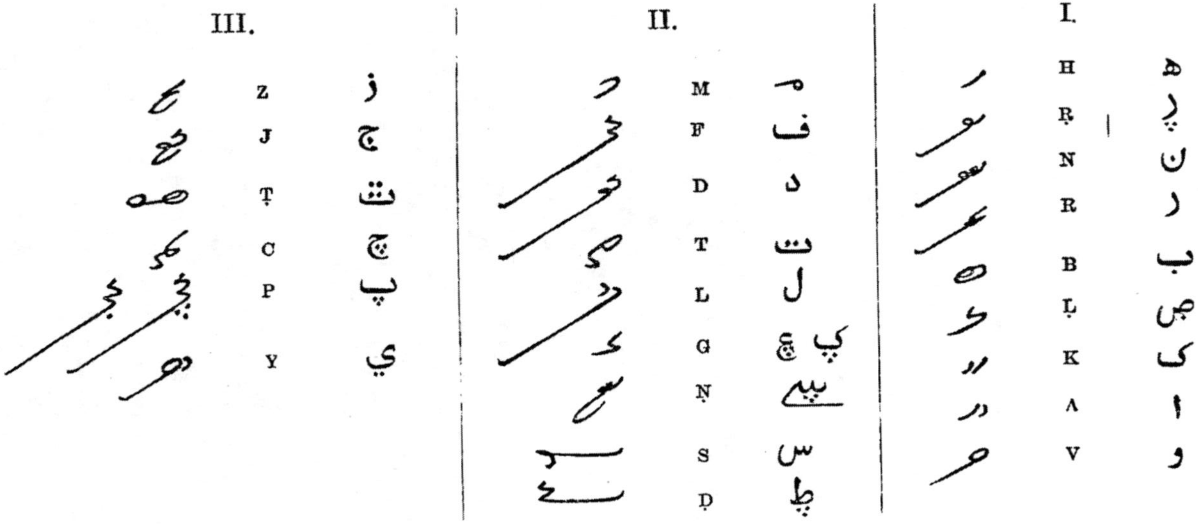

APPENDIX D.

MALDIVIAN LETTERS.

In his *Máldivische Studien*, I., 1900, pp. 678–684, Professor Geiger has copied—according to his own transliteration, and with independent renderings into German,* but without giving the Máldive writing—the only two Máldivian Letters (Texts, Transcripts, and Translations, in full) which have been yet published.

It may be well, therefore, to reproduce, *in extenso*, both these Letters, as first printed, accompanied in each case by a Plate in replica showing the Máldive script (see Plates III., IV.).

I.—Málim's Letter. Transcript (original Máldive Letter missing) and literary Translation appear in Christopher's own manuscript of 1838, published in the *Journal, R.A.S.*, 1841, pp. 72–74.

II.—Sultán's Missive. Appears in Bell's *The Máldive Islands* (Ceylon Sessional Paper XLIII., 1881).

To these is now added a third.

III.—Commercial Letter. This exhibits, side by side, the two forms of the Máldive Alphabet: (i.) the Ancient, or DIVES AKURU, and (ii.) the Modern, known as GABUḶI TÁNA.

I.—Maldive Malim's Letter : A.D. 1837.

[The word-for-word Transcript and Translation, given below, written out (with a few trifling errors) by Christopher in his own clear handwriting, were supplemented by a Summarized Translation from the hand of his Editor, Dr. J. Wilson, which was subsequently printed in the Asiatic Society's Journal (*loc. cit.*, p. 74).]

* See *supra*, pp. 49–52, 54–56, for Mrs. Willis's English rendering of the German.

*Transcript.**

The following is a specimen of the language. It is a copy of a letter written by the Máldive Málim of a boat at Colombo to his countrymen at Galle:—

(1)	GÁLIGAI	TIBI	DIWEHÍNGGE	EMME
	At Galle	stopping,	of the Máldives	to all
	KALUNGNAG	ARABU	OḌI	
	the people	of the Arab	boat	

(2)	MÁLIMÍ	KALÉGEFÁNU	SALÁMEN	MIFAHARAG
	the Málim	Chief's	saláms.	Now
	MI	RARHUGAI	HURHI	OḌI FAHARHI
	at this	port	are	the boats:

(3)	ARABU	OḌI	FINLADU	OḌI	WEDUNG	OḌI
	Arab	boat,	Finladu	boat,	Present	boat,
	FAḌIYÁRU	OḌI				
	Fanḍiyáru's	boat,				

(4)	AHAMMÁ	DÍDÍ	OḌI	MÁNDU-GÉ	OḌI	HITI-
	Ahama	Dídí's	boat,	Mándu-house	boat,	Bitter-
	GAS-DARHU-GÉ	OḌI	MÍFAHARAG			
	tree-corner (house)†	boat.	At present			

(5)	EMME	KALUNG	GADA WE	EBA TIBÚWEWE
	all	people	in health	remain.
	TIYÁ	RARHUGAI	HURHI	
	At your	port	(which) you have	

---

* For the Málim's Letter, Christopher, in his manuscript, employed diacriticals; transliterated Máldivian nasal both as N and NG; the mute ʌ at the end of words by G; Ṛ by RH, or by doubling the connected consonant; and T final by I.

His editor, Dr. Wilson, converted Christopher's silent G into italic *G*, as well as using italics instead of subscribed dots for cerebral consonants; inserted a short diagonal stroke at foot between duplicated consonants; and changed I into short Ĭ.

Geiger abandoned NG for single N, and I for the original T final; adopted N with superscribed dot (here printed Ń) for final semi-nasal; substituted apostrophe (') sign for mute ʌ; and R with small superscript v for RH; restored diacritical dots; and utilized hyphens freely.

† Christopher has rendered MÁNDU-GÉ and HITI-GAS-DARU-GÉ correctly, except that DAṚU means "under." M. HITI-GAS = S. *kọhomba-gaha, Azadirachta Indica.*

Abdul Hamid Dídí writes:—These "Houses" (GÉ) are both in Málé Island. MÁNDU-GÉ is, at the present time, the residence of the ex-Sultán's brothers (MÁNDU-GÉ MANIFUḶUN). HITI, "bitter"; GAS, "tree"; DAṚU (or DORU), "under" = together: "the House under the Bitter Tree."

(6) KABARENG FONUWÁTI MI RARHUGAI
the news you must send. At this port

HURHI KABARU MI FONUWÍE
(which) there is the news I hereby send.

(7) WILÁTUNG AU BOḌÁ SÁHIBENG ATUEWE
From Europe a new Governor has arrived.

WILÁTU RASGE
Of England the King

(8) MARUWEJJEWE LANKA GINA FARHUNG
is dead. Lacs many in strings

SALÁMEN MI RARHU MAS VIKKÍ
saláms. This port's fish we have sold:

(9) HIMITÍ MAS HANG DIHA HAI
the Himití fish for seven tens and seven

RIYÁLAYAG MÁLE ATOḶU MAS
dollars; the Málé Atoḷu fish

(10) FAS DOḶOS HATAKAG FÁDING-FUḶU
for five twelves and seven; the Fáding-fuḷu

KIRÁ MAS * SÁḶÍS-
weighed fish for forty-

(11) HATAKAG MIHIDANG VIKKAIGENG
seven. Thus having sold it

TIBI AGÍMIWEWE † LANGKA GINA
we are stopping for the price. Lacs more

(12) FARHUNG SALÁMEN MI LIYUNÍ MITANGWÍ
strings saláms. This is written here

BÁRUSFATI DUWAHUNG
on Thursday the day.

(13) MÁI KALÁGE RUSSEWÍYÁI SAUDA
If God permits (or pleases) in fourteen

DUWAHU AḶUGAḌU FURÁNEMEWE
days I shall have sailed; †

(14) HITAI HURHI MEVE
I have the desire.

---

* See *supra*, p. 52. † See *supra*, p. 53.

*Translation.**

The meaning of the above letter appears to be as follows:—

The Málim of the Arab boat to all the people of the Máldives stopping at Galle. The Chief's greeting.†

The boats now at this port are the Arab boat of Finladu, the Offering boats of Faḍiyáru and Ahamma Dídí, and the boats of Mándu-gé and Hiti-gas-darhu-gé.

All the people are in good health.

Send what news you have at your port. I hereby send what news there is at this port.

A new Governor is come from Europe. The King of England is dead.

Very many greetings.

We have sold at this port, Himití fish for seventy-seven dollars, Málé Atoll fish for sixtý-seven, and Fádingfuḷu fish weighed (?) for forty-seven: having sold the fish, we are waiting for the price.

Very many greetings.

This is written on Thursday. If God permits, I shall sail in fourteen days; such is my wish.

II.—Missive from the Sultan of the Maldives: A.D. 1795.

[This Missive of A.H. 1210 and its Translation are reproduced below, with the Notes which accompanied it, virtually as they were printed in *The Máldive Islands* (*loc. cit.*, pp. 78–81). Supplementary matter is given in footnotes.]

It may strengthen the position assumed by Albert Gray (*Journal, R.A.S.*, Vol. X., 1878) regarding the affinity of the Siṇhalese and Máldive languages (whilst of interest on other

---

* Geiger's Translation (1900) is as follows:—

Uebersetzung: Der Kapitän des Arabischen Schiffes (sendet) an alle in Galle weilenden Máldivianer Grüsse. Die Boote, welche gegenwärtig in diesem Hafen sich befinden, sind die Arabischen Boote, die Boote des Finladu, die Boote mit den Geschenken, die Boote des Richters, die Boote des Ahmed Didi, die Boote des Mándu-Hauses und die Boote des Hiti-gas-darhu-Hauses. Alle Leute sind zur Zeit wohlauf. Ihr sollt die Neuigkeiten schicken, die ihr in eurer Stadt (erfahren) habt; ich schicke (auch) die Neuigkeiten, die wir hier (gehört) haben. Aus England ist ein neuer Gouverneur gekommen. Der König von England ist gestorben. Viele tausend Grüsse. Wir verkauften an diesem Platz Fische (und zwar) solche aus Himití für 77 Dollars, solche aus dem Mále-Atoll für 67, solche aus . . . für 47 . . . . Tausend Grüsse. Ich schrieb dies hierorts am Donnerstag. Wenn es Gott erlaubt, werde ich noch 14 Tage bleiben. Das ist meine Absicht. (Geiger, *Máldivische Studien*, I., 680.)

† See *supra*, p. 52.

grounds) to insert here a *facsimile* of one of the Annual Missives of the Máldive Sultáns of the Eighteenth Century, with a Transcript in Roman characters, an English Translation, and some Explanatory Notes.

As will be seen, the proportion of words in this Letter clearly traceable to Siṇhalese, or Sanskṛit, sources is large, amounting to at least 65 per cent.

AS-SULṬÁN HASAN NÚR-UD-DÍN

*Transcript.**

HUWA'L GHANI

(1) SUVASTÍ SIRÍMATA MAHÁ SIRÍ-BARI KUSA FURADÁ

(2) NA SIRÍ KULA SADA IRA SIÁKA SÁSTURA AUDÁNA KA

(3) ʌTIRI *AS-SULṬÁN HASAN NÚR-UD-DÍN ISKANDAR* KAʌ TIRI BOWANA

(4) MAHÁ RADUN KOḶUBU GORUNUDÓREWE KIYÁ RASGE-FÁNA(ʌ) MITA(ʌ)

(5) LAʌKA HÁS FAṚUʌ *SALÁM* MANIKUFÁNUMEʌGE KOḶU-BUGAI IHU U

(6) ḶUʌVI RAS-RAS-KALUʌNÁI MI DIVEHI RÁʌJÉGAI IHU UḶUʌ

(7) VI RAS-RAS-KALUʌNÁI RA*ḤMAT*RIKAʌ BEHEʌṬEVI FADAIʌ ME MANI

(8) KUFÁNÁI TIMAʌ MANIKUFÁNU HIʌFUḶUGAI *RAḤMAT* BAHAʌṬAVAIGEʌ HUʌNE

(9) VÍME MANIKUFÁNUMEʌ KIBAIʌ EDI TIBÍMÁVE MI DIVEHI RÁʌJEIʌ OḌI

(10) YE DÓÑE(ʌ)† BEHIGEʌ GOS MANIKUFÁNA(ʌ) *KHABARI* VÉ TANAKU TIBI NA

---

* Bell (*The Máldive Islands*, 1882, p. 78) followed Christopher's system of transliteration generally, except in using (i.) Ṉ (*anuswára*) for his NG, where some nasal pronunciation seemed required, and (ii.) the apostrophe (') where it seemed to be mute.

In the Editor's footnotes to Geiger's *Máldivian Studies*, as well as the present reprint of the Sultán's Missive of A.D. 1795, each Máldive character has been transcribed by an equivalent *single* Roman letter, *irrespective of pronunciation*. Máldive AVIENI sign, shown as ʌ, bears various sound values, according to its usage in Máldivian, whether nasal, duplicative, or simply a mute termination (ʌ). For RH, Ṛ is adopted. Words, or portions, written in Arabic are printed in italic capitals.

† Several other spellings (*e.g.*, DÓÑIYE, DÓNÑE); but all with Ñ (presumed palatal, or variant cerebral), singly or second. Máldivians usually style their Voyaging Vessels FURADI OḌI, or DATURU OḌI.

(11) MA E BAYAKU GEADAVAI E MÍHUAGE HAIHÚNJEAA BEALÁVUMÁI MI DIVEHI

(12) RÁAJEA(A) *ADÁVÁATERIAKU* MANIKUFÁNA(A) EGIAJE NAMA E BAYAKA(A)

(13) MANIKUFÁNUMEA NU-RUSSEVUMEVE MANIKUFÁNUMEANÁI ARAFÓDIGEA-

(14) NUVÁ KUḌA HADIYÁ KOḶA-KÁI *AḤMAD* KUḌA BAḌÉRI KÉVÍ TIÁ FONUAVÍMU MI A

(15) ḶÁ DEANEVI KAME(A) KURAAVAI MI AḶUA KIBAIN *TAKSÍRU*(A) VIAS *MU'ÁF*

(16) KURAAVAI AAVALU MÚSUMUGAI FURUVÁ-KAMA(A) EDI VAḌAIGEA HUANE

17) VÍME 1210 *SANAT*.

*Translation.**

He (God) is bountiful (*lit.*, the richest) !

Hail! *Sultán Hasan Núr-ud-dín Iskandar*,† Mighty Monarch of the Universe, a Kshatriya, endowed with beauty, possessed of great wealth, who imparts wisdom, (born) of illustrious race resembling the sun and moon, conversant with arts and sciences, of unsullied (fame), to the Ruler, namely, the Governor of Colombo,‡ countless (*lit.*, many million-fold) salutations !

---

* The German Translation of 1900 runs :—

Uebersetzung : Heil ! Von dem glorreichen, hoch-berühmten, hochweisen, aus edlem Geschlecht entsprossenen, dem Mond un der Sonne vergleichbaren Herrscher, dem heldenhaften Krieger, Sultan Hasan Núr-ud-dín Iskandar, dem Krieger, dem Grosskönige der Erde an den König des Gouverneurs in Colombo von hier viele tausend Grüsse. Wie zwischen dem früheren Könige Eurer Excellenz in Colombo und dem früheren Könige dieses Máldivischen Reiches Freundschaft bestanden hat, so tragen wir auch zu Eurer Excellenz Freundschaft im Herzen, und wir wünschen (das Gleiche) von Eurer Excellenz. Sollte irgend ein Boot oder Fahrzeug dieses Landes verschlagen werden, so sollst du, wenn es ein Eurer Excellenz bekannter Platz ist, die Leute holen und für ihr Wohlergehen sorgen. Wenn Eurer Excellenz jemand bekannt wird, der diesem Lande fiendlich gesinnt ist, soll Eure Excellenz es nicht dulden Obwohl es der Würde Eurer Excellenz nicht entspricht, habe ich dir durch den Unterschatzmeister Ahmed ein kleines Geschenk geschickt. Wenn er einen Wunsch äussert, sollst du ihn erfüllen, wenn ein Versehen von seiner Seite vorkommt, sollst du es verzeihen. Mit dem ersten Monsun erwarte ich seine Zurückkunft. (Geiger, *loc. cit.*, 683–684).

† "The Máldive Sultáns have assumed the fulsome cognomen *Iskandar*—applied by Arab and Persian writers to Alexander the Great (*Iskandar al Rúmi*)—perhaps by virtue of supposed descent from the wide-ruling *Iskandar Dhul'lkarnein* ('the two-horned'), a traditional Persian King of the First Race, contemporary of Abraham, and tenth descendant from Noah." (*The Máldive Islands*, p. 76.)

‡ See *supra*, p. 56.

As the former Rulers at Colombo — Your Excellency's predecessors—and the former Rulers of this Island Kingdom (Máldives) preserved mutual friendship, Your Excellency and Ourselves have borne (reciprocal) friendship in our hearts. May this (amity) continue on Your Excellency's part!

Should any *oḍi* or *dóni* (Máldive boats) be driven ashore at any place with which (Your Excellency) is acquainted, (We request that Your Excellency will kindly) send for those (shipwrecked) persons, and enquire into their wants.*

(Further) should Your Excellency be aware of any persons ill-disposed towards this Island Kingdom, (We, also, request that Your Excellency will be pleased to) show them no countenance.

For Your Excellency's acceptance we send—all unworthy though it be—a small present by the hands of (Our Ambassador) *Ahmad Kuḍa Baḍéri Kévi*.†

(We beg Your Excellency will kindly) issue directions that his requests be attended to.

If he commit any fault (We hope that Your Excellency will) pardon it.

(We trust that Your Excellency will) allow him to return in the favourable monsoon. ‡ A.H. 1210 (A.D. 1795).

Reply of the Dutch Governor.

[The Reply of the Dutch Governor, J. G. van Angelbeek, to the Missive of the Sultán, despatched from Colombo on December 2, 1795, is couched in equally friendly terms:—]

AAN DEN GELUKKIGEN *SULTAN HASSEN NOOREDIEN ISKANDER.* KONING DER MALDIVOS.

Ik heb de eer gehad Uwer Hoogheids brief, en de daar nevens gezondene geschenken, uit handen van Uwer Hoogheids Zendeling, *Agamadoe Koeda Banderie Kewie*, wel te ontvangen; waar voor ik Uwe Hoogheid zeer vriendlijk bedanke.

Dat Uwe Hoogheid geneigd is vriendschap met my te onderhouden, strekt my tot veel genoegen; en ik zal niet nalaaten, zoo veel mogelijk, alles toetebrengen, wat deeze vriendschap duurzaam kan maaken.

Nevens deezen biede ik Uwe Hoogheid zoodanige goederen aan, als by de ingeslootene Notietsie vermeld staan, met vriendelijk myner geneegenheid te willen akcepteeren.

---

* See *supra*, p. 57.

† This "Assistant (*lit.*, Small) Treasurer" was sent also in 1793 and 1794.

‡ See *supra*, p. 58.

Voorts bid ik God, dat Hy Uwe Hoogheid gelieve 'te zegenen met gezondheid en voorspoed, en Uwer Hoogheids Regeering steeds gelukkig te doen zijn, tot noch een reex van jaare.

Kolumbo, den 2nd December, 1795.]

*Notes.**

(i.) The magniloquent *birudas*, "great swelling words of vanity," employed by the Sultáns in their Annual Missives to the Ceylon Governors, have strangely waxed and waned since the commencement of the Eighteenth Century.†

Sultán Íbráhim Iskandar (A.D. 1721–1749) was content to affix to his name RANNAVALÓKA MAHÁ RADUN.‡

In 1750, under Sultán Mukarram Muhammad Imád-ud-dín, Máldivian official bombast reached the height beginning SUVASTÍ, &c.,§ and attained its zenith some twenty or thirty years later.||

Re-action then ensued; and in letters subsequent to 1805 *circa*, the Sultán's Arabic titles were followed merely by the epithets KULA SUNDURA KAATIRI BOWANA MAHÁ RADUN—"expressions" which Christopher considered "unexplainable at the present day."¶

(ii.) SUVASTÍ MAHÁ RADUN.—Adopting [provisionally] the translation given above, the Sultán's title may be rendered into Sinhalese as follows :—*Sẹpa vévá : ṣrimatvú : mahá ṣrí dharannávú : prajñá pradhána karannávú* (*kalyáṇa*

* In the elucidation of these *birudas* valuable aid was received, in 1881, from the late learned scholars Waskaḍuwe Subhúti Unnánse, Dhammálóka Unnánse, of Ratmalána, and B. Gunasékara, Mudaliyár. Chief Translator to Government.

Suggestions very kindly offered by A. Mendis Gunasékara, Mudaliyár, appear in some of the present footnotes to the Notes.

† By gracious permission of the Ceylon Government, Mr. Bell was enabled to have all surviving *originals* of these Missives (i.) photographed and (ii.) lithographed to exact size, at his own charges. Some of the Missives are choice specimens of calligraphy, written both in red and in black characters. There are many gaps. The earliest Missive in GABULI TÁNA characters discovered in the Dutch Records Office, Colombo, is dated 1713 ; the latest 1825. They await editing.

‡ First appears in extant Missive of 1732. Prior Missives seem to contain no *birudas*.

§ His first Missive (September, 1750) opens: SUVASTÍ SIRÍMATA MAHÁ SIRÍ NAVARANNA KÍRITI AUDÁNA.

|| Variant epithets, dropped later, are: RAN-MÍBA, DANÁLA, VÍRA-SINGA, AUDA, which occur combined with more usual *birudas*.

¶ The epithets mean: "Great Ruler of the World, a Kshatriya of pure race."

dáyakavú) : *ṣrí vaṇsa ęti : hira sañda bañduvú : pratyaksha ṣástra dhárivú : ṣubhra* (*kírti*) *ęti : Kshatriya vaṇsa ęti : lókayé Mahá Rája.*

(iii.) MAHÁ SIRÍ BARI.—S. *mahá ṣrí-bhári*, "possessed of immense (*lit.*, great weight of) glory (or wealth)." *Cf. siri bara* in preamble of mediæval Siṇhalese inscriptions.*

In place of BARI some Missives give DIRI, which may = S. *dula*, "glittering," "splendid," through *dili*.*

(iv.) KUSA FURADÁNA.—Taken [provisionally] as = S. *kuṣa pradhána*. Besides the meanings (*a*) *prajñáva*, "wisdom," or (*b*) *kalyána*, "goodness," assigned here to KUSA, the compound will also bear the sense (*c*) S. *jala pradhánavû*, "Lord of Waters," *i.e.*, the Ocean, and (*d*) "Chief of *Kusa* (*Dwípa*)," a division of the universe.† Some Missives read KUSHA.

(v.) SADA IRA.—The order of Sanskṛit compounds is followed ; *ira* (for *hira*) *sañda* = *sañda ira*.

(vi.) SIÁKA SÁSTURA.—For SIÁKA, Subhúti Unnánse proposed Hindí *sisána*, "clever" ; rendering the compound (*a*) *daksha anuṣásakavú*, "skilful teacher," or "commander," (*b*) *dhúrta janayáta satruvú*, "enemy of wicked men."

Dhammálóka Unnánse, deriving SIÁKA from the Sanskṛit *sáyaka*, "bow," translated (*c*) *dhanurdhravú*, "skilled with the bow."

B. Gunasékara, Mudaliyár, suggested (*d*) *Shiáka saturá* (*satru*), "eṇemy of the Shias," the Máldivians being Sunnís ; (*e*) S. *siya*, "own" + *aka* (Sanskṛit *aksha*, "organs of sense"), "subduer of (his) passions" ; (*f*) *siya* + *aka*, "eye" = *pratyaksha*, and *ṣástura* = *ṣástruvú*, "experienced teacher." ‡

---

* *Cf.*, too, *Ṣríbhara* (*lit.*, "bearer of wealth or glory"): one of the *birudas* of a Seventh Century Pallava King, probably Narasiṇhavarman I. (*Epigraphia Indica*, X., p. 5). A. Mendis Guṇasékara, Mudaliyár, would derive DIRI from the Sanskṛit *dhíra*, "learned," "brave" ; which seems preferable.

† As the Máldive Rulers style themselves in Arabic, on their Coins, AS-SULṬÁN UL BAR WA'L BAḤÁR, "Sultán of Land and Sea," the epithet KUSA FURADÁNA may, perhaps, be better translated "Lord of the Ocean" (S. *jala pradhánavú*).

‡ Taking SIÁKA SÁSTURA AUDÁNA KAATIRI together, A. Mendis Gunasékara, Mudaliyár, would translate : "The Kshatriya (Ruler, famed for) heroism (or glorious achievements, secured by the power) of his (Sanskṛit *swakiya*) arms (Sanskṛit *sastra*)."

(vii.) AUDÁNA. — Perhaps = Sanskṛit *avadáta*, "white," "unsullied."* Appears almost invariably in immediate connection with KÍRITI, "renowned" (S. *kírti*, "fame").

(viii.) BOWANA.—Older Missives give the truer form BUWANA (S. *bhuwana*, "world," "universe").†

(ix.) RASGE-FÁNU.—In early Missives of the Eighteenth Century sometimes written RADUNGE-FÁNU; RASGE-FÁNANSE.

FÁNU, FÁNANSE. —S. *vahansé*, honorific affix, by consonantal change through *vanansé*.

(x.) MANIKU-FÁNU-MEN.—Euphemistic plural-singular.

(xi.) FADAIA-ME.—"As," "in the manner" = S. *paridden*, by rejection of liquid medial consonant: ME = S. *ma*, intensive suffix.

(xii.) HIA-FUḶU-GAI.—"In mind," locative = HIT (S. *hité*) FUḶU (honorific) GAI (GÁTUN, "near"), by euphonic assimilation.

(xiii.) BEHIGEA GOS.—S. *bęhigana* (*bahinavá*, "to descend") *gos*: Pyrard, BEHIGUE, "sailing with the wind and current": Drake's (old English) "spooming along before the sea."

(xiv.) ARAFÓDIGEA-NUVÁ.—"In all humbleness," "unworthy though (the giver and the present) be."

Alternative forms in older Missives: ARA HÓDÍ, ARAI HODÍ, ARANU HÓDE, ARAINU HÓDE.

Cf Pyrard, VEDON A ROUESPOU [VEDUN ARUVAIFU], "the present paid to a delegate of the Sultán"; and Máldive Málim's Letter, VEDUN OḌI, "Present boat."

(xv.) BAḌÉRI. — Originally confined to the "Treasurer," or Keeper of the Royal Stores (S. *Bhánḍágáriká*). The title, like *Banḍára*, *Banḍá*, in Ceylon, gradually acquired a wider use, though at first restricted to persons of high birth.

(xvi.) KÉVÍ.—Perhaps = NÉVÍ, "tindal."

(xvii.) AḶU-GAḌU, AḶU-GAḌU-MEN.—The ordinary designation employed by Máldivian Sultáns and nobles when writing of themselves in the first person.

---

* Whence Sanskṛit *avadána*, "glorious," "heroic" (see *supra*, p. 57, [3]). *Avadána* also means "dividing."

† BOWANA MAHA RADUN. *Cf.* Sanskṛit *bhupati náyaka*, "Chief of Kings" (A. Mendis Gunasékara, Mudaliyár).

(xviii.) GAḌU, KOḶU, FUḶU.—Honorific suffixes, generally implying connection with Royalty.

(xix.) AAVALU . . . HUANEVÍME.—Periphrasis for the simpler expression, occasionally found in these Missives, DATURU (Hindústání *játrá*) AVAS-KURAAVAI, "(kindly) hasten (his return) voyage."

VAḌAIGEN.—*Cf.* the respectful use of Siṃhalese *vaḍinavá*, as applied to Buddhist Priests, &c.

*Consonant and Vowel Changes.**

Some ruling Vowel and Consonantal changes from Siṃhalese into Máldivian are noticeable in this Missive:—

(i.) *Consonants.*

Siṃhalese *ṭ* becomes Máldive Ṛ : S. *paṭa*; M. FAṚUA; R: S. *piṭatvenavá*; M. FURUVÁ.
Siṃhalese *d* becomes Máldive H : S. *dás*; M. HÁS.
Siṃhalese *n* becomes Máldive Ḷ : S. *unna*; M. UḶUA.
Siṃhalese *p* becomes Máldive F: S. *pradhána*; M. FURADÁNA.
Siṃhalese *v* becomes Máldive F : S. *evanavá*; M. FONUAVÍMU.

(ii.) *Vowels.*

Siṃhalese *a* becomes Máldive E : S. *danvanavá, balavanavá*; M. DEANEVI, BEALÁVUMÁI.
Siṃhalese *a* becomes Máldive I : S. *tamun*; M. TIMAA.
Siṃhalese *a* becomes Máldive O : S. *evanavá*; M. FONUAVÍMU.
Siṃhalese *a* becomes Máldive U : S. *ihaṭa, karavanavá*; M. IHU, KURAAVAI.
Siṃhalese *i* becomes Máldive U : S. *innavá*; M. HUANEVÍME.
Siṃhalese *u* becomes Máldive A : S. *tamun*; M. TIMAA.
Siṃhalese *u* becomes Máldive O : S. *bhuvana*; M. BOVANA.
Siṃhalese *e* becomes Máldive I : S. *mé, tibenavá*; M. MI, TIBÍ.
Siṃhalese *o* becomes Máldive U : S. *no-rusanavá*; M. NURUSSEVUMEVE.
Siṃhalese *ę* becomes Máldive E; A: S. *hęngenavá, tęna*; M. EGIAJE; TANAKU.

---

* See *supra*, p. 135, for James de Alwis's similar comparison, and *passim* for Geiger's.

(iii.) *Exotic Words.*

Independent of *Siṇhalese*, many words, purely foreign, or of probable foreign origin, occur:—

Persi-Arabic.—*Iskandar, salám, raḥmat, khabar, adá, hadíyá, taksír, mu'áf, musímu, sanat.*

Tamil.—DÓÑE (T. *tóṇi*), MITA (*cf.* T. *michcham*), RAS (*cf.* T. *arasaṇ*), OḌI (T. *óḍam*), AḶÁ, AḶUN (*cf.* T. *áḷ*).

Malay.—EDI (? Malay *ada*, "be").

Portuguese.—GORUNUDÓRE* (Dutch, *Gouverneur: cf.* S. *Governadóru*).

III.—Maldive Commercial Letter: A.D. 1875 circa.

The Letter in GABUḶI TÁNA (of which a line-for-line Transcript in DIVES AKURU † is given to right on Plate IX.), though short, and purely a "Business Communication," will not, as doubly reproduced, be without some service towards a comparative study of the Old and Modern Máldive Alphabets.

It was written in the Seventies of the Nineteenth Century, by Ali Dídí Dorhiméná-kilagefánu, a Máldivian nobleman then resident at Galle,‡ where his son, the present Prime Minister, Ibráhim Dídí Dorhiméná-kilagefánu, and one grandson, Ahmad Dídí Kuḍa Dorhiméná-kilagefánu, were educated.

---

* GORUNUDÓRE, "Governor." The latter portion is not (as presumed in 1882) = T. *turai*, "lord," &c.: the complete word is a corruption, doubtless through Portuguese, of the Latin *Gubernator*. The transliteration greatly exercised the Máldivian State Secretaries; for the first part of the word appears in Missives under a variety of forms (*e.g.*, GOVORANA, GORUNA, GORNA, GOVAN, GOUN, and a dozen others), more or less close. Of the "Commander" at Galle, they made KUBUDÓRU.

† The two texts only differ in the DIVES AKURU version omitting the Arabic heading, and inserting SALÁM at the end in place of the signature (illegible) at foot of the GABUḶI TÁNA writing.

‡ Ali Dídí died in 1878. "Much of his (Ahmad Dídí, a relative of Sultán Muhammad Múin-ud-dín, A.D. 1799–1835) ability was inherited by his son Ali Dídí (recommended by the Sultán in 1850 to the notice of Lord Torrington), who became a domiciled Ceylon subject, and resided at Galle until his death." (Bell, *The Máldive Islands*, p. 37.)

*Transcript.**

AL-HAMDU-LILLAH

(1) DOṚIMÉNÁ-KILAGEFÁNUṚGE SALÁṚ
Of Dorhiméná-kilagefánu the salutation

(2) HUṚṬEVE *MUHAMMAD* MARAṚKÁRA DEKALU
is (sent) to Muhammad Marakkár, two persons.

(3) ṚNA(Ṛ) ISFINISGE AḌAṚTUO
Of the Spanish Agency

(4) A ÁGU BÓṬU(Ṛ) GENÁ HAḌULUGE
in the steamer † (which was) brought for the rice

NÁLU
the freight

(5) E MÍHUNA(Ṛ) NU-DÍGEṚ TIYA UḶE
to those persons not given that doing

(6) NÍ KÍṚWEGEṚ-HÉ ADU SIṬÍYE
why to-day a letter

(7) (T) EBA FONUVIYÉ NÁLÍHA(Ṛ) HIGÁDÁ
they have sent, proceedings will have

(8) NAMÉ KIYÁ E RUFIYÁ E
to go forth saying. That money to those

MÍHUṚNA(Ṛ)
persons

(9) LIBÉNÉGO(T) AVAHA(Ṛ) HADÁṚEVE
of receiving soon (the means) make.

(10) MI SIṬÍ LIUNÍ MAÍ(Ṛ) 17
This letter is written on May 17th. ‡

---

* The preference of the writer, like that of the author of the FADITA FO(T) (see *supra*, p. 163), for Ṛ, as, on the other hand, of the official scribe who penned the Sultán's Missive of A.H. 1210 (A.D. 1795) for AVIENI (A), may be contrasted, in interesting confirmation of the unsettled orthography of Máldivian words, permitting *alternative use* of these letters, according to fancy.

† See *supra*, p. 66, note *. ÁGU is not onomatopoetic for "cargo": it is from Hindústání *ág*, "steam" (*cf. ág-ká-alat*, "steam engine"). Other Hindústání derivatives are AḌAṚTUO, NÁLU (*cf.* Arabic *naul*, "freight"), NÁLÍHA (*cf.* Persian *nála-gí*, "complaint").—B., *Ed.*

‡ Year not given, but probably about 1875, or earlier.

Translation.

Praise be to God, the Most Highest!

The compliments (*lit.*, *salám*) of (Ali Dídí) Dorhiménákilagefánu to Muhammad Marakkár Brothers (or Company).

Owing to the non-payment of the freight due on the rice brought by the steamer of the Spanish Agency, they (the Agents) have sent a letter to-day enquiring why it has not been paid, and intimating that legal proceedings will have to be instituted.

Please, therefore, take necessary action, so that they (the Agents) may get the money soon.

(Dated) May 17.*

PLATE I.

Journ. R.A.S. (Ceylon), Extra No., 1919.

W. Geiger. *Māldivische Studien I.*

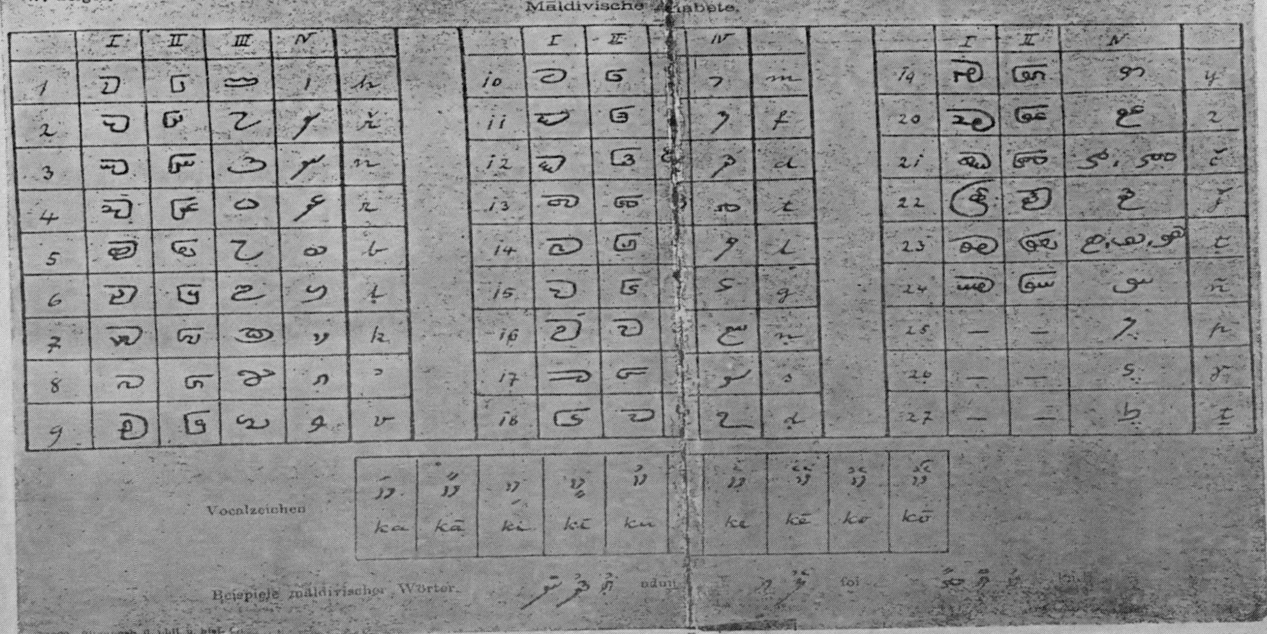

Apothecaries' Co., photo.

MĀLDIVE ALPHABET.

Survey Office half-tone block.

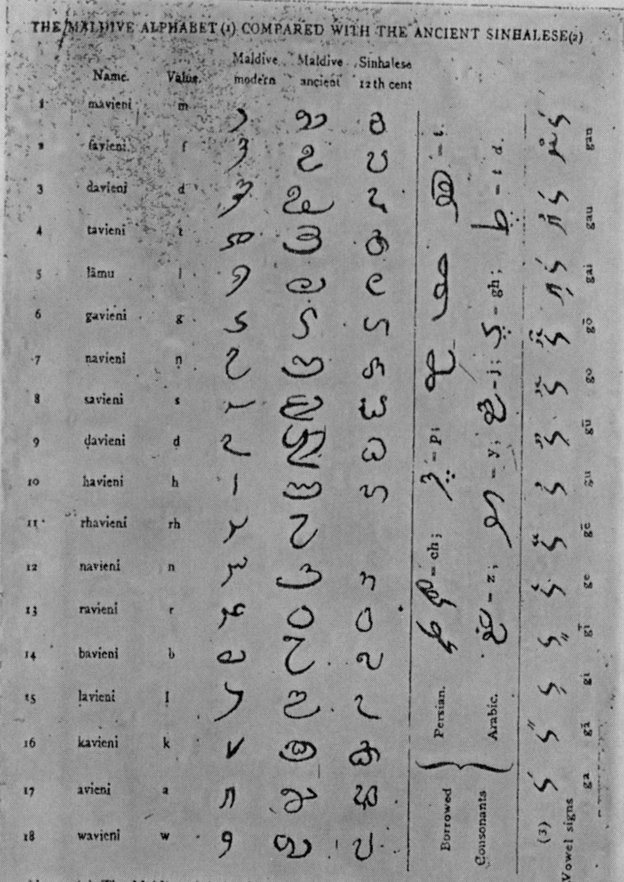

NOTE. (1) The Maldive alphabet is taken from Christopher's list, carefully compared with his facsimile of a Maldive letter. (J. R. A. S. Vol. VI.)

NOTE. (2) The Sinhalese letters are taken from a photograph of the inscription of Nissanka Malla (A. D. 1191.) discovered at Anurādhapura in 1874.

NOTE. (3) The vowel signs are called *fili*, or severally, *aba*, *ābā*, *ibi*, *ībī*, *ebe*, *ēbē*, *ubu*, *ūbū*, *obo* and *ōbō*, *fili*:

"Only six consonants can take the sokun (•) over them, and consequently these only can terminate a syllable; they are a, ṇ, n, rh, s, & t, and in this case with the exception of s, their sounds receive some modification: a becomes g; ṇ or n sometimes take the sound of ng: t is sounded like a very short i: and rh merely takes the sound of the following consonant, giving an emphasis to the syllable it terminates: but when rh terminates the word it is silent, and appears wholly unnecessary, except for the division it causes, but the natives cannot understand writing without it." Christopher in J. R. A. S. VI. 45. There is no inherent vowel 'a'; accordingly every consonant has either a vowel sign or the *sokun:* in the latter case, if the consonant cannot take the *sokun*, it is changed to one which can. The initial vowels are formed by the quasi consonant 'a' with the appropriate vowel sign, and the second of two vowels following a consonant is expressed in the same way, thus 'gai' is written 'g' with the vowel sign 'a' followed by the quasi-consonant 'a' with the sign 'i'.

Apothecaries' Co., photo. Survey Office half-tone block.

MALDIVIAN LETTER.

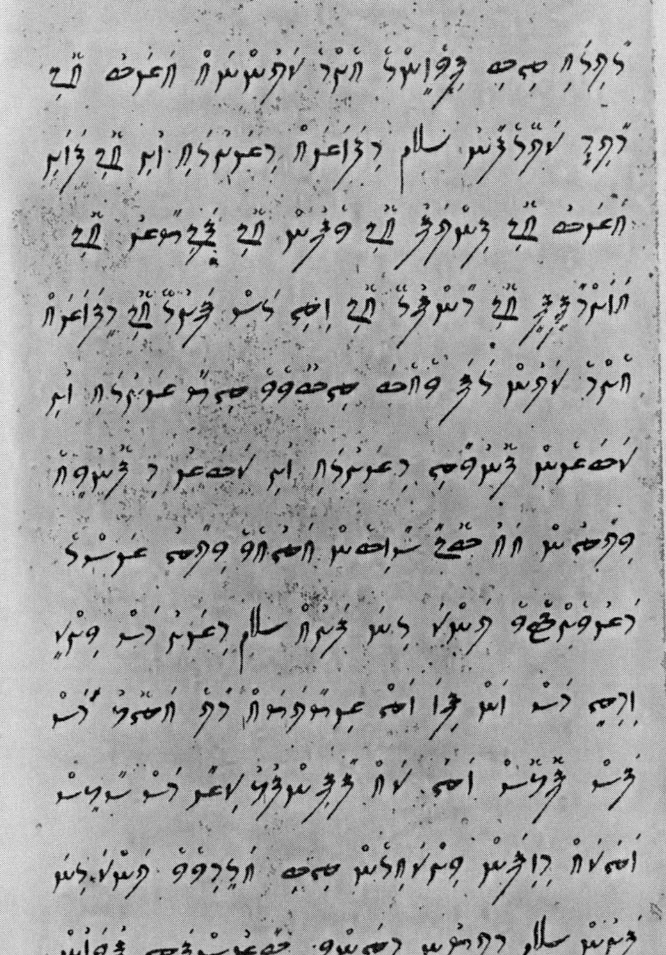

Apothecaries' Co., photo. *Survey Office half-tone block.*

Apothecaries' Co., photo. *Survey Office half-tone block.*

PLATE V.

1.

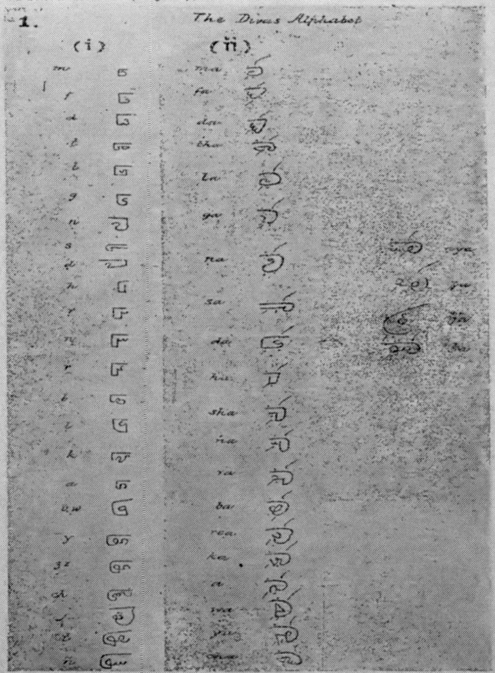

2.

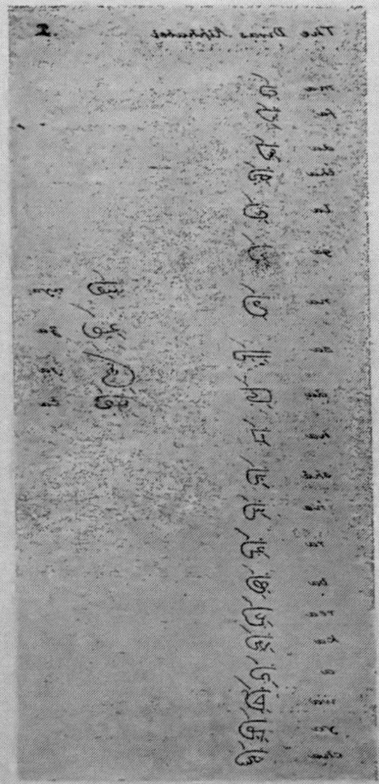

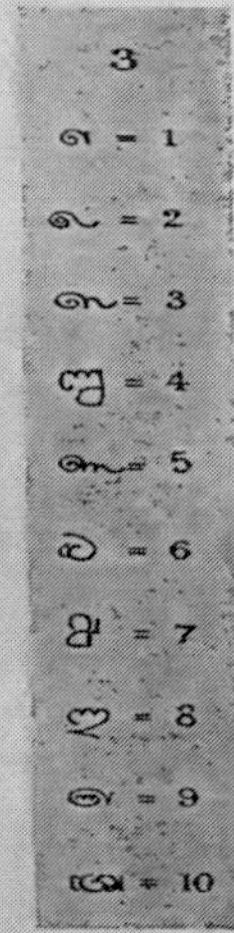

Apothecaries' Co., photo.

1, 2. MÁLDIVE ("GABUḶI TÁNA") ALPHABETS. 3. SIŊHALESE "LIT AKURU."

Survey Office half-tone block.

*PLATE V.**

4.

1 =
2 =
3 =
4 =
5 =
6 =
7 =
8 =

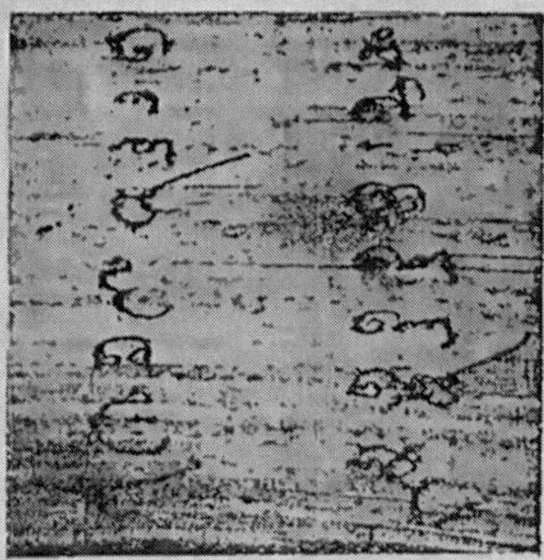

= 9
= 10
= 11
= 12
= 13
= 14
= 15

4. SIṆHALESE "LIT AKURU."

[*These run from 1 to 60.*]

The figures in Column 3, Plate V., are more correctly styled "Siṇhalese Numerals."

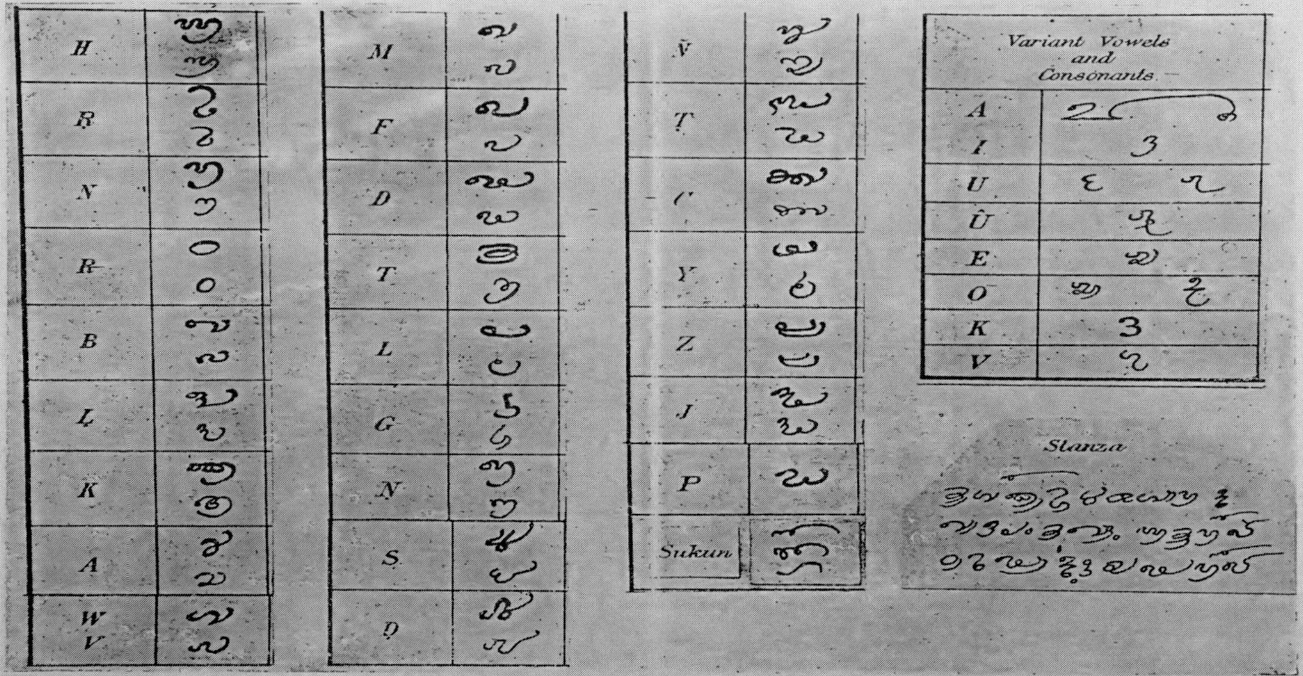

Apothecaries' Co., photo. "DIVES AKURU," OR OLD MÁLDIVE, ALPHABET. Survey Office half-tone block.

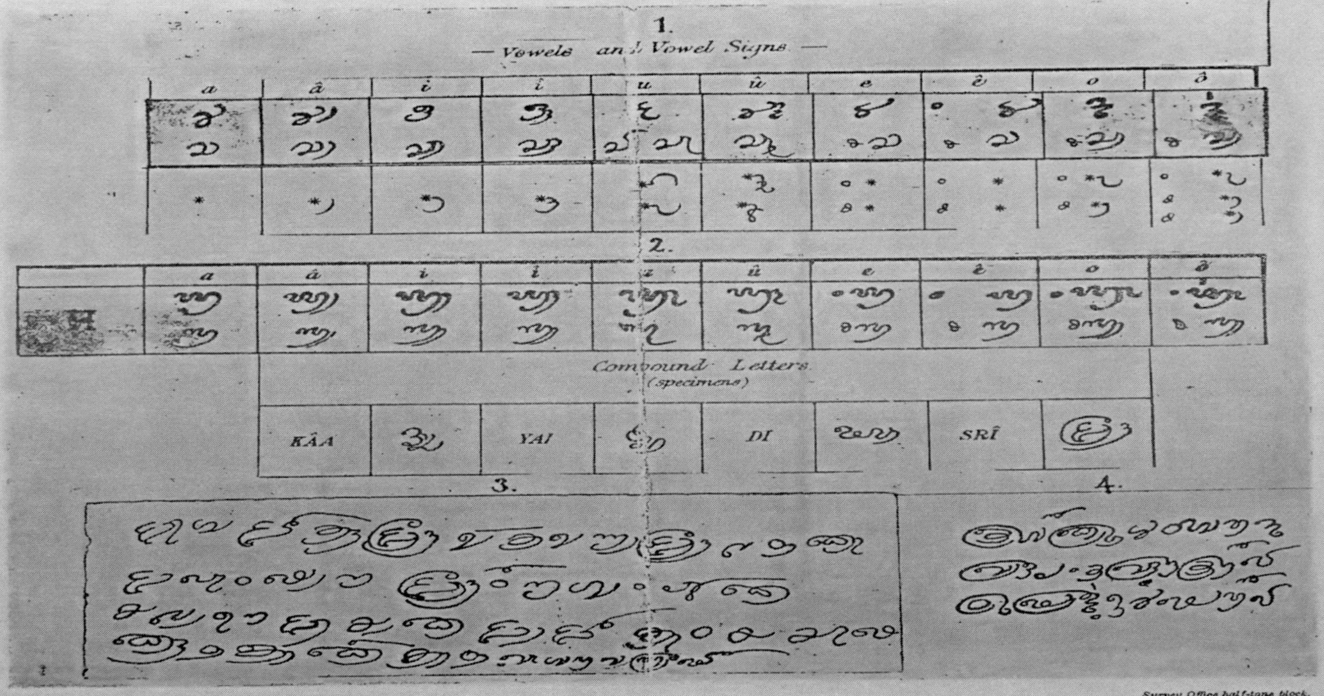

Apothecaries' Co., photo.

"DIVES AKURU," OR LD MÁLDIVE, ALPHABET.

Survey Office half-tone block.

Apothecaries' Co., photo. Bottom. OLD "GABULI TÁNA" MANUSCRIPT. Top. Survey Office half-tone block.

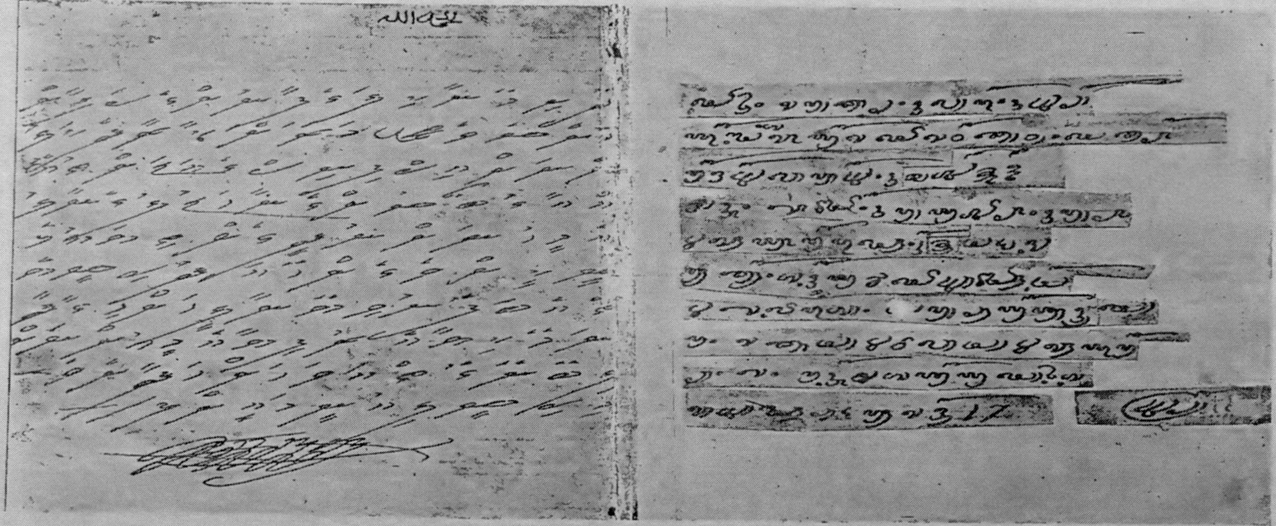

Apothecaries' Co., photo. "Gabuli Tána." MÁLDIVE LETTER. "Dives Akuru." *Survey Office half-tone block.*